The Communist Parties of
Western Europe

The Royal Institute of International Affairs is an unofficial body which promotes the scientific study of international questions and does not express opinions of its own. The opinions expressed in this publication are the responsibility of the author.

The Institute and its Research Committee gratefully acknowledge the comments and suggestions of Kenneth Devlin, Professor Alfred Grosser, and Dr George Urban, who have read the manuscript.

The Communist Parties of
Western Europe

Neil McInnes

Published for
The Royal Institute of International Affairs
by
Oxford University Press
London New York Toronto
1975

Oxford University Press, Ely House, London W.1

GLASGOW NEW YORK TORONTO MELBOURNE WELLINGTON
CAPE TOWN IBADAN NAIROBI DAR ES SALAAM LUSAKA ADDIS ABABA
DELHI BOMBAY CALCUTTA MADRAS KARACHI LAHORE DACCA
KUALA LUMPUR SINGAPORE HONG KONG TOKYO

ISBN 0 19 218311 7

*Printed in Great Britain by
Ebenezer Baylis & Son Limited
The Trinity Press, Worcester, and London*

FOR JULIE

Contents

Preface

It was in 1974 that it first seemed that before 1980 there could well be communist ministers in office in France, Italy, Spain, Portugal, Greece, Cyprus, Finland, Norway, and Iceland. Just conceivably, they could be sharing power in all those nations at once, that is to say, over more than half the area of Western Europe. Not only were communists in all those countries (as well as in others where, however, their chances seemed remote) committed to winning shared power by constitutional means, but they had already done so in several small nations (Finland and Iceland) and seemed within an ace of doing so in several large nations (France and Italy). That they had acceded to office by less regular, but still peaceable, methods in Portugal only made it likely that they could do the same in comparable circumstances elsewhere (as in Spain). Their success, or plausible hope of it, in one place seemed to increase their chances in other places, until the thought of half Western Europe under communist-backed coalitions became realistic enough to stir enthusiasm, dismay, or outright anxiety in various quarters.

Equally possible, nothing of the sort might happen in Western Europe in this decade. It is a standard and fallacious method of writing diplomatic reports and journalistic commentaries to run together disparate scraps of information into a trend whose verisimilitude affects an air of inexorability. At the very time the communist bid for power over much of the Continent came to be taken seriously, a gathering economic crisis was making communist rule less likely— or, at least, not making it any more likely, as is popularly supposed. For one thing, the communist parties have said often enough (and one presumes they are sincere, because it is the fruit of bitter experience) that they will not come to office to administer the affairs of the bourgeoisie during a recession nor to serve as hostages in a government that enforces austerity on the working class. So, whatever explanations they gave publicly for the economic crisis that set in in Europe in 1974, the communists began to give signs of being in no hurry to win portfolios, whereupon in Italy and France there reappeared the old doubt whether they really wanted to win power at all. Secondly, the weakening of the West European economies created the occasion for the Soviet Union to win concessions (for instance, favourable trade arrangements and credit) from embarrassed "bourgeois" governments. To replace those governments with communist-led coalitions would simply substitute awkward dependants for troubled enemies, which is never sound strategy. Besides, it would gravely disturb the superpower balance in a vital region just when Moscow and Washington were seeking to consolidate the détente. To the extent that Moscow helps determine the CPs' policies, it would not be wholeheartedly in favour of a rush for ministerial office. Lastly, the economic crisis in Europe could well diminish the chances of a peaceful, democratic transfer of power to the communists—or to anyone else—by recreating as in the past the conditions for authoritarian régimes decidedly opposed to communism, as well as to trade unions or opposition of any sort. The series of conspiracies in Italy in 1973 and 1974 made that point clear.

Even granted a favourable economic climate, the thought of an imminent accession to office by communists in nine or ten nations depended on some bold guesses. It depended on overestimating communist strength in dictatorships where, in the absence of elections, fears passed for statistics. For example, communist electoral support in Greece was estimated by American sources on the eve of the 1974 poll at 15 per cent, whereas in the event a broad communist-led alliance won only 9·45 per cent of the votes and eight parliamentary seats out of 300. Estimates of 21 per cent for Spain and 23 per cent for Portugal, from the same sources, were not accepted as accurate by the cautious leaders of the relevant CPs. Forecasts of communist success in other countries were merely extrapolations from previous electoral figures, whereas it will be shown below that there is a tantalizing paradox that confronts all West European CPs: the nearer they get to power, the further it recedes from them at the last moment. Finally, the forecasts in question all related to the fortunes of electoral alliances between communists and socialists or radicals (since nowhere could a CP win a majority by itself), and therefore they assumed the solidity of such essentially unstable coalitions. The outburst of recriminations between French socialists and communists in 1974 called in question that assumption by illustrating a principle described below: namely, that communists and socialists compete for the same electorate, and the advance of one is usually at the expense of the other—and hence an occasion for reproaches and for accusations of treachery.

Nevertheless, and with all those qualifications, a new idea has

appeared in Europe, the notion that widespread admission of communists to democratic governments is once again possible. (One says
"once again" because communists already shared power, just after
the War, in France, Italy, Belgium, Luxembourg, Austria, Greece,
Norway, Finland, Denmark, and Iceland.) Now, politics is the art
of the possible in this sense, too, that possibilities have actual consequences there. The acceptance of what was formerly impossible as
henceforth plausible changes the political scene. It changes the weight
or 'credibility' of a party that it comes to symbolize one possible
future for the nation, whereas it was previously dismissed as an improbable contender for even a particle of power. Especially does it
modify the stature and political effectiveness of parties that were till
now ostracized (or chose to ostracize themselves), or even persecuted,
for their leaders suddenly to be seen as ministerial timber. Once such
a party gains potential, there must be a fresh deal of the cards, after
which all the other parties find that they have new hands too. Such a
redistribution of political forces occurred over much of Western
Europe in 1974, even if the reasons for it were as insubstantial as has
just been suggested.

This book will not explain why that happened when it did, for the
sufficient reason that it was not the communists' own work. As ever
in human affairs, hazard played a leading role. The communists
made no contribution to the downfall of fascism in Portugal or to the
overthrow of military rule in Greece or even to the sudden collapse
of the Francoist régime's prestige (which was rather the work of anti-
communist Basques). It was the coincidence of those events with the
progress of communist strategy in France and Italy that brusquely
(and perhaps briefly, for one must stress that we are in the domain of
mere possibilities so far) put West European communism in a new
light. What this book can show is that that light is an ambiguous one,
a light that illuminates less than it deceives. In other words, the principal themes will be an analysis of communist support that reveals
how heterogeneous, mercurial, and unpredictable it is; a description
of communist party structure that emphasizes the presence of three
separate forces that can pull in different directions, namely the party
bureaucracy, the Bolshevik workers, and Soviet power; and finally, an
account of communist policies that shows how they confuse forceful
social criticism with an archaic and incoherent populism.

Such a description, to the extent it were accepted as accurate,
might tempt some to conclude either that the CPs were politically
impotent or that they could only ever function in office as socialist

parties of a special sort. That is why it is commonly argued that parties invoking revolutionary Marxism-Leninism have no future at all in Western Europe, whatever appeals they might conserve in the developing world.[1] That is not the conclusion to which the following chapters will argue. To be sure, violent revolution such as the CPs preached in Western Europe up until the last war is now rejected by CP leaders, not always with horror so much as with a nostalgic twinge of shame such as one feels for generous youthful errors;[2] and if *their* sincerity be doubted, there is the more compelling fact that their parties are full of people who have joined on the understanding that revolution is not on the agenda. Nevertheless, intentions can matter less than the consequences of our actions, and a likely consequence of communist actions is that they would unleash events for which communists would disclaim responsibility but which would constitute 'revolutionary situations'. The upshot of such situations is unforeseeable, and especially so for a political party that blunders into them, as the CPs seem intent on doing, with divided support, an incoherent doctrine, unreliable allies, and the liability of the Soviet connection.

Perhaps one can say, without falling into the charlatanry of political prophecy, that although so much about the CPs makes their future unpredictable, it is fairly sure that they will *matter* more in the decade ahead, more, that is, than during the days when they were 'exiles of the interior'. As participants in the political process and as seeming contenders for ministerial power, their support, structure, alliances, policies, and foreign connections will be directly relevant to European national politics, to the unity of Western Europe and to the American alliance—much more relevant than in the days when they were total, external opponents. Consequently, it is needful to familiarize ourselves with those things, instead of accepting the caricatures of the CPs put out by themselves as well as by their opponents. No apology, then, need be made for the fact that the examination of CP support and structure in the early chapters of this book will seem meticulous to readers impatient of figures. Those who are more interested in what is less interesting about political parties, to wit their declared programmes, are free to hasten to the later chapters, but in the political struggles of the next few years in Western Europe it will be helpful to know precisely to what extent and in what sense the CPs are 'working-class parties', or 'monolithic organizations', or 'Soviet instruments'—let alone 'social-democrat parties of a new type'. A study of those questions will discover a possibility just as real

as that of the CPs winning office over much of Europe within the
decade: the possibility that the attempt to use the Leninist party
machine for purposes it was never designed to meet, with different
forms of social support and with a new relation to the Soviet Union,
will lead to political failure that could assume either farcical or tragic
dimensions.

Paris,   N. M.
November 1974

1 Luciano Pellicani, *Dinamica delle rivoluzioni* (Milan, 1974), p. 322-4.
2 Santiago Carrillo, *Demain l'Espagne* (Paris, 1974), pp. 136, 260, 187.

I The size of the communist phenomenon

What follows is written on, and will test, the hypothesis that there exists a specific entity, West European communism. Communists themselves, publicly at least, maintain that there is only 'world communism' but in reality this no longer exists, having fragmented not only along the lines of the Sino-Soviet split but along other fault-lines described below. Students of the subject would be more likely to question whether West European communism, let alone world communism, has enough unity to allow of systematic treatment; and indeed most work on the CPs deals with national parties in their domestic context. A CP in the government, as the Icelandic party was until May 1974, seems to have little resemblance to a clandestine Soviet agency in Turkey, and yet the ease with which the Portuguese party passed overnight in 1974 from the latter status to the former—and the similarity between its policies in office and those of bigger West European CPs in or near office—shows an underlying unity. Despite evident differences in size and local importance, the history of one party can illuminate another's. Some disputed passages in the PCF's past become clear in the light of what the Norwegian party was doing at the same time,[1] and Maurice Duverger has argued that socialist CP relations in an old, independent democracy like Finland are relevant to events in much bigger countries.[2] Students of the mighty Italian and French CPs dismiss, with the scholar's equivalent of great-power chauvinism, as footling any reference to the Luxembourg CP; but this book is written from another point of view. Still, the notion of 'Western Europe' is so vague in every sphere from geography to culture that one would have no interest in exaggerating the similarities between CPs in the region and not noticing glaring differences. It is just that these differences do not always lie where one would expect.

The political phenomenon of CP membership occurs mainly—as to 94 per cent—between the Elbe River and the Pacific in the fourteen nations (one-third of humanity) that are governed by CPs. The other 6 per cent of the world's 47m. CP members, that is, about 2·8m. men and women, belong to 65 CPs around the world, of which 48 are illegal or semi-clandestine. With the virtual annihilation of the

Indonesian CP after 1965, the only substantial parties among them were in Japan, India, Chile, and Western Europe. Western Europe indeed has the bulk of them, just over 2m., grouped in 23 CPs that range in size from the 1·5-m.-strong Italian party down to sects of a few hundred in Ireland. Some 90 per cent of Western European communists belong to parties in Italy and France although those two nations make up less than 30 per cent of the total West European population. The other 10 per cent belong to parties that, though small, can represent significant political forces in small countries, such as Finland, Iceland, and Cyprus, or can exercise recurrent crucial political influence, as happens in Sweden and Norway, or else possess an unmeasurable political potential in countries where they must now operate illegally, such as Spain and Turkey.

The figure of 2m. for Western Europe's CP membership relates to the first years of this decade. At other recent dates the figure would have been very different. In 1930, for example, it was not one-tenth of that. At that time there were only two notable West European parties, the German CP with 124,000 members and the French party with just over 38,000; the other parties were small groups, of which the largest was 6,000 strong. In contrast, in the first years after the war, Western Europe's score of CPs had over 4m. members. The reasons for these wide fluctuations will be discussed later.

Around the central core of party membership there occur other communist phenomena, ranging from strictly controlled party subsidiaries, such as youth organizations, to more or less consistently influenced trade unions, and ultimately to the most substantial manifestation of communism, the communist electorate, which can in certain cases extend to over one quarter of the voters. Some of these things are hard to measure. For that matter, imprecision begins with the apparently simply fact of party membership, because unlike most other parties, the communists frequently regard membership statistics as a party secret. Worse, they sometimes regard them as party propaganda, so that where figures are vouchsafed, they are certainly exaggerated.

Even the enumeration of the CPs has become a matter of approximation. Not all of them now call themselves the 'communist party of such and such'. Where they have taken another name, the old one, 'the communist party', can be seized upon by ultra-Left groups claiming loyalty to a tradition supposedly betrayed by the CPs. This happened in West Germany and in Sweden. When the West German communists emerged from clandestinity in 1968, they did so as a new and constitutional party, Deutsche Kommunistische Partei, without formally dissolving the illegal Kommunistische Partei Deutschlands. The latter name was appropriated by at least three ultra-Left groups, so that West Germany had one DKP and three KPDs. In Sweden, where the CP changed its name in 1967 to 'the Left Party-Communists', a group formerly known as the Marxist Leninist Communist Federation (Kfml) in February 1973 took over the title Sveriges kommunistiska parti.

Again, some CPs have split in recent years, and both splinter parties might cling to the official name. Judgement as to which of them is the *real* CP might differ. That happened in Belgium, in Greece, where there were 'exterior' and 'interior' KKEs, and in Spain, where the two factions not only kept the same name but published rival papers with the same name. As a limiting case, the bulk of a CP—its leaders, members, and voters—can leave the international communist movements (for there are more than one now) and yet continue to represent in domestic politics everything that communism ever meant in that country save a connection with Moscow. That latter distinguishing mark might be left to a rump party. That happened in Denmark.

With those reservations, then, the CPs of Western Europe are the following.

West European Communist Parties

Country	Name and Abbreviation	Membership
Italy	Partito Comunista Italiano (PCI)	1,622,861
France	Parti Communiste Français (PCF)	240,000–260,000
Finland	Suomen Kommunistinen Puolue (SKP)	48,000
West Germany	Deutsche Kommunistische Partei (DKP)	39,344
Britain	Communist Party of Great Britain (CPGB)	28,000
Greece	Kommonistikon Komma Elladas (KKE)	28,000
Austria	Kommunistische Partei Österreichs (KPO)	25,000
Spain	Partido Comunista de España (PCE)	5,000–20,000
Sweden	Vänsterpartiet-Kommunisterna (VPK)	15,000
Belgium	Parti Communiste de Belgique (PCB)	15,000
Cyprus	Anorthotikon Komma Ergazomenou Laou (AKEL)	12,000
Holland	Communistische Partij van Nederland (CPN)	12,000
West Berlin	Sozialistische Einheitspartei Westberlins (SEW)	8,000
Denmark	Danmarks Kommunistiske Parti (DanKP)	7,000
Switzerland	Parti Suisse du Travail (PST)	3,000

Country	Name and Abbreviation	Membership
Norway	Norges Kommunistiske Parti (NKP)	2,000–5,000
Portugal	Partido Communista Portugês (PCP)	2,000–3,000
Iceland	Altydubandalagid (AB)	2,000–2,500
Turkey	Türkiye Komünist Partisi (TKP)	2,000
San Marino	Partito Comunista di San Marino (PCSM)	1,000
Luxembourg	Parti Communiste de Luxembourg (PCL)	500–1,000
Eire & Ulster	Communist Party of Ireland (CPI)	300
Malta	Communist Party of Malta (CPM)	100

Sources: Membership figures are the latest available, though the PCP figure refers to before Apr 1974; several months later the PCP claimed over 100,000 members. New figures, or estimates, appear annually in World strength of the communist party organisations, published by the US Department of State, and in Yearbook on international communist affairs (Stanford, Calif.). Cf. also F. Fetjö, Dictionnaire des partis communistes et des mouvements révolutionnaires (Paris, 1971) and W. Berner & others, Sowjetunion 1973 (Munich, 1974). A common independent estimate for the PCF is 330,000–340,000, which includes 68,000 'stagiaires' (Est et Ouest, no 523, pp. 6–7); the figure given above is from Unir, no 76, 1973.

Membership figures must be interpreted not only in relation to the population of the country in question but in relation to local customs about joining political parties of whatever sort. The Italians, since fascism, have been meticulous joiners, which the French have never been; that fact accounts for part of the large difference between the size of CPs in two countries of comparable population and comparable susceptibility to communism. Indeed, if the French CP had the 400,000 members it lays claim to, it would be bigger than all other French parties put together. The PCI, in contrast, has no more members than the Christian Democrat Party.

Naturally, formal membership does not indicate much about the degree of political involvement with a party. This point is only worth mentioning because it was in connection with CPs that the expression 'card-carrying member' was thought to be especially meaningful. In reality, a card might need to be endorsed with twelve monthly stamps, of which the cost is related to the cardholder's income. So there at once are thirteen different degrees of formal membership (a fact that explains some discrepancies in estimates of party strengths), not to mention degrees of regularity in attendance at cell meetings and in the discharge of other party obligations. Still, although the seriousness of CP members about their duties is commonly overestimated, there is no question that they are in general more committed to political activity than the members of other parties. Thus membership figures, even as approximate as they must be, give significant information in relation to CPs.

They do not, however, measure directly a CP's success in achieving its objectives because a CP differs from most other political parties in this—that it does not always want to be big. (Nor do parties of 'notables'.) The original Leninist prescription for a CP was for a small party: 'better fewer but better.' Later on, different estimates of the political situation in Western Europe recurrently incited the CPs to expand their membership rapidly, but a period of expansion could be followed by a deliberate effort to reduce membership for the sake of 'quality'. For example, the PCF, after claiming, no doubt inaccurately, to have enrolled its millionth member in 1946, spoke, through the person of Léon Mauvais, of enrolling millions more: 'a party that must be counted in millions . . . we must open wide the ranks of our party; recruit and recruit more still.' Yet already in 1947 Mauvais had to admit that some of his comrades, 'on the pretext of vigilance, are objectively restraining recruitment . . . [preferring] quality to quantity'.[3] Such comrades were to receive support a year later when the Cominform, the movement's international organization, called on the PCF to restrain recruitment for the sake of efficacy: 'The rapid growth of a party has the effect of lowering the degree of [political] consciousness of its members and of damaging in some ways the quality of the party.'[4] The membership of the PCF thereafter continued to decline from its 1946 peak, until 1953. Membership then increased for the first time in seven years, but within a few months the organization secretary, Auguste Lecoeur, was denounced and dismissed on the charge of having practised 'opportunism' and lowered the quality of the party.

Therefore the variation in a CP's membership is not necessarily a measure of its fortunes, as the party values them, because a rise in membership can result not only from a favourable political environment but from a deliberate choice to enrol members more freely; and conversely a decline in membership may be seen as an improvement in quality. Needless to say, the choice to recruit more members will be accompanied by the adoption of the sort of policies that attract members (participation in elections, co-operation with other parties), whereas the decision to streamline the party will come with harder, less popular policies (isolation, revolutionism, violence).

These considerations have less relevance to the Italian CP than to other West European parties because its then leader, Palmiro Togliatti, resolved at the time of his return to Italy at the end of the war to make the PCI a *mass* party 'as well as' a Leninist party of militants. Whereas, in the years that followed, other CPs sought to influence front organizations and to cultivate sympathizers, the PCI absorbed many of its front organizations and enrolled its sympathizers. That was why it could grow between 1943 and 1951 from 5,000 or 6,000 to over 2·3m. members, even to 2·6m. counting its youth federation. Togliatti's definition of the PCI as a mass party has never been disavowed, so deliberate choice could not be the reason for the subsequent loss of hundreds of thousands of members. This is another explanation of the difference in size between the PCF and the PCI.[5]

Youth Organizations

Deliberate choice is especially relevant to the size of a CP's youth movement. Indeed the very fact that a party *has* a youth movement can be an index of its current policy. CPs have seldom been particularly concerned with the young as such, denying that they faced any social problems different from those of their class. Besides, like other political parties, the communists have had difficulty in maintaining control over 'their' youth movements, which have been prone to deviations, whether these be labelled by the leadership Trotskyist or Maoist or, on the contrary, 'Italian', i.e. relatively liberal.

The PCI had no special youth movement during the period of its meteoric growth after the war, preferring to absorb the young into young people's cells within the party or even into cells without distinction of age. A Communist Youth Federation was set up in 1949, and that fact was interpreted as related to the hardening of the party line during the Cold War: special ideological training for young members was part of a quest for quality rather than quantity. That Federation claimed to have 463,000 members in April 1951 and 450,000 still in 1954, but that did not signify any net expansion of communism in Italy since the party's overall membership was already falling by then. Membership in the youth federation slumped after the Hungarian insurrection of 1956 and had fallen to around 150,000 in 1966, and to 70,000 two years later. This did indeed signify a retrogression of communism among the young. That became clear in 1968 when Italian communism was outflanked on the Left by a variety of ultra groups. As that agitation subsided, the PCI claimed to be recruiting thousands of young people who had been 'politicized' by the disturbance of 1968 but who quickly tired of the undisciplined ultra groups. That is no doubt true, but all organized political parties benefited in the same way and it is possible that the Italian

Christian Democrats recruited even more of these disillusioned revolutionaries.

The PCF, which had had stormy experiences with its youth movements in the 1920s and 1930s, emerged from the war claiming 93,000 members in its various youth organizations, but their combined membership was admitted by the party to have slumped to 40,000 by 1954. The party-controlled Mouvement de la jeunesse communiste was revived in 1956 by combining these organizations, but its membership was claimed by the party to be only 50,000 in 1959 and 1967. This is a decline of communist influence because in that period the children born in the postwar demographic wave came of an age to join this movement, while the number of students in French tertiary establishments increased fivefold. The PCF was in reality making no effort to expand its youth movements, being more concerned with their ideological orthodoxy, as clashes with its own communist-student movement in 1963 showed. Thus the PCF too was caught with insignificant support among the young when the events of May and June 1968 produced a situation that the ultra-Leftists regarded as potentially revolutionary. Worse, the PCF was caught with no understanding of what was happening among the young at that time and was reduced to denouncing youthful activists as 'Left-fascist'.

After 1968 the PCF tried to overcome its traditional suspicion of the young, exposed as they are to the infantile maladies of ultra-Leftism, and to increase its audience among them. It claimed to have succeeded in attracting 10,000–15,000 additional members to its youth movement by 1971. If the Mouvement de la jeunesse communiste really did group 60,000–65,000 young people at that date, that was not many; there would be at least 60,000 children of workers alone in tertiary education at the time. The PCF no doubt benefited, as did the PCI, from a certain move back towards political discipline after the heady days of 1968 but there is no guarantee that these gains were lasting: the CPs have been the first stage in a passage from anarchic activities towards *other* disciplined parties, as is shown by the fact that so many leaders of the ultra movements are ex-communist, and in particular graduates of communist youth movements.

The youth movements of the other West European CPs, such as could be members of the Moscow-true World Federation of Democratic Youth, have since 1968 been small and everywhere challenged by, outflanked on the Left by and usually outnumbered by youth organizations of an ultra-Left sort.

Trade Unions

There are no communist trade unions in Western Europe. It was never the intention of Lenin, or apparently of his successors, that there should be. Thus there are no unions formally subordinate to a local CP leadership, as is the case with communist youth organizations or other direct subsidiaries of the party. And of course, as the figures for CP membership show, there can be no significant trade union organizations of which a majority of adherents are party members. What does exist and what is in accord with Leninist precept is the infiltration (white-anting, *noyautage*) of trade unions by communists, which can extend all the way from the activities of CP factory cells at the base of a union, to the conquest of key positions in the union leadership. That type of phenomenon is not measurable, firstly because the trade union phenomenon itself is measurable only with the widest margins of error (guesses at the membership of the largest communist-influenced trade union federation are to the nearest million), and secondly because it is a question of influence and thus subject to differing estimates.

Trade union membership is known only approximately for two reasons. There is the same ambiguity about membership as with political parties: how many stamps on a card make an active member? Secondly, trade unions consistently exaggerate their membership because much of their effectiveness depends on their size relative to other unions and on judgements of their 'representativity' by employers and public authorities. Even if one could measure the size of trade unions in which communists are active at the base (as in Britain and Finland) or which are more or less accurately described as 'communist-controlled', 'communist dominated' or 'communist-led' (as in Italy and France), there would still be doubt about what we were measuring. In Cold War polemics, it was assumed that we would be measuring the communist phenomenon, or one aspect of it. If a trade union confederation claimed 3·4m. members and a majority of its office-bearers were known to be CP members, that was taken to mean that West European communism had the disposition of 3·4m. supporters. In reality, apart from some isolated (and, from the communist point of view, disastrous) incidents in which communists sought to use unions in which they had influence as political cannon-fodder, e.g. as troops in street battles or in political strikes, there has been doubt about the extent to which 'communist-dominated' unions *behave* as communist, *act* communist. Plainly, this is a matter to be discussed along with CP alliances and influences, instead of taking figures of certain trade union memberships as measures of communism.

From the formal point of view, what Leninist doctrine does require of communists who have gained a decisive influence within a trade union organization is that it should be affiliated to an international trade union movement owing allegiance to Moscow. That was once the Profintern; since 1945 it has been the World Federation of Trade Unions. However, that latter body split in 1948 and 1949, when the International Confederation of Free Trade Unions hived off from it, and the WFTU has virtually disappeared from Western Europe. The only union confederations belonging to it are those of Cyprus, San Marino, Italy, and France; one fraction of the Austrian union federation also is a member of the WFTU, though the federation itself belongs to the ICFTU.

Therefore, although the WFTU claimed that 134,299,050 workers were members of affiliated unions in 1969, it could only claim that 5·9m. of them were in Western Europe. (The majority belong to more or less fictitious unions in communist-governed countries.) That 5·9m. is arrived at by adding together the clearly exaggerated claims of the Italian and French confederation that belong to the WFTU; the Cypriot, San Marinesque, and Austrian members are numerically negligible.

The Italian organization in question is the Italian General Confederation of Labour (CGIL). Out of Italy's 20m. workers, unions of various sorts claim to have unionized about 40 per cent, or over 7m.; there is reason to suspect that no more than 5m. are effectively in trade unions. Of them, the CGIL claims to count 3·4m. in member-unions, but the real figure might be as low as 2·5m. That would still leave the CGIL as Italy's biggest union organization, since the CISL (Confederazione italiana di Sindicati lavoratori) is estimated to have between 1·5 and 2·5m. members, and the UIL (Unione italiana del Lavoro) influenced by the Social Democrats and the Republicans, might have around 1m. members. The CGIL is extensively influenced by CP members among its leaders, though they must exercise their influence in agreement with socialists among that same leadership.

The French counterpart is the Confédération générale du Travail (CGT), which claimed in 1970 to have 2·3m. members, of whom over one-tenth were retired people. Government estimates put its membership at 1·3–1·5m. Only 25 per cent of French workers are unionized, so the CGT is even more predominant among organized labour in France than the CGIL is in Italy, but it too faces a growing challenge from other organizations, notably the Confédération française démocratique du Travail (CFDT). The CGT is more extensively influenced by communists than the CGIL, but its leadership is not exclusively communist. Its *membership* certainly is not, since even if all French communists were trade unionists, which they are not, they would not constitute one in ten of CGT members. In the 1973 elections opinion polls showed that 42 per cent of CGT members did not vote for communist candidates. Therefore the CGT, for all that it is the plainest case in Western Europe of communist influence over a stable mass organization, must be ranked among the allies of communism and not, as in Cold War polemics, among the manifestations of communism.

Front Organizations

No measurement of the communist phenomenon would be adequate if it left out of account the numerous 'front organizations' that communists influence in va1ying degrees, whether these be organizations they have created themselves or associations they have 'infiltrated'. ('Front' here means façade. It is the term used by opponents to designate what communists themselves call 'mass organizations'. In contrast, communists use 'front' in its military sense to designate—as the united, popular, or national fronts—what are discussed later as the communists' alliances.) While it is important to grasp the methods and the limitations of communist 'entrism' and 'fronts'—for they illuminate the communist obsession with organizational work and they explain some of the recent history of communism—it is at the same time important to note that any pretence at accurate measurement of this sort of communist influence can lead to ludicrous results. It did so during the Cold War. One drew up lists of organizations in which communist influence was patent or suspected; such lists could rapidly get to be hundreds long and the number of their members and sympathizers could get to be reckoned in hundreds of millions. But in doing so one risked losing sight of what one was supposed to be measuring. If one imagined that one was measuring the spread of communism or describing the operations of a conspiracy, one had fallen prey to an illusion that most (not all) communists laboured under. The belief that communism was advanced by the front organizations and that their progressive spread could be measured was the error of the Stalinists and the McCarthyites.

During the confrontation between the Soviet Union and the western democracies, it became a communist quirk to outlay immense efforts to bring non-communist associations, which might even be non-political associations, to pass an occasional resolution, or send an occasional message of greeting, that contained approval for Soviet objectives and/or condemnation of American ones. It was essential that such actions be only occasional, because if they were regular and if thereby communist domination became obvious, the association in question was held to have lost its usefulness as a front. The point was to get approval for Soviet policy from organizations that were apparently not communist or in which known communists were a minority. This largely futile activity was sometimes rationalized in a theory about 'taking over' a society by stealth or at least of planting men in key positions ready to take over various parts of it when the hour came. That theory was taken seriously only by organization-obsessed communists, and by opponents ready to list as 'communist' a whole organization that had once or occasionally been thus contaminated. Many estimates of the size of the communist phenomenon have been based on such thinking.

Although the veritable industry of tracking down communist-infiltrated organizations[6] has subsided, lists are still produced of scores of organizations[7] of students, peasants, singers, doctors, officers of the army reserve, war widows, actors, returned soldiers, and teachers that are 'controlled'—it is usually added lamely 'in varying degrees'—by communists. Such lists are necessarily incomplete and soon out of date, because what they point to is not a measurable or progressive trend but a constant characteristic of CP behaviour, 'entrism'. As one of the most assiduous detectors of such organizations says,

there are countless committees for topical purposes, such as an amnesty in Portugal, for Greek democracy, for the defence of political prisoners in Iran, and many others. Their exact number can be determined only with difficulty because frequently they disappear as quickly as they mushroomed up.[8]

The reason for that instability is the changing requirements of Soviet foreign policy, since the fronts and the strategy of infiltration were intended to serve not the interests of the local party but the needs of Soviet foreign policy. Of course, the promotion of that foreign policy was *one* of the interests of the local party but unless it aspired (as none in Western Europe has since 1945) to ride to power on Soviet tanks, it could be *only one* of them. Its other interests not only were not served by the fronts but—as the Trotskyists and other ultra-Leftists have always warned in pointing to the dangers of 'entrism'—were actually hampered by them. That is because by seeking to manipulate organizations without the knowledge of their members, the communists were themselves manipulated, in the sense that they became entangled in the society they sought to revolutionize. No group can 'throw a red net over society' without being absorbed by that society. In seeking to politicize everything, communists lost much of their political efficacy and became what their Leftist opponents call a party of order. What the conspiratorial communists imagined they were doing in white-anting organizations by stealth, and what the McCarthyites feared they were doing, was in fact impossible.

This was true too of those front organizations of which the communist control was never disguised, in that they were managed by a secretariat run by communists or located in Eastern Europe, but which sought to become vast mass organizations. The best known ones were the World Peace Council, the World Federation of Democratic Youth, the International Union of Students, the International Federation of Democratic Women, the International Association of Democratic Lawyers, the International Federation of Resistance Fighters. Some of them apparently became enormous: the women's federation claimed 140m. adherents in the 1950s; the democratic youth numbered 85m. in 1955; and a predecessor-organization of the World Peace Council collected 400m. signatures for the Stockholm Appeal in the early 1950s. Such figures mean little because most members and signatories were in the communist countries and were thus of unverifiable value. It was verified, however, that one 'world federation of teachers' which claimed to have 4m. members in the Soviet Union had no Russian-language edition of its official publication.[9] Again, a World Peace Council document, the Vienna Appeal, got 100m. signatures in China in 1955, not one of which, presumably, would have been available four years later when Peking quarrelled with Moscow.

The West European parts of such organizations were a minority but, no doubt, they were the only parts that mattered to the organizers: the 1m. Italian adherents to the women's federation, the 14m. French signatories of the Stockholm Appeal, for example. Yet they turned out to be of little more value than the communist bloc parts. Within a few years, all these bloated organizations were rent by internecine strife (over Yugoslavia, over China, and then over a confusion of issues); they were challenged by rival organizations or used as a forum for anti-Soviet propaganda; they lost the monopoly of protest to local non-communist organizations (as in the campaign against the Vietnam war, where communist-controlled peace movements were eclipsed in Western Europe); and finally they were let fade away. Not only was the enormous enterprise of communist-run fronts—which some had mistaken for the progress of communism—proven to be such stuff as dreams are made of, quite lacking in social substance and political fibre, but they created grave difficulties for the local CPs that were supposed to 'run' them. They caused crises within those parties, and that in turn ruined the prestige of the fronts. The instability of the fronts, and their damaging effect on the political action of CPs, were implicit in their origin, as instruments for the successive phases of Soviet foreign policy.

The fronts arose in the period of the United Front, starting in 1921. That was a period of open political collaboration between the CPs and socialist or other democratic parties, so that it made sense to seek to extend communist influence in circles with which the party was officially collaborating. Collaboration with the leaders could be combined with efforts to seduce those led into the CP; the front's main function for the local party—whatever its purpose for Soviet foreign policy—was as a recruiting ground. It was in the united front period of the 1920s that Willi Munzenberg perfected the organization of the fronts, starting with the Workers' International Relief, an organization that ostensibly sought food, clothing, and medicines for the starving Russians but actually sought expressions of support for the Soviet government. Towards the close of this united front period, Otto Kuusinen expounded the theory of the fronts at a meeting, in 1926, of the Comintern executive committee:

The first part of our task is to build up not only communist organizations but other organizations as well, above all mass organizations sympathizing with our aims, and able to help us for special purposes. We already have such organizations in some countries, for instance the International Red Aid, the Workers' International Relief, etc . . . Besides this, we need a number of more or less firmly established organizational fulcrums, which we can utilize for our further work . . . We must create a whole solar system of organizations and similar committees around the Communist Party, so to speak, smaller organizations actually working under the *influence* of our Party, not under its mechanical *leadership*.[10]

While it reflects the organizational obsession of communists (the belief that politics is not about the promotion of policies but about the formation of committees), this doctrine at least rationalized consistent practice: the white-anting of institutions with which the party was collaborating. It ceased to be rational when, in 1928, the Comintern broke with the united front strategy in favour of violent opposition, isolation, and the clash of 'class against class'. Thereupon, the surreptitious manipulation of non-communist organizations (or of non-communist majorities in communist-run associations) might produce the occasional statement in support of Soviet foreign policy but it could not advance the *other* interests of the local party. Except for the execution of an actual coup d'état, political parties can make no enduring gains from unconscious support. The fronts were therefore eclipsed during this phase and only came back to the forefront of CP policy when the popular front period began in the mid-30s. The fronts then reached a pinnacle of effectiveness, both from the point of view of Soviet foreign policy and for the purpose of winning membership, votes, and prestige for the local party, in connection with the Spanish Civil War and the struggle against Nazism. Eclipsed again during the period of Stalinist collaboration with Hitler, the fronts prospered mightily in the period of the joint fight against the Axis and in the immediate postwar years. It was in 1945 that were founded the WFTU, the World Federation of Democratic Youth, the international Union of Students, and the World Federation of Democratic Women; in 1946 followed the associations of journalists and scientific workers.

This period of communist collaboration with the democratic parties ended with the onset of the Cold War, and immediately the fronts were in trouble. They lost many of their non-communist supporters, as when unions and youth organizations not controlled by communists split off from the WFTU and the youth federation in 1948 and 1949. They continued to claim a huge membership but their actual West European constituents were rump associations that might put out, sporadically, an encouraging telegram to the Soviet government but which could only complicate life for the local party. The complication came from the fact that a party that was pursuing a hard line of absolute opposition to capitalist democracy had to depute members to front organizations that were an integral part of capitalist democracy and were required to remain so, in order that their expressions of friendship for the Soviet Union might have some significance. Those seconded members were thus exposed to contradictory stresses and, from representing the CP in other democratic organizations, they were soon in danger of representing those democratic organizations within the CP. Their support in the front, moreover, seemed to give them a power base that might be used against the party leadership, so that they were suspected of conspiracy. This situation lay behind, as the common factor, successive crises in the French party, associated with the trials of André Marty and Charles Tillon, Marcel Servin and Laurent Casanova, and finally Roger Garaudy.

The mechanism was described from outside the party in 1954 in these terms:

This party pattern of communication and of decision-making has almost inevitably produced a division in the party leadership between those who man the internal party apparatus and those who staff the mass organizations controlled or influenced by the party . . . The mass leadership [i.e. members deputed to the fronts] . . . is dependent on a clientele which has expectations that often conflict with the requirements of party tactics. There is a plane of cleavage between the party organization and the organizations which it controls; and the party leadership which operates at this point [i.e. in the fronts] has a power base that often makes possible a certain amount of independence vis-à-vis the internal party leadership. Since the leadership at this point [in the fronts] is often pulled in conflicting directions, and furthermore has an easier exit, it is more prone to defection than are the central party functionaries.[11]

The PCF, because of its prestige in the movement and because of Moscow's confidence in its leadership, was consistently required to staff the major international fronts. That may be why it was the party most plagued by these tensions, until its leader—after arranging the expulsion or denunciation of colleagues who had been contaminated by serving in the fronts—admitted the existence of these difficulties. It was in 1960 that Maurice Thorez said,

Sectarian and dogmatic tendencies can be most prejudicial to the development and action of mass organizations. These organizations have a very important role to play. To require them to adopt all the communist party slogans is to deny their character, to narrow their possibilities of action, to hamper their growth, and seriously to undermine the value of democratic mass organizations. Basically, it is to confuse the vanguard with the masses; to deny the guiding role of the party under the pretext of affirming it.[12]

That was what Thorez's successive opponents had argued against him at times when the PCF was inconsistently trying to manipulate fronts and at the same time follow a 'sectarian' line. By the time Thorez conceded the point, the party had been shaken and the fronts had been emasculated by these crises. They were soon to be ruined, as instruments of Soviet foreign policy, by the eruption within them of a new sectarianism, that of Peking, which sought to use the Russian-made fronts for the defence of Chinese foreign policy. At that point, the local parties, which had never made gains from the fronts beyond the occasional use of them as recruiting grounds, and Moscow, which had changed its foreign policy to one that could not possibly be advantaged by sharing the fronts with Peking, were in agreement to let the fronts die. The World Peace Movement lost much of its importance as soon as the Soviet Union really wanted peace, which it knew was to be negotiated in Washington and not secured by 'peace campaigns'. The PCF, which had run those campaigns in the west, let the Peace Movement lapse to the humble status of just one out of forty-eight French organizations pleading for peace in Indochina, a cause in which the party was, in any event, lukewarm and outclassed by other Leftist political forces. Few of the fronts in Western Europe were actually disbanded; rather, they faded away like the Italian women's front, Unione delle donne italiane, which had boasted 1m. members in the 1950s but fell to less than 200,000 a decade later. Moreover, and this is an important fact about it and other PCI fronts, at that latter date its membership was concentrated, as to 70 per cent, in the Red Belt, that region of central Italy where the CP holds municipal and regional-government power and where an absolute majority of the population votes communist. The vestigial fronts of the PCI that survive in the Red Belt now serve quite another function, not that of supporting Soviet foreign policy or of extending PCI influence, but of social integration. For the first time, some of them have become, in limited regions, bona fide associations of sportsmen or housewives or peasants linked by a common attachment to communism, i.e. not fronts at all. As to the PCF, it has been said that by 1973 it had only one front left, the CGT.[13]

When the western parties resumed the policy of open collaboration with socialists and other left-of-centre parties it would have been possible for them to revive the fronts without involving themselves in the difficulties of the Stalinist era. However, the rise of new power centres in the CPs, which do not see the defence of Soviet foreign policy as the main function of the party, made that unlikely. The parties were still willing to work through any association, political or not, that might help recruit members or win voters but this would be an open, public activity aimed at promoting the local party's affairs, whereas the front was surreptitious activity aimed at defending

Soviet Russia. That point was made clear in a classic statement of the purpose of fronts ascribed to Georgi Dimitrov at a time when he was a Comintern official:

We must always keep it before our minds that someone who sympathizes with us is in general worth more than a dozen militant communists. A university professor who, without being a party member, fights for the interests of the Soviet Union is worth more than a hundred people with a party card ... The writer who, without being a party member, defends the Soviet Union, the trade union leader who stands outside our ranks and yet defends the international policy of the Soviet Union, are worth more than a thousand party members.[14]

One could not say more plainly that fronts exist for the defence of Soviet policy and not for the advancement of the local CP in the only way that could matter to it, that is by winning actual members. That communist leaders in Western Europe are in the 1970s more interested in the latter than in the task Dimitrov assigned the fronts will be shown later. What matters here is to establish that the fronts, for all the astronomical statistics about them produced by communists and anti-communists alike, never told us anything about the size of the communist phenomenon and even less about its gradual progression. The biggest of them were nine-day wonders connected with Soviet foreign policy and not with the spread of communism, which they probably impeded.

The Press

The first duty of revolutionaries, said Lenin, is to start a newspaper. In discharging this obligation, the West European communists provide a measure of their influence, or at least they would if declining circulations had not led them in recent years to conceal the facts. The enormous circulations of the postwar years have plummeted. Numerous communist papers have failed and others survive with difficulty, supported by subsidies from members, or from other activities, or (in Sweden and France) from local governments, or perhaps (in West Berlin and Austria) from foreign governments. Communist dailies are extant in seventeen countries, as is shown in the table of recent circulations. Granted that there could be no dailies in countries where the party is clandestine or in countries where it is a negligible sect, the only absence from the table is Norway. Norway had an official party daily, *Friheten*, which attained a circulation of 131,000 just after the war. In 1967 it was converted into a weekly with a circulation of 4,500.

Place of publication	Name	Est. circulation
Rome and Milan	*L'Unità*	350,000
Rome	*Paese sera*	90,000
Palermo	*L'Ora*	15,000
Paris	*L'Humanité*	105,000[1]
Marseilles	*La Marseillaise*	120,000[2]
Lille	*La Liberté*	98,000[2]
Limoges	*L'Echo du Centre*	62,000[2]
Helsinki	*Kansan Uutiset*	43,000
Düsseldorf	*Unsere Zeit*	40,000[3]
London	*Morning Star*	50,000
Luleå (Sweden)	*Norrskensflamman*	3,000
Vienna	*Volksstimme*	40,000
Nicosia	*Kharavyi*	15,000[2]
Amsterdam	*De Waarheid*	17,000
Copenhagen	*Land og Folk*	6,000
West Berlin	*Die Wahrheit*	12,000
Geneva	*Voix ouvrière*	8,000
Rejkjavik	*Thjodviljinn*	8,000
Luxembourg	*Zeitung vum Letzeburger Vollek*	2,000[1]
Brussels	*Drapeau rouge*	10,000
Lisbon	*Avante*	—
Athens	*Avghi*	—
Athens	*Rizospastis*	—

[1] Opposition estimate, *Unir*, no 90, 1974.
[2] As claimed to advertising agencies.
[3] Became daily only in Oct 1973. The figure is that claimed for the previous weekly edition.

All these figures represent sharp declines from the postwar years. In the 1950s the *Daily Worker* sold 125,000 copies; *Kansan Uutiset* sold 59,000; *Volksstimme* over 40,000; *De Waarheid* 25,000; *Land og Folk* 16,000; *Thjodviljinn* 12,000; and Stockholm had a communist daily with a circulation of 65,000, *Ny Dag*, in addition to two provincial communist dailies. *L'Unità* had a peak circulation of 488,000 in 1949. Despite the fact that communist or allied dailies disappeared in Milan, Rome, Bologna, Naples, and Florence, thus creating a gap that the central party paper might have filled, its circulation fell to 435,000 in 1953. It slumped to 367,000 in 1956 and has barely held steady since then. Nevertheless, the three extant communist dailies with their total of just under half a million copies constitute 8–10 per cent of the Italian daily press. In addition, the PCI publishes various weeklies, some of which attain notable circulations: *Noi Donne*, for women, prints 280,000 copies.

The PCF in the postwar years had two dailies in Paris and fifteen in the provinces. A generation later it had four, of which the three provincial papers were symbiotic on the Parisian organ, *L'Humanité*. '*L'Huma*' had already seen circulations of half a million in 1936 and attained a peak of almost 1m. in 1947. Its sales then fell steadily to under 200,000 in 1968, at which point the figure was no longer made public. Oppositional sources within the party estimated the circulation at 105,000 in 1974. At that level, the communist newspaper inevitably was experiencing the difficulties familiar to other French newspapers with a small circulation. Warnings that it might have to cease publication were given by the leadership. Whereas between 1948 and 1964, *L'Humanité* could afford to subsidize the fellow-travelling daily *Libération*, in the 1960s it was itself subsidized by the party's popular and less political *L'Humanité dimanche* (which appears on Wednesday, despite the name). When the sales of *L'Humanité dimanche* declined in turn, from half a million to 350,000, despite the fact that hawking it is one of the most popular chores of party membership, *L'Humanité*'s existence was in jeopardy. It was then that French government financial help became available to it and two other small Paris newspapers.

Apart from newspapers, the PCF publishes several theoretical weeklies and monthlies and—much more successful—periodicals aimed specifically at children, women, and farmers. This publishing group is completed by two book publishing companies, a news agency, commercial printing presses, and distribution services.[15]

In addition to these public organs, CPs have a peculiar internal press, the news-sheets put out by the cells and sections. Most of them are roneoed but some are printed. Statistics on this subject are fragmentary, particularly as to the regularity with which such publications appear. For the PCF it is claimed that 10m. copies of cell papers appear in a year, in addition to 15–18m. section papers. Less than half the cells in the party undertake to produce a news-sheet but the others do a large volume of paper work.

The decline in the number and the circulation of communist publications in Western Europe must be seen against the background of the difficulties, and the subsequent concentration, of the publishing industry in general and in particular of party-political newspapers as distinct from newspapers of information or entertainment. The decline in the popularity of the party-political newspaper, which has deprived several social-democratic parties of an official organ, has sorely hurt the CPs because theirs are the most party-political of all newspapers. That is, they are partisan, repetitive, dogmatic, full of jargon and ritual formulas, like any party-political paper only more so than most. Above all, they are the most given to censorship. When that entailed trying to ignore such notable events as Soviet armed intervention in Hungary and Czechoslovakia, or differences between Moscow and Peking, a shrinking of their audience was inevitable.

Whatever the causes, the decline of the communist press tells us something not only about the extensity of the communist phenomenon but also of its intensity. To read and sell the party paper are the prime duties of party members. More than that, party members are supposed not to read any other paper: 'One must be suspicious of those [members] who buy another paper instead of the communist daily'.[16] Studied ignorance of non-communist sources of information and a willingness to be satisfied with the censorship and allusiveness of the communist press (i.e. to practise 'esoteric communication') were the mark of the western communist in Stalinist times. That not one in two or three of present-day CP members takes the party paper, and that almost all of them supplement it with other publications and with radio-television, tells us as much about the decline in the intensity of the communist phenomenon as the fall in circulations tells us about its diminished extensity.

The Communist Electorate

The most precise measure of the communist phenomenon, because public and independent, is the electoral performance of the parties' candidates. The significance that voters attach to casting a ballot for communist candidates to national parliaments (the only sort of election in question here) might well vary greatly from place to place, from time to time, and even from person to person. However, as the adage of French republicanism has it (anticipating an axiom of psephology), 'On ne pèse pas les voix, on les compte'. That is to say, each vote counts for one, whatever its motivation. A study of communist voters' motivations (or rather: a quest for correlations between communist voting and certain objective conditions) will be left till later, until we have recorded the brute facts about communist electorates.

Since nine European nations are associated in the European Community, which has remote and ambiguous confederal objectives, there might be limited and speculative interest in adding up communist votes and communist representation in those countries. If one international parliament had been elected at the end of 1973 for West Germany, France, Britain, Italy, Holland, Belgium, Luxembourg, Denmark, and Eire, with each nation applying its current electoral law (and not, as those communists who favour direct election of a European parliament demand, with all the nations applying an identical proportional-representation electoral law), and if voters had behaved as they did in their last national elections, then the assembly they elected would have 276 communist members out of 2,987 delegates, or 9·2 per cent. If members sat together according to political affinity, the communist block would be one of the smallest in the house; indeed, only the extreme Right, with about fifty representatives, would be smaller. The conservative block would be somewhat bigger than the communist; the Christian Democrat and Centre blocks would each be more than twice as big; and the social-democratic contingent would be five times as numerous. This imaginary parliament would have been elected by 148m. valid votes, of which 15·2m., or 10·3 per cent, would have been cast for communist candidates.

Returning from that hypothesis to the performance of communist candidates in national elections, the table shows the most recent results.

Country	Date of election	Communist votes	% of vote	Seats won	Out of
Cyprus	July 1970	79,280	39·7	9	35
Italy	May 1972	9,085,927	27·2	179	630
France[1]	Mar 1973	5,156,619	21·2	73	490
Finland[2]	Jan 1972	438,387	17·1	37	200
Iceland[3]	June 1974	20,922	18·1	11	60
Luxembourg	Dec 1968	402,610	15·5	6	56
Greece[4]	Nov 1974	464,331	9·4	8	300
Sweden	Sept 1973	274,929	5·3	19	350
Holland	Nov 1972	329,973	4·5	7	150
Denmark	Dec 1973	110,809	3·6	6	179
Belgium	Mar 1974	169,668	3·2	4	212
Switzerland	Oct 1971	50,831	2·7	5	200
West Berlin	Mar 1971	33,930	2·3	0	11
Austria	Oct 1971	62,000	1·3	0	183

Norway[5]	Sept 1969	22,494	1	0	150
West Germany	Nov 1972	114,000	0·3	0	496
Britain	Mar 1974	32,741	0·1	0	635
Eire	Feb 1973	466	0·04	0	144

[1] Votes in first round; seats are allocated after second round.
[2] Results of the SKDL (Finnish People's Democratic League) electoral coalition.
[3] Results of the People's Alliance.
[4] Results of the communist 'united Left'.
[5] In Sept 1973 the NKP was part of the Socialist Electoral Alliance, which got 242,000 votes (11·2 per cent) and won 16 seats, of which one went to a communist.

No obvious pattern emerges from those figures, nothing that would dispense with investigation into the history of each individual country. Even when one takes the evolution over recent years of the communist vote as a percentage of votes cast, no one pattern emerges. In some countries the communist vote has increased, in others it has declined, in others it is steady. One needs to group these countries into five distinct categories to arrive at the most limited generalizations.

1. One country where the CP, though legal, does not fight elections.

CYPRUS. The Cypriot CP, called AKEL since 1941, runs in elections in agreement with the governing party, the Patriotic Front. Although it received 42 per cent of the votes of the Greek electorate in 1960, and about 40 per cent a decade later, it was allocated only five seats out of thirty-five in the earlier year and nine in the later. If in 1970 it had contested all seats, it could have been the biggest group in the Cypriot parliament, but its delicate position as an entirely Greek party in an ethnically divided nation, and as pro-Soviet at a time when Moscow opposes *enosis* with Greece, leads AKEL to hold fire.

2. Countries where the communist share of the vote is so small that almost any freak candidate might do as well, so that variations are difficult to interpret.

BRITAIN. The CPGB has had no representative in the Commons since 1950. Its small part of the vote has seemed to fluctuate in accordance with public feeling about Soviet foreign policy; e.g. between the elections of 1966 and 1970 came the invasion of Czechoslovakia.

	CPGB votes	%	MPs	Out of
July 1945	102,780	0·4	2	640
Feb 1950	91,815	0·3	–	625
Oct 1951	26,640	0·08	–	625
May 1955	33,144	0·1	–	630
Oct 1959	30,896	0·1	–	630
Oct 1964	45,086	0·2	–	630
Nov 1966	62,112	0·2	–	630
June 1970	38,431	0·1	–	630
Mar 1974	32,741	0·1	–	635

The failure was general (in 1964 all thirty-six communist candidates lost their deposit) and it was progressive: the votes won in 1970 were fewer than in 1922, when the CPGB got 52,000.

SWITZERLAND. On the contrary, in Switzerland, where public feeling about Soviet foreign policy would be roughly what it was in Britain, the PST has won more voters, but without increasing its small percentage of the valid votes.

	PST votes	%	Deputies (out of 200)
Oct 1947	49,353	5·1	7
Oct 1951	25,659	2·7	5
Oct 1955	25,060	2·6	4
Oct 1959	26,346	2·7	3
Oct 1963	21,088	2·2	4
Oct 1967	23,208	2·9	5
Oct 1971	50,831	2·7	5

BELGIUM. Although the CPB's electorate is well below what it was in the years immediately after the war, it has not declined in a decade.

	CPB votes	%	Deputies (out of 212)
Mar 1961	164,000	3·1	5
May 1965	236,333	4·6	6
Mar 1968	170,627	3·3	5
Nov 1971	164,195	3·1	5
Mar 1974	169,668	3·2	4

WEST BERLIN. In the all-Berlin elections of October 1946, the local CP won 285,475 votes in West Berlin, or 13·7 per cent of the western electorate. It boycotted the elections in the western sectors in December 1948 and December 1950, and although it has taken part in subsequent elections it has never won representation in the Senate of West Berlin.

	SEW votes	%
Dec 1954	41,375	2·7
Dec 1958	31,572	1·9
Feb 1963	20,929	1·4
Mar 1967	29,925	2
Mar 1971	33,930	2·3

3. Countries where the communist vote, though small, shows a distinct rising trend.

HOLLAND. The CPN, a small organization that is treated as a political pariah and which refuses to co-operate with other CPs, has made what seem to be significant electoral gains.

	CPN votes	%	Deputies (out of 150)
Mar 1959	144,542	2·4	3
May 1963	173,457	2·8	4
Feb 1967	248,000	3·6	5
Apr 1971	246,299	3·9	6
Nov 1972	329,973	4·5	7

LUXEMBOURG. The persistent advance of the small CPL has made it one of the half-dozen CPs that can win over 15 per cent of the votes at a national election. Indeed, in some municipalities in industrial towns the CPL has won as much as 28 per cent of the votes.

	CPL votes	%	Deputies (out of 56)
Jan 1959	220,425	9·1	3
June 1964	330,909	12·5	5
Dec 1968	402,610	15·5	6

DENMARK. After winning one-eighth of the votes in the first election after the liberation, the DanKP lost influence until 1966, but then began to recover.

	DanKP votes	%	Deputies	Out of
Oct 1945	255,236	12·5	18	149
Oct 1947	141,094	6·8	9	150
Sept 1950	94,523	4·6	7	151
Apr 1953	98,940	4·8	7	151
Sept 1953	93,824	4·3	8	179
May 1957	72,315	3·1	6	179
Nov 1960	27,298	1·1	–	
Sept 1964	32,390	1·3	–	
Nov 1966	21,536	0·8	–	
Jan 1968	29,706	1	–	
Sept 1971	39,564	1·4	–	
Dec 1973	110,809	3·6	6	179

4. Countries where the communist vote, once significant, has declined sharply.

WEST GERMANY. As recently as 1949 the KPD could win 1,362,000 votes (5·75 per cent) in a West German election, entitling it to fifteen seats in Bonn. In some regional elections in the late 1940s the KPD won over 10 per cent. By the Bundestag elections of 1955, its share had fallen to 2·2 per cent, with 606,000 votes, and it lost the right of representation in Bonn even before it was outlawed as unconstitutional. Re-emerging from clandestinity, the communists won 197,000 votes, or 0·6 per cent in the Bundestag elections of September 1969. This fell to 150,000, or 0·3 per cent, when the DKP contested the elections of November 1972 in its own name, admittedly while recommending that voters support the Social Democrats in certain sectors.

AUSTRIA. The KPO, like the KPD, entered the 1950s representing more of an electoral force than any but the top half-dozen CPs today, but it declined thereafter. It has had no deputies since 1969, when its four representatives were defeated.

	KPO votes	%
Nov 1962	135,482	3
Feb 1966	19,000	0·4
Mar 1970	47,000	1
Oct 1971	62,000	1·3

NORWAY. From a postwar peak of some importance, the NKP was in constant electoral decline until in 1973 it contested an election inside an alliance, the SV (socialist electoral federation), which was surprisingly successful.

	NKP votes	%	Deputies (out of 150)
Oct 1945	176,535	11·8	11
Oct 1949	102,722	5·8	–
Oct 1953	90,422	5·1	3
Oct 1957	60,060	3·3	1
Sept 1961	53,678	2·9	–
Sept 1965	27,996	1·4	–
Sept 1969	21,517	1	–

In September 1973 the SV won 242,000 votes, or 11·2 per cent, and sixteen seats, in a House of 155, of which one went to the president of the NKP.

SWEDEN. In Sweden, the stabilization of the communist electorate after a long decline appeared earlier than elsewhere.

	SvKP/Vpk votes	%	Deputies	Out of
Sept 1944	318,466	10·5	15	230
Sept 1948	244,826	6·3	8	230
Sept 1952	164,194	4·3	5	230
Sept 1956	194,016	5	6	231
June 1958	129,319	3·4	5	231
Sept 1960	190,560	4·5	5	232
Sept 1964	221,746	5·2	8	233
Sept 1968	145,172	3	3	233
Sept 1970	236,653	4·8	17	350
Sept 1973	274,929	5·3	19	350

5. Countries where CPs are consistently one of the largest electoral forces, if not the largest.

ICELAND. Whether alone, as from 1946 to 1956, or in the People's Alliance, the Icelandic communists have held their ground despite the pro–Peking defections of the 1960s.

	SUP/AB votes	%	Deputies	Out of
June 1946	13,049	19·5	10	52
Oct 1949	14,077	19·5	9	52
June 1953	12,422	16·1	7	52

	SUP/AB votes	%	Deputies	Out of
June 1956	15,859	19·5	8	52
June 1959	12,929	15·3	7	52
Oct 1959	13,621	16	10	60
June 1963	14,274	16	9	60
June 1967	13,402	13·9	10	60
June 1971	18,055	17·1	10	60
June 1974	20,922	18·1	11	60

FINLAND. The Communist-run SKDL electoral machine held a quarter to a fifth of the Finnish electorate until the setback of 1970.

	SKP votes	%	Deputies (out of 200)
Mar 1945	398,618	23·5	49
July 1948	375,820	20	38
July 1951	391,362	21·5	43
Mar 1954	433,528	21·6	43
July 1958	450,506	23·2	50
Feb 1962	507,124	22	47
Mar 1966	502,713	21·2	41
Mar 1970	420,894	16·6	36
Mar 1972	438,387	17	37

FRANCE. The PCF contested only four legislative elections in the Third Republic, winning its best percentage, 15·3, in 1936. Yet it emerged from the war as France's biggest political party, claiming the suffrages of over a quarter of the votes.

	PCF votes	%	Deputies	Out of
Oct 1945	5,005,336	26	161	586
June 1946	5,199,111	26·1	153	586
Nov 1946	5,489,288	28·6	169	621
June 1951	4,910,547	25·6	99	627
Jan 1956	5,532,631	25·7	144	596
Nov 1958	3,882,204	18·9	10	465
Nov 1962	3,992,431	21·7	41	485
Mar 1967	5,039,032	22·5	73	485
June 1968	4,435,357	20	34	485
Mar 1973	5,026,417	21·2	73	490

ITALY. The PCI took part in only one election before fascism, that of 1921, when it polled 4·6 per cent of the valid vote. It came out of fascism with the support of one-fifth of the electorate and has progressed ever since.[17]

	PCI vote	%	Deputies	Out of
June 1946	4,356,686	19	104	556
June 1953	6,120,809	22·6	143	590
May 1958	6,704,454	22·7	140	596
Apr 1963	7,763,854	25·3	166	630
May 1968	8,557,404	26·9	177	630
May 1972	9,085,927	27·2	179	630

How the Communist Electorate Varies

Because of western communism's ideological commitment to the Soviet example, and because of its evident organizational connections with the international communist movement, it has often been thought that its electoral audience would be determined by western feeling about that example and that movement. When West Europeans were well disposed towards the Soviet Union or full of admiration for the Red Army, communist candidates would do well at elections, but when an election supervened on the morrow of some unpopular Soviet action, some display of *Panzerkommunismus* or tank-communism, then communist candidates would do poorly. Whatever its foundation in fact, that expectation was cultivated precisely during West European election campaigns—by the opponents of the communists, who saw an advantage in identifying the communists with unpopular Soviet policies: 'Ils ne sont ni à gauche ni à droite, ils sont à l'est!' exclaimed Guy Mollet. Since many West European elections have been fought with little other ideological content than anti-communism, if these arguments were electorally effective, one would expect to see the history of world communism reflected in the electoral returns. The statistics do not show that.

Communism indeed found its first mass electorate in Western Europe in the wake of the victories of the Red Army, after several years of alliance between western democrats and Soviet communists, at a time when inaccurate ideas about the nature of Soviet society were popular (were in fact officially propagated) in the west. Since then, it is easy to find cases where that electorate has been sharply reduced by revulsion against some Soviet action. A striking case is the Swedish election of September 1968, held within weeks of the invasion of Czechoslovakia by the Warsaw Pact nations. In desperate efforts to dissociate itself from that action, the VPK was the first party in Sweden to denounce the invasion and it did so more vehemently than any other CP in the west. Its president, C. H. Hermansson, stigmatized the invasion as 'shameful' and he urged the Swedish government to recall its ambassador to Moscow, in protest. He compared Soviet actions with those of the United States in Vietnam, which were particularly obnoxious to Swedish opinion at the time. The governments that had sent armies to Czechoslovakia replied by calling Hermansson an 'intemperate squealer', a 'petty bourgeois', and the like. Nevertheless, the Swedish communist electorate shrank by a third, a circumstance that had a decisive and unexpected effect on the election results.

Another case of that sort concerns the West Berlin communists. When elections were held in the city in December 1958, weeks after Khrushchev's Berlin ultimatum of November, the SEW vote contracted by a quarter. In February 1963, when the first elections were held since the building of the Berlin Wall, the SEW vote hit a low point, scoring less than half the votes it had won eight years before.

Still, even in those striking cases, the tables show that within a short space of time the Swedish and West Berlin communists had made an excellent electoral recovery. And in general, more West Europeans voted communist in the years 1972–3 after a series of Soviet actions that were roundly condemned in the west, than in 1945–6, in the days of diplomatic friendship. Communists won more votes in Austria, Denmark, Switzerland, Italy, France, Sweden, Iceland, Luxembourg, and West Berlin after the invasion of Czechoslovakia than before. The steady progress of the PCI vote in election after election lends no colour to the view that Italians are more or less inclined to vote communist depending on their feelings about the Soviet Union. Nor was the impressive stability of the Finnish communist electorate from 1945 to 1966 evidence for that. In France, where popular reaction to the Soviet suppression of the Budapest insurrection in 1956 was of an extreme violence, the impact on the communist electorate was slight and brief. Public opinion polls showed a certain hesitation among communist voters some weeks after those events but within four months there was no trace of them. The partial and regional elections of 1957 proved that 'the PCF does not seem to have suffered much from its tribulations'.[18]

More than that, there are cases where a communist electorate seems to thrive on such 'tribulations'. After the invasion of Czechoslovakia in 1968, one CP that positively approved of that operation, the Luxembourg party, had to face elections shortly afterwards. It increased its vote by about a quarter and, with 15·5 per cent of the votes cast, became a major political force in the Grand Duchy. Just to show that this was no accident, it went on to score significant gains in municipal elections throughout 1969.[19] Both the local party and Moscow were quick to contrast the electoral failure of the Swedish communists, who condemned the invasion, with the success of the Luxembourgeois communists, who had staunchly supported it. That fact was thought to weaken the case of western communist leaders who claimed that, whatever their true feelings, they were obliged to denounce the invasion in order to protect their electoral position.

This apparent insensibility of West European communist electorates does not show that Soviet actions have no impact on western communism, but we are looking for it in the wrong place when we look first to the electoral returns. Paradoxically, it is the members of CPs, not their voters, who react with dismay and revulsion when Soviet actions are incompatible with western standards of political behaviour. It is the size of the party membership, and its unity, that are sorely affected, but not its ability to win votes from electors who are, after all, less interested in foreign affairs, including the affairs of the communist world, than are intellectuals and party activists. In relation to events in the world communist movement, it is CPs that are sensitive and unstable, whereas communist electorates arc relatively steady. Such things as de-Stalinization, the secret report of Khrushchev, the insurrections of East Germany, Poland, and Hungary, and the invasion of Czechoslovakia have decimated and split western parties, whereas they have often left voters indifferent. Sometimes in such cases the anti-Soviet opposition within a party has sought a prompt electoral test—and has been wiped out. It is only if the split goes so far as to divide the party into warring factions that it can, after a certain delay, have a harmful effect on the communist vote, as the following examples show.

Whereas the Khrushchev report struck a communist intellectual like 'an electric shock . . . I was exalted, crazed, and my thoughts darted in three directions: anger, hope, and a beginning of self-critical reflection',[20] the majority of French communist voters dismissed the debates as a remote matter of history and theory. By the time that the Hungarian insurrection, shortly afterwards, took its toll of PCF membership, the party had lost more than half its membership in ten years—and yet it commanded an undiminished part of the electorate. The troubles of 1956 started an internal opposition to the PCF leadership, which persisted for years but without ever being able to make an electoral impact. In contrast, the Danish party was rent by the controversy over Hungary and de-Stalinization, and the division worsened throughout 1957 until it came to a head in 1958 with the expulsion from the party of its leader, Aksel Larsen—who took most of the membership with him. It was only then that the DanKP failed electorally, becoming a rump organization without parliamentary representation. The Dutch party had the same experience. Despite the extreme violence of the Dutch reaction to the Hungarian repression (the riots in Amsterdam have been called, somewhat fulsomely, 'the anti-communist Terror'), the CPN did well in the next elections, but when it was rent in 1958 by a struggle between Paul de Groot and the 'Revisionists', its electoral support fell by almost half.

The Hungary fury had cost the party many members and readers [of *De Waarheid*] but only had little impact on its electoral following; the expulsion of the 'Rightists' had the reverse effect: little loss of members or readers, but a loss of almost half the voters. A party that carried a heavy foreign liability was, for many Left voters, apparently less unattractive than a party rent by discord.[21]

Similarly with the western repercussions of the events of August 1968. Voters' reactions were as we have seen ambiguous, but the dispute over Prague split the Spanish CP in two; it produced a revolt of Stalinists in the PCF (including the resignation from the polit-buro of Jeannette Vermeersch, widow of Maurice Thorez and long the party's queen-mother); it exacerbated and brought to a head the revolt within the PCI around *Il Manifesto*. Yet none of that had any electoral echo. When the supporters of *Il Manifesto* went to the polls in 1972, they were annihilated. It was only the Austrian party, which had been gravely split to the point of numerous expulsions and resignations from the central committee, that failed at an electoral test, when it lost half its electorate and its last representatives in the Vienna city council.

The point is not that European communist electorates are eternally stable, as was imagined by some despairing opponents in the 1950s. (They may well be more stable than any *other* part of the electorate in countries like France and Finland, however.) The point, rather, is that they are less affected by the sort of outside events we have been discussing than are the parties themselves. The electorates do change, for all that, and they can change in spectacular ways after seeming for years to be immutable. It is just that they have their own laws of change, which are not those of the CPs. This is another way of saying, what is familiar, that many people who vote communist are not communists and thus will be indifferent to some things that fascinate communists, whereas they will, unexpectedly, join in general, non-communist movements that might well be condemned by party members.

The Icelandic party, though shaken internally by the Sino-Soviet quarrel and by the invasion of Czechoslovakia (which it condemned), managed to limit its electoral losses in 1967. Thereafter it benefited from the wave of anti-western nationalism that swept Iceland during the 'cod war'. Though it took an isolationist stance within the international communist movement, refusing to recognize the pre-eminence of either Moscow or Peking and maintaining friendly relations only with the Rumanian and other Nordic CPs, the Icelandic party was electorally identified with the most determined opposition to the capitalist West European countries that contested Iceland's extension of her fishing rights. So, along with its 'left-liberal' dissidents, it won over a quarter of the votes and one-quarter of the seats at the 1971 elections. It thereupon joined a government coalition, becoming the only CP in Western Europe to hold office. Significantly, its representatives took the Fishing and Industry Ministry, as well as the Health and Social Security portfolio. Thus a CP shaken by disputes that concerned communists, but not most voters, won electoral victory and public office because of its stand on a matter that had nothing to do with communism but which keenly interested the electorate.[22]

More commonly, communists stand to suffer from such movements of opinion, as the PCF did from the Gaullist tidal wave of 1958. There had been a warning of this disaster in 1951, when the votes lost by the communists went in part to the Rassemblement du Peuple français, the Gaullist movement of the day. The warning was ignored, and the party persisted in ultra-Stalinist policies that disturbed many members but which were compatible with an electoral recovery, once the Gaullist RPF lost ground. There is evidence in public opinion polls in early 1958, long before the return of de Gaulle, that this recovery was based on a misunderstanding, that Frenchmen were voting communist for reasons that were not reflected in the policies the party was proposing.[23] That became clear in June, after de Gaulle's return, when one-third of the electorate that had been voting communist for ten years deserted the PCF candidates. An apparently stable electorate that had been regarded as a foreign body in French national opinion for a decade, and a calcified one at that, suddenly melted before a movement of opinion that affected it in common with other parts of the electorate. (For Gaullism, it must be recalled, hurt not only the communists but all the other parties of the Fourth Republic.) Our table, which shows only legislative elections, does not bring it out that this electoral loss was abundantly confirmed in subsequent referendums in the Fifth Republic, when the CP continued to be disavowed by its electorate. As a percentage of voters on the rolls (our tables refer to percentages of votes cast), the PCF electorate was reduced to about the size it had had in 1936, so that all the acquisitions of the Resistance and the Liberation were lost. Thereafter, the party made an electoral recovery but the next wave of French public opinion, in May and June 1968, for which the PCF was once again no better prepared than other parties, demonstrated the fragility of that recovery, for the party lost 12 per cent of its electorate. Thus it was twice proven that a party that was supposed, in political polemic and in some more serious study, to be at the mercy of the fortunes of world communism could survive, electorally, communist crises that shook its own foundations, and yet could be seriously affected by local issues that impinged on all local parties. Specifically, the PCF lost large parts of its electorate not because Thorez was a Stalinist in the age of de-Stalinization or because it apologized for Soviet *Panzerkommunismus*, but because it had no policy to deal with the constitutional problems of the Fourth Republic, or with the difficulties of decolonization, or (in 1968) with the destabilizing social consequences of rapid economic progress. In that, it closely resembled other French parties. The 'foreign body' was participating in, was integrated into, national political life more than it knew.

The case is not unique. Comparable losses at the polls were sustained by the Finnish party in 1970, on top of smaller losses that should have served as warnings in 1962 and 1966. Here again, the cause was not the party's relations with the Soviet world, though these are necessarily very close in Finland's case—close enough to have led to serious division within the SKP from 1969. The cause, rather, was that the Finnish communists were unable to cope—and seeing that they participated in a governing coalition from 1966 to 1971, it was their direct responsibility to cope—with the social consequences of rapid economic advance. That part of their electorate that had always been a 'protest vote' from people indifferent to, perhaps even ignorant of, the problems of the communist world deserted communist candidates for a new Poujadist movement that split off from the peasant party. The main beneficiary of the setback of the Finnish communists in 1970 was the Country People's Party led by Veikko Vennamo, a demagogic radical movement that overnight claimed 10 per cent of the electorate. The Finnish communist party which, within its SKDL electoral machine, had held 20–23 per cent of the electorate since the war was cut back to 16–17 per cent, thanks to social and economic developments at home in which it was participating more than it knew—while it spent time on internecine disputes about the rights and wrongs of Soviet policies.

To say, then, that CP members find it harder to take the zigzags of party policy than do communist voters is to say that the electorate is ideologically indifferent, or less sensitive than the party, while leaving open the question of changes in that electorate due to other political, social, and economic factors. But if the electorate is less responsive to ideology, it is worth noticing that to a certain extent the party ideology is responsive to electoral success and failure. This is commonly, and with plausible reasons, denied. To *what* extent CPs adjust their policies to the electoral returns, i.e. to what extent they are, after all, parties like other democratic parties, is a question that requires prior examination of the power centres inside CPs and of the constraints under which policy is formulated; those problems are studied below. Already it must be pointed out that, though CPs do not trim their sails to the electoral wind to anything like the extent of other western parties—say, the US Republicans or the West German Social Democrats—they do adjust their aim. They would have to, if only for the reason that successful elections lead to an increase in enrolment in the party; and the converse: unsuccessful elections lead to a loss of membership. A party that has to digest a massive inflow of new members is liable to adapt its policies, whatever the ideological constraints. And a leader who suffers electoral defeat must face increased ideological opposition within the party. There is good reason to think that the PCF, after its electoral setbacks at the hands of Gaullism, decided to accept the de-Stalinization it had been refusing since 1956 because the contrast between its electoral failures and the successes of the de-Stalinized Italian party became too glaring. Responsiveness to electoral performance is increasingly a feature of West European communism, as will be shown later, even if the Leninist structure of the parties sets limits to that responsiveness.

The process has gone far enough—it is a process known as integration or participation—for the size of the electoral aspect of the communist phenomenon no longer to be seen as primarily determined by the relations of western communism with the international movement.

Notes

1 Haakon Lie, *Hvem kan vi stole på? En dokumentasjon om Norges Kommunistiske Parti under den tysk-russiske alliansen* (Oslo, 1974).

2 *Le Monde* (hereafter *LM*), 18 May 1974.

3 Jacques Fauvet, *Histoire du Parti communiste français*, ii (Paris, 1965), pp. 215–16.

4 Ibid.

5 The PCE also has foresworn Leninism and aspires to become a mass party (*VIII Congreso del Partido comunista de España* (Bucharest, 1972), p. 310.

6 Witold S. Sworakowski, *The Communist International and its front organizations* (Stanford, 1965) is a research guide to the extensive literature on the subject. Also James D. Atkinson, *The politics of struggle: the communist front and political warfare* (Chicago, 1966).

7 A regular survey appears in the *Yearbook on international communist affairs*, published by the Hoover Institution, Stanford. For a recent list of such organizations in France, *Est et Ouest*, no 484, pp. 5–6.

8 Babette Gross, *Frankreichs Weg zum Kommunismus* (Zurich, 1971), pp. 85–6.

9 Atkinson, p. 170.

10 *Inprecor*, no 28, p. 429. Italics added.

11 Gabriel A. Almond, *The appeals of communism* (Princeton, 1954), p. 170.

12 Speech at the Moscow Conference of 81 Parties, November 1960 (Proceedings, Moscow & Paris, 1961).

13 André Laurens & Thierry Pfister, *Les Nouveaux communistes* (Paris, 1973), pp. 170–3.

14 Cited from a PCI training manual in H. Bärwald & H. Scheffler, *Partisanen ohne Gewehr* (Cologne, 1967), p. 23.

15 On the PCF press, André Barjonet, *Le Parti communiste français* (Paris, 1969), pp. 103–4 & 119–32.

16 The remark is attributed to Georges Cogniot at a central committee meeting of the PCF by Charles Tillon, *Un Procès de Moscou à Paris* (Paris, 1971), p. 96.

17 The table omits the 1948 election which the PCI fought in a cartel with the socialists, called the Popular Democratic Front, which won 31 per cent of the votes.

18 Fauvet, p. 298.

19 Heinz Timmermann, *Die nichtregierenden kommunistischen Parteien Europas*, Berichte des Bundesinstituts für ostwissenschaftliche und internationale Studien (hereafter Berichte), no 28, 1972, p. 15.

20 Edgar Morin, *Autocritique* (Paris, 1970), p. 190.

21 A. A. de Jonge, *Het Communisme in Nederland* (The Hague, 1972), p. 136.

22 Krister Wahlbäck, 'Politik på Island', in Ingemar Lindblad et al, *Politik i Norden* (Stockholm, 1972).

23 Jean Ranger, 'L'Evolution du vote communiste en France depuis 1945', in F. Bon et al, *Le Communisme en France* (Paris, 1969), pp. 235–6.

2 Who are the communists?

Before seeing who the communists are, and who votes communist, one must note that one never steps into the same CP twice. From the 1920s the French party was known as 'le parti passoire', the sieve party, meaning that it was constantly turning over its membership, losing new recruits shortly after making them. The phenomenon was called 'fluctuation' and was later seen in all the CPs. Efforts to measure it have been common, including unsuccessful attempts to prove that some major parties were stabilizing their membership by overcoming fluctuation. The chronic instability of West European CPs is important because if the people that constitute their membership this year are not the same people as made up their membership two years ago, and even less four years ago, then this shows that communism is a phase through which a minority of Leftists pass. It is not a party in which many Europeans can make a spiritual home. In that, it contrasts with some other political parties and notably the party from which communism sprang, West European socialism. The socialist parties were stable formations; entry into them was thought to be a life-choice; they based promotion on seniority; they constituted steady markets for socialist insurance schemes, friendly societies, and similar businesses. The CPs are very different.

It is not possible to specify the precise turnover in CP memberships since most parties do not publish exact membership figures, let alone break them down by length of membership. It is known, however, that turnover is high in the clandestine parties, as it is in all illegal political activities. Fairly accurate guesses about the rate of turnover in major parties that vouchsafe some information on membership are possible. For example, the PCF announced that it dispatched 454,005 membership cards in 1968 (though only half might have been actually taken up and paid for) and it dispatched 454,640 cards in 1972. The gain in membership in those four years was therefore about zero. Yet the party had announced making 44,000 new recruits in 1969, 45,000 in 1970, 30,000 in 1971, and 48,000 in 1972—a total of 167,000. For the 167,000 that joined, an equal number quit in four years. If the current membership were indeed

340,000 (see above), then about 50 per cent of it had been turned over in four years. (Mortality would be a negligible factor in a young party in contemporary France.) If, as is more likely, the actual membership is around 250,000, then 66 per cent of it had been turned over ('fluctuated') in four years. That is an extraordinary degree of instability for a political party.

Taking a longer period of the PCF's history, and thereby ironing out whatever effect the excitements of 1968 might have had on the period just studied, it appears from PCF statistics that in the fourteen years 1959-72 the party recruited over 535,000 new members but added only 25,000 to its total membership. Thus it was taking an annual draft of over 38,200 new members to keep up party strength, so great were the annual defections. That intake is equal to 11 per cent or 17 per cent of membership, depending on how it is estimated.

It could be, mathematically, that the people defecting each year were those who joined last year (or in the same year, a few weeks or months before). A party that immediately disappointed or repelled so large a part of its recruits would have little cause to boast of its growing audience as the PCF does, but at least it could claim to be stabilizing its membership and reducing fluctuation: some 80-90 per cent of its membership would not be turning over but would be spending long periods in the party. But in that event, the average age of the party would rise. Precisely that has happened to the CPs of Sweden, Norway, Austria, and West Berlin, which are all old parties. They have resolved the problem of fluctuation—at the same time as they ceased to be vital political forces. However, this is not true of the PCF, because it announces that its average age of membership was the same in 1973 as it had been in 1954,[1] adding that it is the youngest party in France. If fluctuation is high (50-66 per cent of members leave within four years) and the average age remains low, it follows that the majority of the party is recently recruited and soon to defect. There may well be, in addition, a minority that stays in the party for a long period without wastage.

The causes of fluctuation are various. Police repression, and victimization or discrimination at the place of work, have been adduced as reasons why new members, once they identified themselves as communists by undertaking the tasks required of them, might find it dangerous or unpleasant to continue. That would be true of the clandestine parties, especially in Spain and formerly Greece where the police regularly disrupt communist organizations.

A more general cause would be that, even when the tasks of a communist are not illegal or dangerous, they can be exacting. An active cell might require its members to sacrifice several evenings a week after work, as well as Sunday morning, to meetings, recruiting calls, fund-raising, and newspaper hawking. A working person who joined the party because his conditions of work were already so tiring as to make him feel exploited, or a student or intellectual who joined mainly in order to hold 'the card', would find these labours beyond him and would let his membership lapse while retaining a sympathy for communism that could express itself, less energetically, in votes and subscriptions. Yet it happens also, and perhaps just as frequently, that what is repelling in the labours required of a communist is not their burdensomeness but their futility. A recruit who joined the party so as to participate in 'world revolution' would soon discover that nagging other members into paying for monthly stamps on their card, selling a newspaper that few of them wanted to read, or taking part in cell discussions that always ended in endorsing a resolution handed down from higher echelons of the party, constituted activities well short of 'revolution'. A member who joined in the hope of advancing the cause of proletarian self-government, of workers' control of society, would also soon learn that he had come in at the bottom of a fairly rigid and centralized bureaucratic organization, of which the leadership was engrossed in efforts to win power in the state by familiar electoral methods, plus some lobbying for Soviet foreign policy. Such members would be likely to defect after a year or two.

Thus, although fluctuation in some parties may be aggravated by the fact that the party is recruiting heavily among transitional groups (i.e. among the young, students, new immigrants, the unemployed, or workers in trades with a high labour turnover like building, none of whom stay those things for long), the basic and most general cause is that the party is disappointing the expectations of new members. Since it awakens those expectations itself—with some help from bourgeois or fascist governments that use the communist bogeyman in their political propaganda—the cause of fluctuation, then, is the discrepancy between the CPs' revolutionary oratory and their conservative practice or political inefficacy (which are the same thing, for the revolutionary).

Fluctuation has consequences that mark off the communist from other parties. In all West European countries ex-communists are far more numerous than communists. Those of them who quit or let their membership lapse out of lassitude may go to swell the communist electorate. So, for all that fluctuation might seem to be a disadvantage for the party, it is constantly replenishing a large pool of communist sympathy, votes, and financial help (students and professional people sometimes contribute heavily, out of guilt for their reluctance to work within the party). At the same time, the disappointment of expectations also breeds the characteristic phenomenon of ex-communist anti-communism, one of the most virulent forms of political antipathy known in western society. Those who see communism as 'the god that failed', and who were capable of conceiving a *political* god in the first instance, are apt to be singularly unsympathetic critics. They are familiar in the democracies but no less in Spain or Greece. In the latter country, one of the organizers of the persecution of the communists on behalf of the regime of the colonels was an ex-communist.

Another consequence of fluctuation is that it facilitates, though it does not cause, those abrupt changes of policy at which CPs used to be adept. It was one of Lenin's criteria for a bolshevik party that it should be capable of such sudden tactical adjustments. A party that is constantly turning over its membership at a faster rate than other parties will have less 'memory'. Its members will consent to do, say, and believe the contrary of what was being said, done, and believed in the party a short time before, because they are not the same members. Indeed, the earlier members may have quit *because* of the change of line, and the new may have joined for the same reason. That leaves intact the question of why and how the leadership, which is substantially constant, changed policy but it suggests how that leadership has at its disposal a following for successive and conflicting policies.

These remarks have less force in the 1970s than in the first fifty years of western communism, for the parties today practise fewer zigzags than previously. Thus they require less versatility of their members. Nevertheless, because fluctuation remains a constant feature of CPs, it is important for the student of the question— exactly because the student approaches it with the *history* of communism in mind—to remember that most communists know little or nothing of that history. They are young and freshly recruited (and soon to defect). By the end of the 1950s most West European communists were hearing little or nothing in their party about Stalin. By early in the 1960s they were learning nothing of the Khrushchev report (especially inside the French party, which has never published it or acknowledged its authenticity.) By 1968 most of them had been told nothing about Hungary and thus could be surprised by Czecho-slovakia; and in France they knew nothing of any regime but de Gaulle's. More generally and more importantly, by 1973 most western communists had joined the party during its (fairly recent) phase of collaboration with the social democrats. They have joined a party that in their experience seldom if ever used expressions such as 'revolution' or 'dictatorship of the proletariat' but which practised, as far as they had seen, an 'electoralism' not markedly different from other western parties. The point is relevant to many disagreements about the significance of communist policies. Hostile critics, or simply students well familiar with the party's history, are apt to argue that it 'really' is still what it always was, a revolutionary party, whereas more sympathetic observers, or simply students well familiar with its present constitution, reply that it 'really' is what its recently recruited members can be brought to do—which does not include revolution.

Regions

A first approximation to seeing who the communists are is to see where they are. In some European countries, they are recruited from sharply delimited regions or communities. Rather than dismiss such cases as oddities, one might look at them more closely, to see whether they show something about the various ways of being communist, something that is less obvious in countries where recruitment is apparently not localized. In Cyprus the CP recruits only among the Greek community. AKEL has no Turkish members, and the Turkish Cypriots have no CP of their own. In Switzerland 71 per cent of communist votes (and a comparable proportion of party member-ship), as well as all five communist members of the National Council, come from the French-speaking cantons although these contain only 20 per cent of the Swiss population. The German-speaking cantons, with over 70 per cent of the population, provide only 25 per cent of the communists; Ticino and the Grisons, which give 4 per cent of communist votes, are also under-represented in the party. The minority of German-speaking Swiss communists comes from the two large industrial conurbations, Zurich and Basle. It is in Geneva that the communists constitute a substantial political force. Belgium is a similar case. Belgian communists are French-speaking Walloons as to 80 per cent, and all the party's deputies are Walloons. The Walloon communists are concentrated in the old industrial and mining regions in the south of the kingdom; among the few Flemish communists, the Antwerp dock workers provide the largest contingent. One senses in those three cases the intersection of economic factors such as urbanization and industrialization (notably in old, heavy industry) with ethnic, religious or linguistic tensions.

Other cases of localization seem to be entirely economic. The DKP recruits largely in the Ruhr and especially in such cities as Castrop-Rauxel and Bottrop, in the old mining and heavy industry areas. In Luxembourg the party is drawn from the populations of the cities and the heavily industrialized south of the Duchy. In Holland the communists used to be found in the large port cities of Amsterdam and Rotterdam and in other industrial centres in the west of the kingdom; their numbers, according to the party, are stagnating there now and increasing elsewhere. In Denmark both the rump DanKP and the Socialist People's Party that split from it are based overwhelmingly in Copenhagen, with much less representation in Jutland and the islands.[2] In Britain the communists are mainly in London, Glasgow, and South Wales.

A different situation exists in Finland, Norway, and Sweden, where there are two distinct regions of communist influence, leading students to speak of two *sorts* of communism. There is the industrial, urban communism similar to that found in the countries mentioned above but also a 'backwoods communism' (*ödemarkskommunismen*). The plainest case is Finland, where about one-third of communist support used to come, in the decades after the war, from the thinly populated, isolated, and economically backward north-east of the country. The active population there used to consist of small farmers who were obliged to eke out their existence with seasonal work as lumberjacks, often in forests far from their homes. 'This split in the job market and the insecurities which follow from it create, in Allardt's terminology, a situation of *diffuse deprivation*, which politically is expressed by radical voting behaviour.'[3] It is expressed, for example, by high participation in elections, when whole settlements march to the polls with the apparent intention of lodging a protest. There is competition for these votes between the agrarian Centre Party and the communists; the representation of social democracy in the north and east is now strikingly weak[4] though it existed there before 1917. These are regions where religious revivalism has been notable in modern times, though the individuals who vote communist are not themselves religious. Economic progress since the war and a reduction of the extreme physical isolation of these remote areas actually increased discontent and introduced new forms of economic insecurity and social instability. The communist vote appears to have benefited from that as long as the communists were not identified with the government, that is, during the Finnish communists' eighteen years out of office after 1948. This type of communist vote is held to be non-ideological, in the sense of not proceeding from any intellectual commitment to socialism in general or communism in particular.[5] Urho Kekkonen, the Finish president, who admittedly comes from the rival agrarian party, has said:

Up there in the north there are many supporters of communism who, when I talk to them I can see, know practically nothing about communism. But they vote for it because they believe that any change whatsoever would bring an improvement in their living conditions.

All the same, even in the backwoods, there is evidence of a link between the communist vote and a pre-1917 socialist tradition.[6]

In apparent contrast to that backwoods communism, one finds in the industrialized south and west of Finland an 'ideological' communism that is expressed not only in voting (electoral participation is in fact lower here) but in a variety of other political and trade union activities. Some two-thirds of the support for Finnish communism has come from these regions. It is not possible to correlate that support with unemployment or insecurity or low incomes or types of industry, because one can find areas showing the identical social and economic characters where there is no large communist vote. Commonly, however, such areas would vote social democrat and *that* is the important correlation. That is, 'industrial communism' has arisen, even more plainly than backwoods communism, on soil prepared over many decades by social democracy. If the communists in the backwoods are protesting against their present situation, the communists of the industrial towns would seem to be pressing an inherited protest, carrying on a tradition formed at the start of Finnish industrialization, even when they admit in public opinion polls that they have no present *economic* motivation for doing so. Immigration from the remote north, which is a feature of continued industrial progress, naturally supplements the communist vote in the south.

The contrast of two sorts of communism is somewhat less stark in Norway, where however there are two regions of communist support. There is the remote north, Finnmark, which is contiguous with the remote areas of Finland and has a common frontier with the Soviet Union. It was indeed liberated by the Red Army, so that the large communist vote in 1945—communists won 23 per cent of the electorate—was an illustration of the 'Red Army communism' common throughout Western Europe at the time. But the communist vote in Finnmark remained strong (1949: 16·5 per cent; 1953, 18 per cent; 1961, 14·6 per cent) when it sank to insignificant proportions in southern Norway. Finnmark has remained the only province where orthodox communism has resisted the nationalist radicalism of the Socialist People's Party that split off from it. The other, and less faithful, stronghold of Norwegian communism is the backward province of Hedmark, where forestry is the principal industry. In contrast to those two regions there is the relatively prosperous south and west where, after a solid communist vote had been recorded after the war (20·5 per cent of the electorate in Bergen in 1945 and 16·5 per cent in Oslo), communism receded sharply. These regions are now the stronghold of centre parties and of religious and teetotal movements that are ideologically and aggressively opposed to communism. Where communism has held on there, it is in regions with a long socialist past and an economy marked by manufacturing industry, mining and, notably, single-industry factory towns, e.g. smelters built near a waterfall where the sense of precarious dependence on one capitalist enterprise might be strong. The contrast in Norway, then, is not between agrarian and industrial communism (indeed there is throughout the country a negative correlation between the communist vote and a settled agriculture independent of forestry) but between communism in remote and economically insecure regions, of which lumberjacking is often the main industry, and communism in areas long familiar with socialism and modern industry.

The two types of communist support in Sweden are not only electoral facts but have come to have political importance, in that they correspond to a political cleavage in the party at a time of crisis around 1970. There are on the one hand pockets of communist support in predominantly and traditionally socialist sectors of Swedish society, such as the dock workers, shipbuilders, typographers, seamen, and building workers of Stockholm, Gothenburg, and central Sweden. These are well paid workers in a prosperous society who, for political reasons, adhere to a tradition of opposition and protest that is almost unknown among farm workers, fishermen, and even food and textile workers in the same regions. On the other hand, there is the communism of the Swedish north, notably in the province of Norrbotten, which is to be found in remote settlements, among timber workers and miners. Whereas the first sort of communism clearly arose, as with all West European communism, within the socialist movement, the second sort, 'Norrbotten communism', has been thought to require special explanation. The relative poorness and remoteness of the province and its dependence on lumberjacking and on the iron ore mines of Kiruna are obvious economic factors, but no less important are the history of religious revivalism and the immigration of Finns, often Finnish communists, from the very regions where 'backwoods communism' was first noted. The local religious phenomenon of Laestadianism with its penances and confessions of sinning is curiously connected with a 'non-ideological' communism, in that people can practise both or can oscillate from one to the other. Many folk in the region are Finnish-speaking, and this community was replenished by an influx of communist refugees after the Finnish civil war of 1918 and again after the peasant-fascist Lapp movement of the years around 1930, which led to anti-communist terrorism in northern Finland. Today Norrbotten communism has solid roots in the trade unions, which communists organized in the timber industry, and in the influence of the daily *Norrskensflamman*, the only one left to Swedish communism. This paper opposed 'revisionist' tendencies in Swedish communism, while Norrbotten produced the militants who held to the Stalinist line against the reforms introduced by party leader Hermansson.

However, one must not contrast this backwoods Norrbotten communism too starkly with the communism of the Swedish south. Norrbotten too was a centre of socialist influence at the start of this century, and *Norrskensflamman* was begun as a socialist paper in 1906. The radicalism of the region first expressed itself as a deviation into anarcho-syndicalism before the first world war and it was *this* current that flowed into communism first in 1918, again at the end of the 1920s. The peculiar economic conditions of this Swedish 'colony'[7] did not lead to the appearance of communism *ex nihilo* but they might explain, together with the influx of Finnish communists, why socialism there should generate successively anarcho-syndicalism, communism, and a persistent Stalinism.

Do constituents or components like those exist in the more widespread communist phenomena of France and Italy? If they do not seem to at first glance, nor did they when communism won substantial proportions of the electorate in north Europe just after the war. The two types of communism described there are reefs exposed only at low tide. It could be that when communism spreads to the point of becoming a national political party, it covers over those strongholds, but they would remain the centres of its strength, the source of its leadership and inspiration. Thus it has been said:

Italy is perhaps the country most comparable with Finland with regard to this aspect. An industrial north and a backward area in the south seem to have contributed to a similar pattern of communist support . . . The creation of the *clientilismo* system in southern Italy and the sudden change in social relations which the movement of the labour force from southern to northern Italy had led to, resemble the situation in north-east Finland. On the other hand, the socialist tradition is present in the industrial areas of both countries. [8]

In regard to France the same suggestion about two sorts of communism has been made. 'The peasants of central Italy and of the Massif Central area in France, both protestors and anti-clerical, belong to the same type of communist voters; the workers in the Milan and Paris suburbs to a completely different type'.[9]

These parallels seem altogether too rough and ready. The communist implantation in central France occurred on territory previously socialist and before that radical; while the Red Belt of Italy, which has been overwhelmingly communist since the war, was overwhelmingly socialist before fascism and was an important base of co-operation and unionism before this century began. Thus the prior socialist tradition, which is what really characterized 'industrial communism' in north Europe, rather than any link with industry, is actually older and plainer in the regions of 'peasant communism' of central Italy and France. Perhaps the mistake is to look for backwoods communism in southern Europe where there are no backwoods. There are regions of lesser industrial development, but nowhere that the railways and other communications do not reach. Since, as we shall see, socialism and communism are especially strong among the workers and employees of the railways, the posts, the gas and electricity services, as well as in education and the building trades, that would help give communism a uniform national coverage, quite different from the duality seen in northern Europe. Indeed, the PCF is the most national of all the French parties, in the sense of having the widest geographical base, while the base of the PCI is rivalled in Italy only by that of the Christian Democrats. That does not mean that these parties do not have bastions of greater strength and regions where occasional advances turn out to be fragile, but it means that it would be difficult, without much meticulous research, to show that the significance of an affiliation with communism was radically different in various regions.

Even if it were true that in some bastions of communism, such as Romagna in central Italy, the people had a radically different history and character, and thus invested *their* communism with a different sense that marked it off from the communism of other (in this case) Italians,[10] one would have to note that their peculiar history and character had first of all carried them to republicanism, anti-clericalism, co-operation, and socialism. That political inheritance later fell to Italian communism for quite specific historical reasons, connected with the situation of the region under fascism and at the time of the liberation.[11] Thus non-political facts such as geographical situation, economic fortunes or local psychology will everywhere be subordinate to specifically political and organizational factors, and consequently the phenomenon of communism will show a uniformity and continuity that are denied in the hypotheses of two different sorts of communism. The most one need concede to that theory as applied to France is that there might well be rural areas that traditionally embrace the most Leftist political party that presents itself there. Several generations ago that meant radicalism, a generation ago socialism, and today communism without, in the last case, there being any reasoned attachment to Marxism. Yet it would be adventurous to contrast that too sharply with a supposedly revolutionary and ideological sort of communism among city workers.[12]

Age

Between the two world wars, the CPs, as I have shown elsewhere,[13] were regularly younger than the corresponding socialist parties, a fact that Lewis Feuer has taken to illustrate his argument that revolutionary movements are connected with, if not based on, a generational conflict. Whatever the value of that thesis, Feuer is right in adding that in the 1960s the communists in their turn were overtaken on their Left by those younger than they.[14] For the CPs aged. They had never paid much attention to, and certainly had never wooed, the young. They were parties of theory, discipline, and experience, supposedly based on class, which has nothing to do with age. They needed only, what they regularly boasted of getting, an infusion of young recruits adequate to replace, after the long training a militant needed, retirements from the ranks of the veterans. That was compatible with a gradual rise in the average age of the party, which made it unfit to understand, let alone foresee, the revolt of the European youth in the 1960s.

This ageing process was extreme in parties that were in political decline. The average age of the Norwegian party since 1964 has been between 55 and 60. In 1968 some 60 per cent of the members of the Austrian party were over 60. The West Berlin party, the SEW, reported at the end of 1967 that 81 per cent of its members were over 40 and 71 per cent over 50. The illegal KPD became very old: in 1966 only one member in twenty was aged under 30. The Swedish party gave no figures but complained that it was ageing because the young were bolting to the extreme Left. Ageing happens in a party that is dying: the young stop joining while the old stay on by ingrained conviction. That process is seen in declining federations within parties that otherwise are not on the downgrade. Thus 67 per cent of the membership of the federation of the department of Corrèze in 1966 was over 40, whereas at that date 57 per cent of the PCF as a whole was in the same age group.[15]

That even a large and vigorous party like the PCF should have had 57 per cent of its members over 40, and only 9·4 per cent under 25, showed that it was ageing too, especially when that structure is set against the age pyramid of the rejuvenated postwar population of France. The Finnish party, similarly, was old: its average age in 1968 was 49. The revolt of the young revealed the dangers of this ageing, when it spawned violently anti-communist ultra-Leftist movements. The CPs thereupon tried to win young recruits, and to promote them quickly within the party. The PCF claimed in 1972 to have reversed the ageing process and to have got back to the age structure of 1954. The DKP, which emerged into legality a party of greybeards, claimed that in 1972 'almost half' its membership was under 40, and by 1973 70 per cent.

It is too early yet to judge of the success of the CPs' courting of the young, but the continued vigour of the ultra-Leftist movements across Europe suggests that party claims are exaggerated, or premature. Certainly, announcements about a lower average age in participants in CP congresses are not a sign of rejuvenation, but a bid to *look* younger by stacking the delegations with hand-picked youngsters. (Since this wooing of the young went on at the same time as an effort to meet the demands of women's liberation movements, the technique of stacking congresses led to the appearance in them of teen-age girls—a circumstance that would make it all the easier for a senior leadership to steamroller a congress without fear of informed political discussion.)

There are signs that the membership opposed some resistance to this sudden intake of young people, and some cells of the PCF were denounced for their anti-youth attitude. Georges Marchais complained that the PCF was blocking the promotion of young people within its ranks, whereupon heads rolled.[16] The Italian party similarly rejuvenated its election candidates from 1968, excluding those that had served in three legislatures, although this meant sacrificing some heroes. The French party followed that example in 1973. These actions must count as window-dressing until it is proven that they have contributed to a rejuvenation of the ageing CPs, which continue to be ruled by an oligarchy aged over 50.

Turning to the age of the communist electorates, it is evident that in France and Italy these are composed of younger voters. 'In 1962 the [French] communist electorate and that of the PSU counted the most young and the fewest old voters; in 1966 the younger groups are those where the inclination to vote communist is strongest.'[17] However a tendency towards ageing in the communist electorate that was not clearly visible when that was written became detectable later. In 1973 the 20–34-year-old group made up only 30 per cent of the PCF electorate, against 42 per cent in 1952, while the over 65 group made up 23 per cent, against 4 per cent.[18] It was no longer the youngest electorate in France. Eighty per cent of the voters of the small parties grouped officially under the heading 'Parti socialiste unifié (PSU)—Extreme Left' were under 50, compared with 64 per cent for communist voters. Looking at the electoral breakdown of the age groups (instead of the age breakdown of the electorates) one sees that in 1973 the PCF got fewer of the votes of the 21–34 group than the socialists or the Right-wing parties (22 per cent, compared with 23 and 32 per cent, respectively), it got the same amount of the 35–49 and 50–64 age groups as the socialists (one-quarter and one-fifth respectively) but less of the over 65 groups. In sum, the PCF's electoral support is young but not the youngest and may be getting old faster than the whole population.[19]

Those estimates of the age of the PCF voters are based on public opinion polls, since the ballot itself is secret. In the case of the PCI electorate we have a more reliable criterion. Italians can vote for the lower house at 21 but must wait to turn 25 to vote for the Senate. Thus in the 1972 elections, there were 3,200,000 more votes cast for candidates to the assembly than for candidates to the Senate. The tandem PCI-PSIUP (Partito socialista italiano di unità proletaria) got 1,168,000 more votes in the former election. Hence out of 3·2m. people aged 21–25, 1·2m. voted communist, or over 37 per cent compared with 27 per cent of the total electorate that voted communist. That same election saw the annihilation of the ultra-Left groups, which hardly scored 1 per cent. The two facts are no doubt related: the defeat of the ultra-Left at the polls explains the high young vote for the PCI, whereas the more modest success of the PCF among young voters corresponds to the slightly better electoral performance of its rivals to the Left.

Sex

The CPs are predominantly male parties as to their membership, electorate, and policies. Probably all political parties in Europe are predominantly male as to their membership and, judged from the point of view of contemporary feminists, as to their policies too, but the CPs are the most male of all. Conservative electorates are in general predominantly female whereas the communist electorate is strikingly male. There is no reason for surprise at these facts, if one bears in mind the roots of communism in the working-class movement, which was usually conservative or indifferent in the field that has come to be known as women's liberation. Yet such facts are now-adays, at a time of feminist agitation, often picked up as surprising or even scandalous, as indicating that a supposedly avant-garde political movement is hypocritical and reactionary. First of all there is no reason, in this matter or any other, to judge the CPs by the standards of the avant-garde. The association of certain avant-gardes of bourgeois origin with the European CPs between the world wars was based on a brief misunderstanding. Since the war CPs have not been innovators in any department, whether political, economic, social, or moral. To approach them with the expectation that they will be spontaneously receptive of new notions in any of these fields is to betray a preconceived idea of them. Least of all would one expect them to be receptive of new attitudes in the matter of women's liberation, where the tendency of Marxist economic doctrines is all the other way: to 'liberate' women from the home was a capitalist manoeuvre to increase the supply of labour, hence to lower its price; to limit births by contraception or abortion was seen as desirable only because capitalism was restraining the output of goods required by a larger population; to practise sexual liberty was to divert energies away from political work, in a direction where they would not disturb the bourgeoisie; and so forth.

Yet on all these subjects the CPs have been evolving in recent years, seeking to soften their rather forbidding air of Victorian masculinity. It is probable that they are not doing this out of conviction but out of electoral necessity. To put it crudely, women became interesting to communism when they got the vote (that was only after the war in France) and they became increasingly interesting as the CPs surrendered other concerns to electoralism. As with the change in their attitudes to the young, the evolution in their policies and practice in matters of special concern to women is belated and reluctant—a question of limping along behind the innovators—and it is so far primarily a matter of façade, e.g. co-opting more women to the central committee or sending a 16-year-old girl as delegate to a party congress. As with the wooing of the young, it is too early to say whether these changes will be rewarding in the way that most concerns the CPs, that is, electorally.

The increase in the percentage of female membership of the PCF is marked:

1946	11·1	1966	25·5
1954	20·2	1972	30
1959	21·9		

Sources: Kriegel, Les communistes français (1970), p. 30; LM, 23 Feb 1973 & 10–11 Mar 1974.

The bulk of this female membership is in the cities. At a time when only one member in four was a woman, the Parisian federation was 37 per cent female. Women in rural areas, even where the communist implantation is old and strong and even when they themselves vote communist, leave membership strictly to the menfolk. If these percentages seem low, it must be remembered that they are higher than in other French political parties. They always were, even before the war when they were insignificant. At a time when other parties were *completely* indifferent to feminist questions, the PCF favoured equal pay and female suffrage and it put women up for election (illegally and fruitlessly). On the other hand, one cannot conclude from these percentages, which are published by the party, that it is attracting many more women. One would need to know the absolute membership figures, and one does not. It could merely be that women were slower to leave a shrinking party.

The PCI reported its female membership at the end of 1971 to be 23·5 per cent. The Swedish party in 1972 had only 26 per cent female membership in a country where feminism is a militant political force, but it still refused to consider forming a women's organization. The party secretary suggested furnishing baby-sitting services in order to increase female activity in the party.[20] Other parties, which provide no information on female membership, presumably have even less to boast about.

The suggestion that the party should supply baby-sitters recalls that these percentage figures mean little if the women members, however numerous, are silent, passive, and mostly absent in a male-run party. One reason they are members even on paper is that it has always been communist policy for men to encourage their wives to join the party, if only because the long hours the man had to give to party work would then be less disruptive of his marriage. That means that many female 'members' are in fact members' wives, whose political role inside the party is nil. Then, as the husband is promoted in the party, his wife might go up the hierarchy with him, which is easy to arrange in a party where the leadership has always been selected by co-optation and nepotism. Thus of nine women members of the PCF central committee in 1967, seven were or had been married to other members of the central committee. This practice received its monarchical expression when Jeanette Thorez-Vermeersch acquired sovereign powers in the PCF during the absences and illnesses of her husband. On the other hand, the number of women who make their own way up in the CPs has always been small. Certainly, female representation in all the echelons of the party has been lower than the female membership and, in the opinion of one female observer, lower than in responsible positions in society at large.[21] The role of women in the Italian party has been even more minimal, and the number of women deputies in the PCI parliamentary contingent has been falling, although it would be easy to manipulate the composition of its list of candidates in a country with proportional representation. The Spanish party, despite its having glorified Dolores Ibarruri, 'la Pasionaria', and made her party president, is aggressively anti-feminist in traditional Spanish style, as its secretary-general admits.[22]

Efforts to reverse the trend are recent and have begun where it is easiest, in stacking party congresses, which are meticulously stage-managed affairs. The PCF boasted of 27·3 per cent female attendance at its 1972 congress, up 12 per cent in twelve years. For comparison, less than 10 per cent of delegates to the Swedish party congress in that year were women. The PCF then put up more women candidates than any other party in the 1973 elections (eighty-three of them), but most were *suppléantes*, i.e. they were second-string candidates who would only get a seat if the elected deputy died.

3

Meanwhile the French party's electorate, as measured by opinion polls, may have been becoming slightly less masculine:

Percentage of women in the PCF electorate

1948-9	38
1952	39
1962	35
1965	39
1966	37
1973	42

The French population in 1973 was 52 per cent female, so with only 42 per cent of females among its voters, the PCF still had a markedly male audience in the country. That is natural, because, apart from any specifically female reaction to general communist policies (e.g. women are usually less sympathetic to parties that speak of revolution or promise considerable social change), the CPs have been hostile or indifferent to reforms that concern, in the first place, women. They have scorned the idea that women might have problems that could not be subsumed under class problems. Faced with the 'petty bourgeois' agitation in favour of family planning, they have declared, 'Against Reactionary Neo-Malthusianism, We Fight for the Right to Maternity'—that being the title of a 1956 pamphlet by J. Thorez-Vermeersch. They have defended family and marriage, and denounced free love, sexual liberty, contraception and abortion with arguments that were conventional, demagogic, and sometimes hypocritical.[23] Where divorce became a live issue, as in Italy, the CP subordinated questions of principle to considerations of political tactics, i.e. to the desire to avoid a clear division between conservatives and secular parties in which the CP might have trouble in seeing where its electoral advantage lay.

The striking of these attitudes has been accompanied by sundry moralisms, such as denunciations of obscenity, homosexuality, promiscuity, and the depravity of *déclassés*.[24] Unconventional points of view on sexual issues have been dismissed as symptoms of the degeneration of capitalism. Thus Berlinguer, secretary of the PCI:

We are not in favour of a society of bigots or puritans but no more are we for a society where anything goes, where there prevails the thesis that every instinct must always be followed rather than rationally controlled. These libertarian theories are pseudo-cultural drugs, as damaging as the drugs that are bought and consumed, and they are also a product of capitalism that increases disorder and criminality, that dissolves and dissipates and destroys every authentic human and family relationship.[25]

Such attitudes came to appear increasingly anachronistic as the CPs came under attack from the libertarians and the women's liberationists. A PCF meeting in 1972 on the role of women was broken up in fisticuffs by squads of apostles of female liberation and sexual liberty while Jacques Duclos intoned from the platform against 'homosexual revolutionaries'. At a more serene level, the PCF was criticized as 'a great defender of bourgeois morality and the family', a defender that proposed the scapegoat 'capitalism' in order to protect the real oppressor, the male, whether worker or capitalist, and that begged the question by promising that socialism would liberate women without any thought being taken of their particular situation. The PCI's Union of Women, which took a cautious line on divorce and abortion, was assailed by women's liberationists, who enticed many women out of it into rival organizations.

External criticism of that sort was perhaps less effective in forcing change than the circumstance that contraception, abortion, sexual education, and divorce became electoral, and then legislative, issues in France and Italy thanks to the initiative of secular, including Right-wing, parties. Once there was narrowly political advantage to be won, or more accurately the risk of narrowly political loss in the event of an unsuitable stand, the CPs hastened after innovators whom they had not anticipated. The PCF proposed a law on abortion that was so juridically vague that it amounted to no law at all and it urgently pressed for reform of the 1920 law on contraception, which it had found no fault with when it was in the majority and in the government before and after the war. Its deputies declined to vote the law on sexual education and its secretary preferred to keep his ideas on divorce and adultery safely vague.[26] In general, the CPs have been uncomfortable spectators of the revolution in morals and there is no certainty that their attempts to adapt to it will be successful, because there are clear signs of resistance in the rank and file to new attitudes adopted by leaders engrossed with electoral expediency. To be sure, the party stands to gain little from efforts to graft a new concern with morals on to a stale social theory, as when a communist psycho-analyst discovers that the necessary prelude to the 'erotic society' is limitation of the power of the monopolies.[27]

Religion

Given the clear philosophical bent of Marxism, one may assume members of CPs to be overwhelmingly irreligious. Some communist electorates have been proven to be so, also. In Finland, where over 90 per cent of the population belongs to the Lutheran Church of Finland,

Those who take an indifferent or negative view of religion support the People's Democratic League (the communist-dominated electoral alliance) seven times as often as religious persons and believers. . . . Persons who view religion indifferently or negatively are five times as numerous among PDL supporters as among non-socialist groups. There were less than half as many religious persons and believers among the People's Democrats as within the non-socialist parties. As far as religion is concerned, the Social Democratic Party voters were closer to non-socialists than to People's Democrats.[28]

It is interesting to note that the negative correlation between religiousness and communist voting in Finland is most marked among workers, and that affiliation with the Marxist party thereafter reinforces irreligiousness.

Similarly in France, where 85 per cent of the population are baptized Catholics, successive opinion polls have shown that the percentage of communist voters admitting to no religion and/or no religious practice was 77 in 1966, 78 in 1967, and 71 in 1972. For socialists, the nearest party on the political spectrum, that percentage hovers around 50 only. Between 10 and 20 per cent of communist voters occasionally practise some religious rite, according to opinion polls in 1966 and 1967, whereas over a third of socialists and two-thirds of all other sorts of voters do so. However, the 1973 survey shows that 28 per cent of French communist voters occasionally go to church, which may indicate that something is changing here. The communist electorate meanwhile remains the least religious and the most atheist. Indeed 47 per cent of French people who admit to no religious connection also vote communist (whereas 26 per cent of them vote socialist). Only 2 per cent of devout Catholics vote communist (but 13 per cent vote socialist). In France as in Finland, on the religious issue the communists stand distinct from the rest of the electorate, from socialist to Gaullist. One would hesitate to say the same of Italy, and for that matter Spain, until it were proven. Those countries probably mark the transition to the other end of the spectrum, Cyprus, where most members of AKEL practise the Orthodox religion, a circumstance that facilitated the collaboration of the communists and Archbishop Makarios.[29]

Just as a minority of believers in Catholic countries vote communist, there is an even smaller number who join the party. They are well advertised exceptions. The PCI lets it be known that Signora Berlinguer goes to mass. *L'Humanité dimanche* (12–18 May, 1971) has reported the case of a woman who goes to seven o'clock mass and then sells the communist weekly in the streets; Roger Garaudy said he used to do the same after attending the Evangelical circle in Marseilles. The DKP has recruited some fifty members of the Evangelical clergy, notably in Hesse.[30] The Finnish communists count members among theological students and the Helsinki clergy. Such cases are no doubt oddities but of a sort that will occur more frequently now that the churches and the CPs have passed, in Garaudy's words, 'from anathema to dialogue'. Like other instances of intellectual confusion, this dialogue has generated an enormous and enthusiastic literature.[31] An initial scepticism about the possibility of 'philosophic mediation' of conflicts between institutions[32] will restrict the author to mention of its external and frankly electoral aspects.

The dialogue is facilitated by the fact that the West European CPs abandoned long since—in the 1930s—the militant anti-religious campaigning still seen in parts of the communist world. Whatever electoral calculations lie behind communist advances to the Christians, the record of the western parties on the issue of religious toleration is so clearly established (and contrasts so sharply with recurrent *Kulturkämpfe* in the Soviet world) that it must be counted part of an adaptation to the conditions of pluralist western society. Moreover, after a phase of tart and possibly legitimate criticism of Vatican politics, the PCI passed to a position of anti-anti-clericalism, to the despair of the secular parties, which currently suspect it of collusion with the Vatican. The Finnish communists, too, have learned to handle the religious sects with consideration in regions where both have a hold over the population. The PCF has not yet managed to make the transition beyond tolerance of a plurality of beliefs to an anti-anti-clericalism, as was demonstrated in Georges Marchais's gaffe about religious schools.

In a letter to a priest in August 1972, Marchais made the deduction that the nationalization of confessional schools receiving public funds, which was proposed in the joint communist-socialist programme, when read in conjunction with the exclusion of priests from state schools which has been a principle of French law since 1866, implied that all the priests in the confessional schools would be dismissed once those schools were taken over. He took the opportunity to broaden the issue by insisting that the principle of the separation of church and state meant that 'no member of any church can exercise a function in the state, and not only in public education'.[33] The expression 'member of any church' was so manifestly excessive that Marchais soon had to retreat to the admission that a communist-socialist government would allow even priests into the public service, provided they did not function there as 'consecrated representatives' of the church.[34] That logic-chopping was unimportant—since the issue was not whether priests could be postmen or whom they would 'represent' if they were—alongside the revelation that on the threadbare debate about *laïcité* the French communists were still victims of an epidemic anti-clericalism. Specifically, they could not see, until the socialist leader François Mitterrand pointed it out to them, that it was one thing to exclude priests from public schools if public and confessional schools existed side by side, but quite another to dismiss them en bloc if all schools were made public by nationalization. The controversy that Marchais unintentionally started gave the communists the occasion to repeat that they differed explicitly from the East European parties in refusing to install Marxism or any other doctrine as official belief. Marchais said: 'People say to us "That will be new! It's not what they have done so far in countries that have passed under communist rule!" Exactly. It will be different.' Pierre Juquin, a member of the central committee concerned with ideological issues, added 'The state will adopt no faith. Neither will it profess any irreligious doctrine. More generally, it will not affirm or deny anything in philosophy'.[35] Yet their confusion and recantations during the debate (recantations which Mitterrand found 'only half convincing') suggested that on the narrower question of relations with the church and its schools, which educate over 17 per cent of French children, the French communists do not yet have a settled doctrine.

There are other signs of indecision in their attitudes to Christians. It is understandable that at the same time as they court a Christian electoral clientele they also keep up their courting of the secularist movement, for there is no pretence at a meeting of minds or of ideological compromise with Catholicism. But in preferring to deal with traditional Catholics rather than the Left Catholics, they betray that they are more interested in cultivating influential leaders who can swing votes than in exploring the terms of collaboration with the Christians who are nearest them.

That explains the failure in this sphere of Roger Garaudy, the party's philosopher-in-residence. He was charged for years with the seduction of the Catholics and seemed to enjoy a certain success, but by seeking sincerely to find Christians ready to collaborate with communists, Garaudy ended up dealing with Left Catholics, who represented only a marginal force inside the church. Realizing that a prelate who consents to be neutral in an electoral contest could bring more votes to a communist candidate than the few hundred ballots of the Left Catholics, the party preferred to deal with 'more representative' Catholics. Worse, it regarded the Left Catholics as a subversive and disturbing force inside a religious community that it would rather deal with as a coherent block under the leadership of its conservative bishops. As the Left Catholics saw, this was a mirror image of the attitude of the communist governments in Eastern Europe, which prefer by far a concordat with the Vatican, and the right to nominate conservative bishops who preside over a religious community held strictly to the observance of a *cult*, to any toleration of progressive Catholics who might invoke the Vatican Councils to argue that Christianity also has a social and political mission. After Roger Garaudy was expelled, the party returned to a less sentimental, more cautious, and in fact strictly electoralist approach to religion. In that respect, the PCF line is once again parallel to that of the other parties. Moreover, when Garaudy revealed after his expulsion that he had always remained, through decades of activity as a communist leader, a religious mystic, his conception of communist-Christian collaboration lost much of its interest, because it was seen to arise in personal conviction rather than in party doctrine.

Though this turn of events disappointed French progressive Catholics, it is worth noting that the 'philosophical' compromise that Garaudy was offering them was intellectually suspect, whereas there is no *merely* electoralist stand a party can take that leaves no imprint on its character. That is to say, there is no tactical line that can be adopted, however calculatingly, year after year through successive election campaigns that does not in the end compromise a political party, involve it in connections it cannot easily break, and commit it to particular policies and alliances in the event of winning power. The evolution from aggressively anti-religious atheism, such as still marks Russian communism and disfigures Albanian communism, to a habit of toleration of multiple beliefs and to recurrent disavowals of the East European model, is a development we will find duplicated in other aspects of the recent history of West European CPs. There is nothing in that, of course, to lessen the probability of serious clashes between the parties and the churches as institutions (e.g. as managers of schools and owners of property) in the pluralist society the communists say they are now reconciled to.

Social Class

The first thing to notice about the social class of the members and voters of the CPs is that the parties are seldom happy about it. They have a preconceived, theoretical model of themselves as class parties of a quite specific sort, and they occasionally admit that, in fact, they do not answer that description. (Or rather, in accord with the practice of never admitting any present fault in communism but only faults in its recent past which are now being corrected, the parties say that their class constitution has been inadequate but is improving.) In trying to see what the facts are, we must be careful not to follow the communists on to their own ground and thus become involved in byzantine quarrels about 'class' such as are a feature of communist polemic. Though much use is made, and not only by Marxists, of the notion of class, it is a vague one. It is, at best, a static classification that can never hope to fit the dynamics of politics. For example, to what class would one assign permanent officials of a party who once briefly were workers but have been professional politicians for decades; or students; or housewives; or retired people; or intellectuals; or land-owning peasants; or the executives of communist business enterprises; or 'brain workers' such as the large and growing stratum of technicians in industry? These are not odd cases. People belonging to those groups make up over half the membership of many West European CPs. They would be difficult to classify on *any* theory of the division of society into classes, but it is quite impossible to squeeze them into a narrow and antiquated classification in which the main division is between proletariat and capitalists.

That difficulty has political consequences. Political power is held, both in East European communist countries and within West European CPs, by groups who operate in the name of the working class. That class is defined as it was by Marx when studying West European societies over a century ago, so it is not surprising that it is not a useful tool when applied to modern West European societies or, even less, to non-industrialized societies such as Russia. So it has had to be supplemented with the Leninist theory about the proletariat's *allies*: awkward categories that will not fit into the Marxist division, like those mentioned above, are denied independent existence and reduced to the status of the proletariat's allies—even if they do not yet see that they should be its allies.

This enables the groups operating in the name of the workers to adjust to situations very different from those envisaged by Marx. But of course there comes a time when the subterfuge will not serve, so great are the discrepancies between social fact and Marxist theory. One variety of CP thereupon justifies its power in the name of *another* class, the peasantry, but this is Maoism and does not concern Europe. There, rather, the attempt has been made to redefine the working class, and, in particular, to raise the political status of its 'allies', even to the point of giving them the leading role and making the workers *their* allies. These redefinitions are not proposed by communists in the interests of social science but in order to rationalize a transfer of political power away from communists who operate in the name of the proletariat to other communists who want power for different purposes and with different allies. That is the political significance of theoretical disputes about the nature of the working class and its relation to technicians, both in Prague in 1968 and inside West European CPs about the same time.

Those who proposed new ideas on the subject were removed from political life in Czechoslovakia by Soviet intervention and their supporters in West European parties were either expelled, like Garaudy, or reduced to submission to the traditionalists. Hence the official theory of the class relations of the model western CP remains as follows. It is composed mostly of workers, its leadership is even more overwhelmingly working class, it is supported politically by the majority of the working class and, where it enters into alliances that make it a national and inter-class party, always preserves the leadership of those alliances in the hands of the working class. The justification for this insistence on the working class is the Marxist theory of its decisive role in the evolution Marx foresaw for capitalist society. The working class he had in mind was, substantially, productive manual workers in privately owned capitalist industry. That notion has progressively been broadened by the CPs to cover a motley but without surrendering the privileged historical importance of the particular group Marx spoke of. CPs would still endorse Lenin's words: 'Only one particular class—namely, urban workers and in general factory workers, industrial workers—is capable of directing the whole mass of toilers and exploited.'

In reality, the CPs do not conform to the model, as they recurrently confess by complaining that there are too few workers in their ranks and in their higher echelons. The small parties clearly do not conform to the ideal but no more do the bigger and more successful ones. No party in a contemporary democracy could win large membership and wide electoral appeal on a narrow working-class basis. Worse, that basis is contracting, and so by insisting on its special importance the CPs are swimming against the tide of social evolution. In France, for example, for every two new workers that come into productive work, there are five additional salaried non-workers. Consequently while the French working class increased absolutely in size by 14 per cent between 1954 and 1971, it became a smaller percentage of the active population. That development is recognized by the European socialist parties, which base their electoral fortunes on the fact that rising living standards and a dwindling proletariat do not hurt the Left vote (they might even reinforce it in Europe), for all that they make that vote less a *class* expression, less proletarian in the sense of the communists.

Reluctance to admit that fact varies between the CPs. The PCF is the most dogmatically proletarian in its approach, no doubt because *ouvriérisme* is a solid French tradition, much older than the PCF itself. Marx had to fight it in the person of Proudhon, Lenin scorned it in Sorel, and the PCF both exemplifies it in its attitudes and respects it among French workers. The PCI, by comparison, is more *interclassista*, more apt to claim the backing of the masses, of the simple majority, rather than the industrial workers among them. The CPGB changed the *Daily Worker* into the *Morning Star* precisely because it saw that a specifically proletarian organ had little place in British politics. In seeking to adapt, the CPs are handicapped by the Soviet party. That party, which is one of the sources of legitimacy and support for the western parties, exercises power in the name of the workers. Indeed it actually boasts of an *increasing* proletarian hold over Soviet society just at a time when the Soviet working class must be losing ground to the scientists and technicians because of the modernization of the economy. As long as the Soviet party holds to that ideology, the western parties will be disinclined to discard their proletarian bias.

In analysing the class relations of the parties, we shall look in turn at their membership, their leadership, and their electorate, because the class origins of each can differ widely.

MEMBERSHIP. A percentage breakdown of the membership of the PCI provided by *Rinascita* (3 Nov 1972) may be compared with a

similar analysis of the membership of the other great Italian party, the
Christian Democrats (*La Discussione*, 26 Mar 1973).

	PCI	CD
Agriculture	17·6	15·2
Industrial workers	39·5	16·6
Middle class	13·11	32·2
Retired	14·9	7
Housewives	11·6	25

That about 40 per cent of PCI members are industrial workers has
been true since the war. In that time, the size of the CP has fallen
sharply, whereas Italy has seen a massive transfer of the population
from farms to the cities; there has thus been a notable decline in the
number of communists among the workers. Whereas one Italian
industrial worker out of five was a PCI member at the beginning of
the 1950s, this is true of only one in twelve in the 1970s. As the
number of Italian farm labourers declined, so did their representation
in the party, but they were replaced by sharecroppers (*mezzadri*) in
regions where the party had local power that could be useful to party
members, that is, in the Red Belt. Counting industrial workers, the
remaining farm workers and the wives and pensioners of those two
groups, the PCI is still as to two-thirds a working-class party, but the
large and growing percentage of the membership that consists of
wives and pensioners, which would be normal for an *electorate*, is a
notable development in what was once the *party* of actual working
men. It is a development that necessarily changes its character.

The party has retained the loyalty of a proportion of the artisan
class (6 per cent of its membership) but elsewhere in the cities it has
not managed to attract the employees, professionals, and middle
classes who proliferate with industrialization and urbanization. Thus
Italy's development into an industrial economy has not favoured the
PCI as much as the Christian Democrats and the socialists. Where
they can recruit the employees and service workers in new industries,
it can only hope to attract the workers and it does not attract many of
them. So it fails to make advances in the industrial north, where just
after the war it had 40 per cent of its members but now has only 28
per cent, and its centre of gravity shifts, not to the poor south, but to
the prosperous but little industrialized centre. That region now
accounts for 51 per cent of its membership, against 42 per cent after
the war.

Galli sums up:

The PCI today is less the party of productive workers and farm labourers than it was immediately after the war. It is more the party of working-class families (housewives, pensioners) than of factory workers. Its points of strength are neither in the most industrialized and most advanced parts of the country nor in the poorest and most backward. It has not at all grown as the party of the workers and of the poor. It has not gained strength either where an already high degree of industrialization progressed further nor where industrialization started after the war. . . . The PCI is strongest not where there are the most workers or where poverty is most general but where the socialist tradition used to be strongest and where, because it has local power, it is a party of social integration.[36]

The attractions of a political party as a vehicle of social integration, or social participation, are less in the rich industrial regions of the Italian north. There it is not only PCI membership that has fallen but that of all political parties, as social life approximates neo-capitalist society. In contrast, the persistence and indeed the growth of PCI implantation in less industrialized regions between the Po and the Tiber where it holds power is to be noted, along with its recruitment of wives and old people in the same regions and with the transformation there of the former front organizations into genuine associations of citizens with similar interests.

The PCI is surely a more proletarian party than any other in Italy, but not enough to make it the exclusive or even privileged agent of that class or to make the representation of the proletariat its main function. Where it is strongest, it does not have a class role at all but attracts members because it confers status, secures jobs, distributes local power, and provides much of the fabric of social life at the regional level.

What little we know about the social origins of the members of smaller CPs is confusing in its diversity, confirming an earlier judgement, that 'the main feature of communism in the west has been the variety and instability of its clientele'.[37] The Luxembourg party is heavily proletarian in membership as in leadership. The Turkish party is not proletarian at all but attracts students and intellectuals. The Portuguese party is believed to be two-thirds workers and one-sixth peasants. The Spanish party, which was a middle-class party during the civil war, is now said to be overwhelmingly working class (though not necessarily strong in the industrialized regions of the country). That is because the PCE's penetration of the student and intellectual strata in the 1960s, which worried the Franco regime more than communist influence among workers, proved to be vulnerable to ultra-Leftist competition. The students deserted, leaving a working-class majority in the divided party. In contrast, the Swedish party, which had long been solidly working class, attracted, and so far has held, a proportion of middle-class and intellectual members. The Finnish party consists predominantly of lower-paid industrial workers and poor rural dwellers. The British party, like most small parties, is an amalgam of industrial militants and middle-class members, with the latter increasing fast since the war. Similarly in West Germany. The DKP claims to draw 35 per cent of its members from factory workers but 28 per cent from clerks (15 per cent), technicians (6 per cent) and students (7 per cent). The remaining 37 per cent are housewives (30 per cent of all members are women), farmers, retired people, and professional folk. This influx of middle-class people, housewives, and brain workers threatens, in the view of the older members, the *ouvriériste* tradition of German communism.

In its anxiety to appear as proletarian as possible, in 1966 the French party presented a breakdown of its membership, but in a way that made comparison with the statistics of Italian and German parties difficult. Thus:

	Per cent
Workers	60·1
Clerks	18·57
Farmers	6·56
Intellectuals	9·0
Shopkeepers & artisans	5·77

Obviously women members, who at that date made up just over a quarter, and half of whom were housewives, have been classified according to the occupation of their husbands. Retired people and party employees (who number thousands and are thus a noticeable percentage of the membership) have been classified according to the occupation they once exercised. In all, about 33 per cent of members are not active in the economy. If we reduce the percentages provided by the party by one-third, we could conclude that about 40 per cent of the PCF, as of the PCI, consists of working men and women. Thus the PCF is overwhelmingly proletarian, provided this is understood to mean that it is a party of working-class families, whereas in the 1920s it was a party of, mainly, workers. That can be seen by noting the decline in the number of cells organized at the place of work, relative to cells organized in the locality of residence. This is a matter of doctrinal importance to CPs, since it was one of the Leninist precepts that a revolutionary party must have its greatest strength in workplace cells, rather than in locality cells, which typify the democratic parties. In 1926 half PCF cells were indeed workplace cells; by 1970 only 26 per cent were, despite recurrent admonitions, drives, and campaigns in favour of them. The decline reflects the influx of women, pensioners, intellectuals, and independent middle-class folk who cannot organize themselves at a place of work.

The agricultural membership of the PCF has been falling, in line with the exodus to the cities and yet the party has not been recruiting in the industrial regions as much as elsewhere. The explanation of that paradox may be the strength of the PCF in the public sector of the economy, which covers the country. The proportion of PCF members who were (or had been, or were married to) workers in private industry appears to be steady around 40 per cent but the proportion in the public services and nationalized industries, whether as workers, clerks, teachers, or technicians, grew from 14·5 per cent in 1954 to 30·7 per cent in 1966. That could help explain, merely by a reference to the party's own immediate interest, why the PCF is a watchful guardian of the conditions of work in the public sector and an ardent apostle of further nationalizations. In sum, then, the PCF, while touching only a small fraction of the working class, is pre-eminently a party of working-class families and is more proletarian than any other French party.

LEADERSHIP. Sovereign authority in CPs is, theoretically, vested in party congresses. However, since congresses are stacked, the social origins of their handpicked members tell us nothing except what the party wants itself to look like. That is why they are, at least according to party representations, markedly proletarian. For example, PCF congresses are composed of 55–60 per cent workers—not members of working-class families but actual working men. In 1964 well over a quarter of delegates to a PCF congress were workers in the metallurgical industry, who would answer precisely the Marxist definition of a worker—the creator of surplus value in large-scale capitalist industry. At the DKP congress in 1971, 68 per cent of delegates were workers. These proportions are higher than in the population as a whole or in CP membership, so that they express a clear determination to *look* working class. Civil servants, who we have seen are an important element in membership, are systematically under-represented at congresses. If this seems to invite the danger that the sovereign assembly of the party might take specifically working-class positions, one must recall that congresses are stacked in another way: permanent party officials and permanent employees of party-controlled bodies, though they may be *described* as workers, make up a substantial part of the attendance. Thus the composition of congresses is designed (a) to build a certain image, and (b) at the same time to ensure the passage of motions originated by the permanent leadership, so that painstaking analysis of their social origins is vain.

Turning to the permanent officials who run the parties in between the congresses, one must distinguish the small from the large and affluent parties. The social composition of the officials of small parties, such as those of Britain, Sweden, or West Germany, defies analysis. These parties consist of an uneasy alliance between working-class and middle-class people, and the function of the leadership is to maintain a balance between these two wings such as will enable it to secure support for the policies it presents. They are prepared for this classless stance by the material nature of their occupations, which consist of intellectual and organizational work amid people of various social origins.

The situation in the bigger parties looks at first to be, and may in fact once have been, very different but curiously ends up strikingly similar. That is because, whatever the origins of party officials, a career inside the CPs of Italy and France is a recognized channel of social promotion. It is one of the ways that working men get on in those societies. It is, amongst other things, of course, one way of escaping the ordinariness and insecurity of proletarian existence by joining an organization that can offer material security, promotion through stages of a long career, prestige in a wide sector of society or even fame and distinction, and a sense of achievement. After a decade or more in such an organization, the fact that an official is a worker by reminiscence is of less importance than whether his current occupations bring him into contact with working-class people—which they often do not. At that point, such officials will see nothing amiss in co-opting or promoting party officials of quite different social backgrounds, such as middle-class intellectuals, if they fit into a cohesive team capable of securing acceptance of party policies among the various social groups the party deals with.

These middle-class people who come into the CP hierarchy are also *getting on* in society, but then all political parties in Europe offer channels of social promotion for the middle class. The CP, and to a lesser extent the socialist parties, are different in offering promotion to workers too. The Right and Centre parties, even when they can plausibly claim to have an inter-class base, such as Italian Christian Democracy or Gaullism, do not offer promotion to the many workers at their base; middle-class members dominate from well down in the hierarchy, upwards. In that sense, then, the CPs are indeed proletarian, in that they promote workers in a way other parties do not—but this is a peculiar sense because we are describing with the name of a class a channel that passes between classes. We are describing a form of social mobility as though it were static. Not to put too fine a point on it, the ideal image of worker leadership for a party of working men does not cover the case of a party managed by ex-workers turned career bureaucrats and by middle-class professionals. The objection, 'How else could a big political party be run?' is an admission of the limited use of *class* analysis in politics, as compared with the use of the notion of *élites*.

If the CPs in Italy and France offer, among political parties, by far the greatest prospect of vertical mobility to working men, they still resemble the other parties by promoting mainly middle-class people, in their case bourgeois radicals. Thus by the time that the promoted workers get to the top of the party, that is into the central committee or into elected public office, they find themselves outnumbered by middle-class politicians. By then, however, it is so many years since they left workers' jobs that the circumstance is not likely to disturb them. It has been calculated that of Italian communists entering the central committee or parliament in the 1950s, only 2 per cent were at that moment salaried employees in non-party jobs. That was not noticeably different from the situation in the Christian Democracy: 0·4 per cent of its top-echelon politicians were salaried employees in that case.[38] Such communists would scarcely have noticed during their long rise to eminence that whereas wage-earners are about 66 per cent of the membership, only 40 per cent of militants at the base are wage-earners (compared with, already at that low level, 45 per cent from the middle class), or that at the level of provincial party organizations, the middle class had won 62 per cent of official posts, leaving only 38 per cent for ex-workers; or that of communist municipal councillors only 27·5 per cent were ex-workers; or finally that of communist deputies elected to the Italian parliament only 25·9 per cent were ex-workers. In the PCI leadership generally, workers-by-reminiscence have held out a little better: they are outnumbered by politicians of other origins by two to one, instead o three to one as with the members of parliament, but the trend there too is for declining representation of the proletariat. Such a party can easily recognize itself in the person of its secretary-general, Enrico Berlinguer, son of a socialist lawyer, scion of a distinguished and noble family of Sardinian landowners, who within a year of joining the PCI at the age of 21 began an uninterrupted career in the party bureaucracy.

The PCF, having taken over the French tradition of *ouvriérisme*, would hardly choose as leader a man of those origins. Its leaders— Thorez, Duclos, Marchais, Waldeck Rochet, and Georges Séguy— all had brief experience of the worker's life before entering into the channels of social promotion offered by the party and the trade union bureaucracy. The PCF offers the best such channel of all the French political parties, so that it can point out that to some parliaments it deputes as many ex-workers as the ruling parties depute company directors. It has happened that the Gaullist and allied Independent Republican contingents in parliament contained not a single ex-worker, despite the undoubtedly large working-class electoral support they enjoyed. For all that, by the time ex-workers get to the top of the PCF, they find themselves outnumbered by people of other origins. Of 30 'éminences' and aspirants singled out for mention in 1973 by two students of the party and for 26 of whom an occupational background was provided,[39] 11 had once been workers, whereas 13 had been or were teachers, technicians, clerks or professional people. Two others had been trade union bureaucrats. Of the ex-workers, only 5 had ever held a job in capitalist industry; the other 6 had once worked in the nationalized industries or public services. Both groups were outnumbered by the 8 teachers.

The social origins of the communist deputies is better known, as the law requires. Annie Kriegel has pointed out a massive shift from workers to teachers in communist candidates in the Seine between 1924 and 1966.[40] It has continued since then, and on a national basis. Whereas of the 41 PCF deputies elected in 1962 less than half (18 exactly) had once been workers, compared with 12 teachers, technicians, and professionals, out of the 73 communist deputies returned in 1973, 27 had been workers once, compared with 30 teachers, technicians, and professionals. Though this is still a substantial proportion of workers, and more than in any other party's representation, the fact stands that the PCF is promoting fewer workers than people of other social origins.

The case of parliamentary deputies is interesting because of, rather than in spite of, the fact that the function of deputy is not as exalted a one in a CP as in most other political parties, where it is usually the peak function. The CP deputy puts his signed resignation into the hands of the party the day he is elected, so that he can be displaced at will; he makes over his parliamentary salary to the party and gets back what it allows him; and he votes with discipline according to instructions. If that means that he cannot claim the prestige of a politburo member who has never even run for office, it also means that the party could put up almost anyone as its candidate. It does not need brilliant tribunes, learned lawyers, or great debaters, so it could afford to exclude all but workers as candidates, if it chose. Where the electorate votes on proportional representation, as in Italy and for some years in France, the party ticket would be elected, no matter what the calibre of its individual candidates. Hence the fact that, nevertheless, the Italian and French CPs promote a minority of ex-workers to the role of parliamentarian proves that in the upper reaches of its membership there are too few ex-workers for it to do otherwise. The party has been taken over at that level by other classes, notably middle-class intellectuals.

Plainly, a party in that situation has evolved considerably since the fourth congress of the Communist International passed a resolution on French affairs that stated:

> In order to give the party a truly proletarian character and so as to keep out of its ranks people who just regard it as an antichamber to parliament . . . it is indispensable to make it an inviolable rule that the lists of candidates put up for election by the party must contain at least nine-tenths communist workers still on the job in workshop, factory or field, and peasants; representatives of the liberal professions can be admitted only up to the strictly determined limit of one tenth.

ELECTORATE. The electoral impact of communism in Western Europe has been primarily upon the socialist diaspora rather than on the electorate as a whole. Communism has been an affair internal to the Left. From Denmark to Italy, we can find scores of constituencies where the total Left vote has been fairly stable since the First World War but where within that Left vote wide fluctuations in the communist vote have occurred. When the communists won votes, they won them from socialists; when there was a swing, the socialists won their own ground back. The bourgeois parties to the Centre and Right have looked on largely unscathed. Where communism has failed to win a significant following, it is an electoral nuisance only to the socialist party; where communism has succeeded mightily, it has at best occupied territory already in the hands of the Second International parties in 1919. This means that communist voting is not correlated primarily with socio-economic factors like class but with a prior political fact, the existence of a socialist electorate.

That latter was not a class phenomenon. Parliamentary socialism in Western Europe was always a Lib.-Lab. affair, a collaboration of middle-class and working-class politicians who could never win the whole of the working-class vote, a significant part of which went to the Right and the poorest part of which often to the extreme Right, and who always won substantial backing in other classes. Communism being an affair internal to that electorate, its class relations will be more complex than its ideal of itself suggests, and they will vary widely from one European country to the other.

The percentage social composition of the PCI electorate compared with that of the Christian Democrats is as follows:

	PCI	CD
Upper bourgeois	0	1·6
Salaried petty bourgeois	12·1	14·4
Independent petty bourgeois	25·3	36
Wage-earners	60·6	44·8
Other	2	3·2

Sources: Rinascita, 3 Nov 1972 (PCI); *La Discussione,* 29 Mar 1973 (CD).

Given that the Christian Democrat vote is bigger than the communist vote, the Catholic party has been attracting a larger absolute number of wage-earners. The other parties, notably the two socialist parties, claim many of these wage-earners too. Hence even the biggest CP in the west, the PCI, is getting a minority of the available wage-earner votes. Nevertheless, it boasts the highest working-class electorate of all the parties.

Galli has correlated Italian party votes, commune by commune, with all sorts of factors.[41] With regard to the PCI vote, he has found a significant positive correlation with: the presence of active CP membership and organization; the presence of the communist-influenced trade union body, CGIL; the circulation of *L'Unità*; a history of socialist voting in years gone by. Moreover, he has shown that the communist vote is positively correlated with income: people vote communist where they are less poor and where television is commonest. The relation to education is, at first sight, odd: illiteracy is correlated with the communist vote, but so is education beyond the primary school. Finally, there is no correlation with the distribution of the population between primary, secondary, and tertiary sectors of the economy.

The first four, and statistically most significant, correlations confirm at once that this is a politically determined phenomenon rather than a direct reflection of class or economic situation. The CP organization is a historical offshoot of the socialist one; the CGIL is a joint communist-socialist organization; the very name *L'Unità* refers to relations between the parties of the Left; and the history of socialist voting is the classical background to communism. Although the very poor in Italy vote Christian Democrat and extreme Right, the communists win the votes of the lowest paid of the Left-voting workers—as though they had invaded the socialist electorate from the bottom. They get the least educated, illiterate workers' votes, but not those who go to the primary schools, which, in Italy, are run mainly by the nuns and thus produce a Catholic vote. Once past the primary schools, however, and once submitted to the educational and irreligious effect of television, the Left vote increases again, and the communist vote with it. The degree of industrialization has no effect. In predominantly agricultural regions, Christian Democracy gets the votes of the farmers while the PCI gets those of the farm labourers and sharecroppers; in industrial regions, the PCI gets many worker votes but the Catholic party gets the votes of specialized workers, technicians, and clerks; if tertiary activities dominate, the PCI gets the lower paid, the CD the better paid employees. The degree of economic development, therefore, does not impinge directly on the vote, but indirectly through the above mentioned factors of income, education, and socialist past. That 'class' is involved is perfectly possible but it cannot be the coarse class divisions of communist polemic *or* the exact notion of the industrial working class drawn from Marxist theory.

A comparable picture of communist invasion of a socialist electorate from a particular angle, rather than direct correlation with socioeconomic factors, is found in Finland. The SKDL vote is predominantly a wage-earner vote: 76 per cent—but no more than the social democrat vote: 74 per cent. Moreover, two and a half times as many workers vote social democrat as vote communist, and one and a half times as many vote Right. Forty-nine per cent of wage-earners vote social democrat, 20 per cent communist, and 30 per cent for the agrarian and Right parties. The sector of the worker vote that the communists have won consists of the poorer, less educated and less securely employed. When the communist vote increases, the social democrat vote falls, as in 1945 and 1958, and vice versa, as in 1948 and 1966.[42] In Sweden, too, the communist vote seems unrelated to economic factors. Some industrial workers in traditionally socialist regions vote communist, others do not,[43] and often the reason is plain in the local history of the split in the social democrat party in 1917.[44] In any event, the VPK electorate is increasingly drawn from middle-income groups.

The electorate of the PCF is historically determined, rather than a direct class phenomenon. It is concentrated in regions with a long tradition of republicanism, radicalism, and socialism, where communism has in turn established itself as the Left contender in generations-old political and social struggles. Because of that concentration, its electorate is working class to a higher degree than any other, but it covers only a minority of workers, between 25 and 37 per cent depending on the election.

A percentage breakdown, by the occupation of the head of the family, of the French population, and of the communist and other electorates about the time of the 1973 elections yielded these results, according to opinion polls:

	Occupation	PCF	PSU & Left	Social-ist	Gaullist & allied	Right
Agriculture	12	4	2	5	13	17
Independent enterprise	7	5	4	6	8	8
Executives, professions	15	3	24	7	13	21
Clerks, lower management	17	15	40	21	16	18
Workers	32	52	22	35	22	14
Inactive	17	21	8	26	28	22
Total	100	100	100	100	100	100

The percentage of workers in the PCF electorate may have been increasing since the war, which would be consistent with the facts that the PCF electorate has fallen as a percentage of the vote, while the worker part of the French population has declined. (The number of workers in France has increased, but 2m. of them are immigrants who cannot vote.) The following table, showing the breakdown of the communist electorate since the war, illustrates the rise in the percentage of workers among communist voters, but it must be noted that successive public opinion polls are never exactly comparable; e.g. agricultural labourers were classed with 'agriculture' in the earlier polls but now go to swell the count of 'workers'.

	1948	1952	1958	1962	1965	1966	1967	1972	1973
Agriculture	22	13	6	5	8	9	9	2	4
Independent									
Executives	6	9	14	6	7	9	8	7	8
Professions									
Clerks									
Civil servants	13	13	20	13	17	21	15	15	15
Lower management									
Workers	37	38	43	51	51	46	49	52	52
Inactive	22	27	17	25	17	16	19	24	21

The main point of this table is that although less than half the people who vote communist in any year are industrial workers, if one adds in agricultural workers and clerks, then two-thirds of the communist electorate is accounted for. Before one concludes from that, however, that 'the French CP is the party of the working class', one must see what proportion of workers and clerks vote communist.

% of votes won by communists (and Gaullists)

	1967	1969	1973
Workers	31 (30)	23 (32)	37 (21)
Clerks, etc	18 (35)	17 (35)	17 (38)

Thus the communists got less than a fifth of the votes of clerks and a quarter to a third of the votes of French workers. One Rightist party, the Gaullists, could get as many or more worker votes, while the total of parties that the communists describe as Right or bourgeois regularly got many more—in the 1969 presidential elections, three times as many.[45]

This is an important qualification to the assertion that the PCF is 'the party of the working class'. That claim (which is on a level with the statement that the Bolshevik Revolution was a 'proletarian' revolution) is a misleading way of saying, what is true, that the PCF has the most working class of all electorates. Even so, more than half its votes come from outside the urban proletariat. Class is obviously involved but it tells no more than half the story.

Looking to correlations between the French communist vote and various social facts, one notes that it is not correlated with unionization. It can be strong where few workers are unionized and weak where many are; even in the CGT, as mentioned above, 42 per cent of union members do not vote communist. The PCF vote does not come from the poorest Frenchmen but increases as we go up the scale of working-class incomes, up to a point, after this it declines. As to education, it appears that a primary education produces a Right vote among non-workers and a Left vote among workers (there are virtually no illiterates in France) but workers tend to vote Left less often as they become more educated. Whereas, whatever the social class, the Right and socialist parties draw a roughly equal percentage of votes from each educational level, the PCF in 1973 got 27 per cent of the votes of those who had only a primary education, 18 per cent of the votes of those with a technical school training, 15 per cent of the votes of those with secondary education, and 7 per cent of the votes of those with a higher education.

The PCF vote is not directly related to industrialization. True, its small peasant electorate is falling even faster than the total rural population, and communist votes among workers increase in line with the size of the factory. But the party roughly gets its national average of the votes in villages, towns, and urban agglomerations. More striking is the division between the private and public sectors of the economy. In 1973 the PCF won 33 per cent of the votes of wage-earners in the public sector, more than any other party, against 27 per cent of the votes in the private sector, less than the Right parties. The dependence of the PCF on the public sector, both state services and nationalized enterprises, for its electorate, its membership, and its leadership has been called its *fonctionnarisation*.

Another qualification to the claim that the PCF is the party of a class is that the opinions of communist voters as revealed to opinion pollsters are, while undoubtedly Left opinions, not class opinions, either in a classic Marxist sense or even in the sense of the PCF programmes. PCF voters do not want revolution and do not believe that the party does either; nine-tenths of them favour inheritance and property; half of them defend inequalities of wealth and income as necessary to economic life; a quarter to a third of them even oppose nationalizations. These facts show that the communist electorate is continuous with the rest of the Left electorate, and they are compatible with the theory that the CP has won a fraction of the electoral base of the old Second International parties. Where it has made gains outside that electoral base, they have proven evanescent.

The New Classes

If West European communism were indeed a political mutation within West European socialism, one would suspect that when social and technological change led to the appearance of new classes, then communism would be unarmed to penetrate them. These new classes would become objects of competition among *all* the political parties. The CP, lacking a socialist base among them, would not be particularly qualified to attract them, even if in Marxist theory it was 'their' party. Economic growth in Western Europe after 1950 led to the appearance of two new classes: a massive sub-proletariat of immigrant workers from countries lacking any socialist tradition, and a class of technicians and intellectual workers. From Sweden to Italy, the CPs failed to penetrate these groups. Indeed, as long as they could they ignored the first and denied that the second existed. This blindness to important social changes resulted in a stagnation of communist influence followed by serious political defeats in 1968 and subsequently. In turn, that shook the parties internally and, in an atmosphere of crisis and diversion, they began to wrestle, so far inconclusively, with the problem of their relations with classes to which a prior socialist connection could not give them the *entrée*.

The new sub-proletariat was susceptible, as far as the law allowed it any political activity at all, to the penetration of native ultra-Leftists. Indeed, where the law denied these poorly paid workers, as foreigners, any political influence, where the trade unions ignored them, where fellow workers discriminated against them on racist grounds, and where all the political parties, communist included, spurned them as non-electors, then the sub-proletariat provided the only solid social base that Maoism, utopianism, and anarchism could hope for in a contemporary industrial society. There followed wildcat strikes and outbursts of violence, for example in Swedish, French, and Italian automobile factories, that took the communists by surprise. The efforts of the communists to take control of these movements led to direct clashes with ultra-Leftism.

The same ultra-Leftists had unexpected success among the other new class, the intellectual workers (and the apprentices of that group, the students), but so did many other parties once the ebb after the agitation of 1968 set in. Embarrassed to discover how little support it had in this class, the PCF bid for its custom by, for example, starting in 1969 a new CGT trade union for 'engineers, technicians, cadres and middle strata' (UGICT), by starting a periodical aimed at the group, *ITC Actualités* (which soon failed), and by defending the wage differentials that favoured it against the egalitarianism of unions under ultra-Left influence. None of this succeeded in recruiting members or voters from the new class, because the CPs were offering it dependent status, akin to that previously granted to the peasant and shopkeeper 'allies' of the proletariat, instead of the central role claimed by those who hold that the techno-structure has replaced labour and capital at the heart of the new industrial state.

The technically trained experts of electro-technics, laboratory research, electronic data processing, chemistry, and precision mechanics were cordially invited to join the CPs—but it was made clear that those parties would remain under the sway of ex-workers and middle-class people trained in law and teaching, who would continue to operate in the name of the old-style manual worker. This refusal to grant promotion inside the party to new sorts of economic agents, even when they were anti-capitalist and in favour of collectivization, combined with the ideological glorification of the metallurgical worker and miner—i.e. the Marxist proletarian—repelled people who would perhaps have been willing to belong to a 'party of toilers and thinkers'. To justify their attitude, the CPs at first denied the statistical evidence for an absolute decline in the number of manual workers and a rapid increase in the number of intellectual workers. When they conceded that the latter were gaining in importance, the most they offered them was an 'alliance' with the 'working class', i.e. the opportunity to be used in tactical manoeuvres in the way non-capitalist groups have been used since Lenin.

When it was seen that the new class would refuse this subordination and that if it joined or collaborated with the communists it would want to have a voice in defining a socialist society and on the strategy aimed at attaining it, opposition arose inside the CPs. In Italy the *Il Manifesto* group and in France Roger Garaudy suggested to their parties that, instead, they should offer the new class of technicians a measure of equality with the classic working class, by admitting them as members of 'a new historical block'. The suggestion was reconciled with Marxist orthodoxy by the argument that these technicians were 'in process of being proletarianized' and thus, in anticipation, could be admitted as honorary members of the working class and granted more of a say in framing its strategy than the old 'allies' like the peasants. The suggestion was rejected by the party leaders, and both the *Il Manifesto* group and Garaudy were expelled. Georges Marchais made clear why, in dismissing as incorrect the expression 'new historical block':

This expression suggests that the mass of the intellectuals and the working class form an integrated whole. Now on the one hand, that does not at all correspond to the facts and will not do so for a long time; on the other hand, it leads one to lump the working class together in a heterogeneous mass and to question its decisive role, its avant-garde role, in the struggle for the transformation of society.[46]

The debate was accompanied by much pseudo-sociological theorizing about class and by abstruse scholasticism aimed at defending, or in contrast in reinterpreting, the Marxist notion of 'the working class'. We need not go into that because, quite apart from the deficiencies of Marxist class theory, we have seen that the CPs are not class parties. Since they represent a minority of the working class and draw at least half their support from other classes, they *could* well have adapted to changes in western societies' class configuration, as Garaudy and *Il Manifesto* urged. That they *would* not was due to the political, not sociological, circumstance that the CPs are managed (as is Soviet Russia) by bureaucrats of mixed social origins operating in the name of a proletarian ideology inherited from the past, and unwilling to cede power to pretenders invoking another ideology.

Intellectuals and Artists

The attitude of the CP to the new class of technical intellectuals was an extension of a consistent attitude to intellectuals from 'the other culture', the humanists and artists with whom communism and socialism have a long acquaintance. The CP consistently welcomed such people, especially if they were famous enough to bring it some prestige, but only on the condition that the intellectuals submitted to the proletarian ideology as embodied in the party leadership. If they would surrender all claim of the class from which they came (usually the middle class) or of the intellectual strata to be anything but the subordinate 'allies' of the working class, then they could even aspire to rise to the top of the workers' party. 'The intellectuals have a place in the party only on condition that they accept, to an even higher degree than the other militants, the total hegemony of the leadership of the party which, by definition, is the incarnation of the working class.'[47] This insistence on the 'even higher degree' of submission required of intellectuals reflected the distrust of politicians (and not only communist politicians) of people ever inclined to turn a party into a debating club or a talking-shop (as the politicians say impatiently), i.e. to go on being intellectuals.

Despite the rigour of these conditions, the CPs attracted a long lineage of intellectuals, often of some distinction.[48] This need not be ascribed to a masochistic desire among middle-class intellectuals to bow before the humble working man. There can be specifically intellectual *reasons* for becoming communist. Communism provides assumptions from which to argue towards telling criticism of West European societies, of the alliance with the United States, of the allocation of investments (called 'profit'), and in general of the social life of those countries where communism is most widespread, such as France and Italy. Yet there can be no intellectual reasons for remaining a member of CPs if the exercise of intelligence implies a care for consistency, for open criticism and free inquiry, for these things are not available within the party. Consequently, since there are reasons for joining but none for staying, fluctuation is high among communist intellectuals, higher even than among workers. It is exacerbated by the fact that intellectuals and artists are capable of joining a party 'for the experience'.

In discussing the appeal of the CPs for intellectuals and artists, one must distinguish widely different situations in various countries. It is one thing for an Italian intellectual to join a vast movement that claims to represent a whole alternative culture, and another thing for a British intellectual to join a small and freakish sect—especially if enough British (and today Swedish and West German) intellectuals join the CP for them to equal or even outnumber the members of working-class origin. Still, not too much should be made of this difference between big and small parties, as is done by those who feel that the British communist intellectual is pathologically 'deviant' whereas the Italian intellectual who joins the party is behaving almost normally. ('If I were Italian, I would join the communist party,' said Jean-Paul Sartre patronizingly.) The gap between middle-class and working-class standards is probably as great, and the gulf between intellectual activity and party work certainly is, in the big parties as in the small. More important, the techniques used by the bureaucratic leadership to maintain the submission of the intellectuals, in the name of the workers, is exactly the same. Consequently the experience ends in being quite similar.

A distinction can, rather, be drawn between the appeal of communism to intellectuals in parliamentary democracies on the one hand, and in countries where democracy is still insecurely established or not at all, on the other. Here the line runs between on the one hand the PCI and the PCE, and on the other hand the parties of northern and Western Europe, be they big or small, such as the PCF and the PCGB. For the Italian since the war, and even more obviously for other Mediterranean communists, the CP can seem to be an instrument for the conquest of democracy and civic rights. The intellectual who joins it in that hope leaves when he finds it is not such an instrument. On the contrary, the French or British intellectual more often joins the party precisely to show his contempt for democracy and civic rights, which he scorns as merely formal or abstract. He leaves when he discovers the value of formal democracy, as against the élitism and 'economism' that attracted him to communism.

That difference might go some way to explaining why the Mediterranean parties, including the clandestine Greek and Spanish parties as well as the PCI, were more successful in attracting intellectuals and let them have more leeway than the aggressively *ouvriériste* PCF. But all such fine distinctions were drowned by the tide of ultra-Leftism in the 1960s, which washed away the intellectual support of the Spanish party in the universities as easily as it swept the Swedish Left into such grotesque fantasies as the worship of Mao Tse-tung's magic eyes.[49] The *Manifesto* opposition to the PCI was overwhelmingly an intellectual movement, and it attacked the party precisely for its compromises with parliamentary democracy.

Mechanically repeating the classic assertions of Lenin and Stalin, who denied any autonomous political role to intellectuals, the parties were taken aback by the worldwide events that reached a climax in Paris in May and June 1968 and which showed that the intellectuals were claiming just such a role and reviling 'les crapules staliniennes', as Cohn-Bendit called the PCF, who denied it to them. The instinctive reaction of the PCF was to intensify its *ouvriériste* attitudes and to keep the working-class elements it controlled aloof from the demonstrations of students. This aroused opposition inside the party and that opposition could invoke support from Soviet Russia. In articles in *Pravda* in 1968–70, it was argued that recent events actually created 'a historical opportunity' for the western parties to widen their social base, by accepting an alliance with the intellectuals. Of course, the Soviet theorists pointed out that the 'leadership of the working class' would have to be preserved but they added that this easily could be done by adopting the theory that intellect was being 'proletarianized'.[50] Intellectuals, who for years had been lumped with 'other social groups' alongside the workers and peasants, began to get specific mention among the exploited whom the CPs sought to attract.

The decline of West European Maoism, in part because of changes in Chinese policies and in part because such extravagances quickly burn themselves out, was greeted with relief by the communists but in fact it did little to reduce their difficulties with the intellectuals.

Other ultra-Leftist forces, and in particular a revivified Trotskyism, consolidated themselves at the same time, and this complicated the relations of the communists with intellectuals. A further complication was that the new Moscow line towards intellectuals required the parties to make concessions to western intellectuals that would involve taking their distances from Moscow. The effort to seize the 'historic chance' of winning the support of the growing mass of intellectuals has made it necessary for the western parties to take stands on art, literature, and even discussion that differ sharply from Soviet policies.

In this, they were hastening a retreat from Zhdanovism—that is, from party tyranny over art and thought in the name of socialist realism and Stalinist orthodoxy—a retreat that had begun with de-Stalinization itself. The PCI had never gone as far in Zhdanovism as the French party, which had its own Zhdanov in the person of Laurent Casanova. Even the French party by 1964 was conceding the necessity for the leadership to be neutral in questions of art, science, and philosophy (but not social or political science). Those concessions were incorporated in the declaration of Argenteuil in 1966,[51] a resolution of the central committee that was to be invoked for years afterwards as the charter of liberties of the communist intellectual and artist. Significantly, that liberty was actually used—by Aragon to protest in *L'Humanité* in 1966 at the condemnation of two Soviet dissidents, Sinyavski and Daniel. The Spanish party denounced that condemnation also, not merely with the voice of an intellectual spokesman but that of its secretary-general, Santiago Carrillo.

It was this movement—native to West European communism and independent of Moscow—that gathered pace from 1968. The occasion for the western parties to show Moscow what was really involved in wooing intellectuals was provided by the censoring and persecution of Solzhenitsyn and by the repression of liberties in Czechoslovakia after August 1968. The PCI was outspoken on both issues, as was Aragon's publication, *Les Lettres françaises*, in both cases to the point of receiving reprimands from Moscow and Eastern Europe. Indeed, Moscow managed to have *Les Lettres françaises* silenced, by banning it inside the Soviet bloc and by pressuring the PCF into withdrawing the funds needed for its publication, in October 1972. But that only made it the more necessary for the PCF, this time in the person of Marchais, to denounce censorship, to defend Solzhenitsyn, and to specify that western communists did not see any 'cultural model' to the east and had a conception of the freedom of intellectuals and artists different from that prevailing in Soviet Russia.

To set this new line on intellectuals and artists in perspective it is indispensable to recall that the western parties have relaxed their censoriousness on earlier occasions, only to restore the hard line when the political climate changed.[52] Moreover, there are still limits to the right to criticize, as the silencing of *Les Lettres françaises* showed, as well as a refusal to say that among the 'shortcomings' vaguely ascribed to the Soviet world is the ruthless and inexorable persecution of intellectuals and artists. Finally, there seems to be no case of western communists anticipating non-communist denunciation of Soviet oppression, even though they must be better informed about the facts. Only when others decry an instance of oppression, do the western parties say 'Me too'—but even then not for *Samizdat*.[53] For all these qualifications, it would be idle to deny the more liberal face the parties now present towards intellectuals and artists. Particular significance might attach to the evolution of western communist attitudes to painting and architecture, and above all the abandonment of opposition to formalism and modernity generally, because these are not just 'views' that might change tomorrow but actual practice exemplified in the parties' buildings, fairs, exhibitions, and publications. A change in *taste* and a toleration of experimentation in art are solid realities alongside *claims* to liberalism in politics and thought.

Although, for these reasons, the life of the intellectual inside a western CP has become more comfortable than it was, there is no evidence that the party is attracting, and holding, any more intellectuals. There is doubt about its sincerity; there has been competition from other sections of the Left since the CP lost its monopoly of criticism of capitalism; and there is a decline in the fascination that communism exercises over intellectuals as it becomes more liberal, more like other parties. Not that it will become quite like other western parties for the intellectual until it revises the basic contract it has always offered the educated non-worker, the terms of which were: the intellectual communist wins a vantage point from which to exercise criticism and analysis of western society in return for an undertaking to suspend the exercise of intelligence over a certain range of problems. The three main problems that were taboo were: 1. the situation in the Soviet bloc; 2. the political strategy of the local party leadership, and 3. the validity of the proletarian ideology and the veneration of manual work and extensive industry.

These three points are not arbitrarily chosen as especially interesting. They relate to the three sources of power and legitimacy in a western CP. As will be shown in an analysis of the structure of those parties in the next chapter, the pillars of a party are Soviet support, the local bureaucracy, and a section of the working class. When intellectuals win the right to discuss those three taboo questions, they will have a stable place inside the party. To this point, they are still fighting for the right to discuss the third, as we saw in the debate about the precedence of the classic, manual-labour proletariat over the new class of technical intellectuals. They have not yet won the vestige of a right to discuss the second. The local bureaucracy is still unquestioned in its political wisdom, i.e. these are still Leninist parties, where the leadership has a monopoly over the right to 'enrich' and 'develop' Marxist theory whereas intellectuals may not commit the crime of 'revising' it but must confine themselves to asking for 'clarifications' from above. As to the first taboo, the situation is fluid. For one thing, the local party bureaucracy is itself seeking to redefine its relations with the centre of Soviet power, for reasons of political necessity and opportunism; it thus tolerates a certain discussion and questioning of the Soviet world by the intellectuals that would never have been allowed before. For another, there is occurring the break-up of a secret doctrine about the Soviet Union that was shared by western intellectual communists for several generations. Since they spent much of their time in the party pondering it, we can briefly recall its tenets.

For a western intellectual to remain with—more, to defend—the CP at a time when everyone interested knew about the concentration camps, slave labour, purges, rigged trials, genocide, and the rest of the Stalinist (and post-Stalinist) nightmare, it was not enough for him to pretend not to know, not to read capitalist newspapers, not to trust non-party sources. Other party members might shut their minds but not the intellectuals. They knew. They agreed, nevertheless, to defend communism on the basis of the half-secret doctrine of the 'besieged fortress'. All these horrors were the result of capitalist encirclement, the fascist threat, then the Cold War. It is important to see, and it becomes easier to see as these events fade into the past, that a moderately plausible case can be made out for the claim that the Stalinist tyranny was in many ways a defensive reaction to perceived external threats, that were imagined to endanger the continuation of an insecure new polity in a nation where centuries of oppression prepared people for resort to authoritarian methods.[54] Of course, for that explanation to explain very much it must start from the fact that the

Soviet leadership from 1917 to this day has envisaged its situation in warlike terms, as an instance of struggle between inexorable enemies. That is, they started out with the conviction they were in a 'besieged fortress' and then had no difficulty in identifying the besiegers, and dictating a war emergency on the home front.

But even at its most persuasive, this justification of Stalinism in terms of Soviet history was never a justification of western communism. Even if you believed every word of it, the most you could conclude would be that you should join a pro-Soviet friendship society, or that you should take up the attitude of American capitalists like Cyrus Eaton or Armand Hammer or European generals like Charles de Gaulle. You could never conclude that you should join a CP—unless you had in mind a second, secret doctrine. Before turning to that doctrine, it is worth dwelling on the *non sequitur* of western intellectuals who explained the horrors of Stalinism as due to objective social and political conditions in Soviet Russia and yet also defended Stalinism in the west, where no such conditions obtained. This illogicality became public when Khrushchev in his report to the twentieth congress of the Soviety party denounced Stalinism but avoided all discussion of its causes by giving it the absurd label, 'the personality cult'. Thereupon western communists explained in chorus that this amounted to evasion of a quest for the real causes. Togliatti,[55] the politburo of the PCF, and the political committee of the CPGB[56] were unanimous that it was un-Marxist and intellectually dishonest to hush up Stalinism as the fault of one man, without looking for its social causes in Soviet society. They apparently failed to notice that their own position was no better than Khrushchev's, for whatever 'social causes' were found would be Russian, not Italian, French, or British and thus could not explain Stalinism (as distinct from non-communist sympathy with Moscow) in Italy, France, or Britain. In other words, a westerner might well believe that Stalin purged the Red Army and the satellite governments because he had plausible ground to suspect an imminent capitalist onslaught. That belief could not reasonably lead a westerner to join a local CP that denied that such purges ever took place and which staged imitation purges, trials, and witch-hunts in its own ranks.

He would not do so unless—and this is the secret doctrine that kept many western intellectuals in the CP—he also believed that the spread of communism to the enlightened west (for which temporary Soviet help might be necessary) would at last liberate communism from its Russian or Slav or East European shortcomings. This is a perfectly respectable thought for a western communist, for it comes from Lenin. Lenin, in the days immediately following the Bolshevik Revolution, not only expected but hoped that a similar revolution would soon follow in a more advanced European country than Russia, whereupon backward Russia would necessarily lose the leadership of world communism. Whatever basis that hope had in the agitated days of 1918–19, when the Third International was being founded precisely to give it substance, it had none when socialism was limited to one country and Soviet power was consolidated. The folly of co-operating with the Soviet state and the Soviet secret police in order to keep alive a Soviet power that one day might serve as protector of a more advanced, more civilized (and hence anti-Soviet) communism elsewhere has been demonstrated from China to Spain via Yugo-slavia. The most recent victims of the illusion were the Czech communists of 1948 who believed that the *coup de Prague* had at last brought communism to power in an advanced, educated, industrial-ized European society where the nightmares of backward Russian communism were unimaginable. Beria's secret police, who directed the interrogation of these very Czech communists when they came to be framed, were there to cure them of that illusion.[57]

That does not prevent the director of the PCF's Centre of Marxist Studies from dismissing Stalinism as 'a specifically Russian pheno-menon' that 'could never happen here'.[58] As the local western party bureaucracies have sought to take their distance from Soviet power, the secret doctrine has been brought out into the open. Enrico Berlinguer in 1972 told the PCI congress that the 'difficulties' that communism is now admitted to have encountered in the east only heighten 'the historical responsibility of the European working class', i.e of the western CPs. That responsibility, he explained, is to show 'what socialism can be in *this* part of the world'.[59] The notion that western Marxists will one day put the backward Russians in their place has kept many an intellectual in the party. Now that it is a public claim it loses the charms of a whispered secret doctrine and must face the objections that can be brought against it after an inquiry into the western parties' dependence on Soviet power, both now and in the hour of their problematic coming to power.

Political Psychology

Those who feel that, after looking at the relations between com-munism and regions, age, sex, religion, class, and occupation, they

4

still do not see *who the communist are* will not find the answer in a study of political psychology. No one would think to argue that the many millions of communist voters in Western Europe are of some special psychological type, but there have been attempts to show that party members are. There is a Cold War literature that embroiders on such themes as, 'The party meets the needs of neurotically hostile people', or 'For individuals unable to escape from these cruel dilemmas and confusions, the party makes possible a positive and constructive image of the self', etc.[60] Apart from the absence of a comparative study of *other* political parties (such as might show, for example, that anyone who joins any party does something for his 'image of the self'), such literature is too plainly based on the prejudice that communism is kinky.

There are no grounds for a clinical psychiatry of communism, or for psychological explanations of how people become communist, or for study of the appeals of communism that are limited to certain sorts of people. The West European communist is not, as such, sick or deviant (not even statistically so, in many regions). If his work in the party develops certain normal human weaknesses, such as implacability and partisanship, it also develops the familiar human virtues of heroism, self-sacrifice, meticulousness, and devotion. The CPs in Europe have offered, and still offer under the dictatorships, the chance to participate in an epic whose scope covers continents and generations. Communism offers serious 'reasons to believe' and it denounces real crimes and injustices. That there is as much and more to be said *against* it does not alter the fact that when men and women weigh up such a matter, their decision is not habitually determined by a personality trait or psychological weakness. Quite the contrary, in France at least, the decision to join the party is the sign of a serious young worker who is settling down, passing one of the rites of manhood, signifying his adjustment to the urban situation after migrating from the countryside, and acquiring a badge of virility and proletarian respectability.[61] Beyond that, it is clear that there is an immense variety of reasons for which, or moods in which, people join CPs in different countries and at different times, and a study of them is liable to be quite uninformative.

It might be more helpful to notice that if there is anything odd here it is the action of joining *any* political party. After all, the faith that causes are promoted by sitting on committees, passing resolutions, knocking on doors, selling papers, and cadging votes is shared by only a minority of Europeans, whom the rest regard as victims of political obsession. Now what is distinctive about communism is that it is the most extreme form of that obsession. It is the most political of all the political parties, not only in that it has most committees, passes the most resolutions, etc, but in that it reduces everything to politics. The party line can extend to every imaginable issue and indeed if the CP's programme does not contain the solution of a problem, then it is not a real problem (as women, youths, and Jews are regularly informed). Communism, said Simone Weil, is 'la politique à l'état pur'.

Thus if one insisted on having a psychological portrait of the communist it would be enough to think of a political activist of any colour, whose engrossment with drafting resolutions, counting votes, and fighting factions was carried to a stage of mild delirium. Except for the policies he espouses, there is nothing else peculiar about the communist. Consequently, pictures of the 'typical communist' of this or that party are apt to inform us only about the ideal type that that party wishes to present to the world, or about the sort of party worker who most easily wins promotion (up to a point, and especially to congress delegations) because he corresponds to the party's image of itself. In reality, there will be many sorts of typical communist because the party, like any party that succeeds in attracting tens of thousands and even hundreds of thousands of members, offers a variety of roles for people to play and a variety of degrees of adhesion.

In other words, there are various ways of being a communist. Firstly, there is the obvious point that one can be so more or less. Secondly, one can be so in different modes: as a political choice because of local problems and grievances; as an 'existential' choice because in one's milieu it is the done thing; as an ideological choice because one is Marxist-Leninist. Lastly, within the party there is a choice of various roles to play, between which one chooses according to one's talents but also according to instructions as the party's tactics change.

These things are true of other parties; it remains to note some peculiarities about communism. As to the more or less, it is a commonplace that parties have an activist node surrounded by a series of coronas, extending to mere sympathizers. In the case of the CP, a large part of members' time—perhaps the greater part—is spent in trying to get other communists to move centripetally: to become more active and more 'class conscious', to come to cell meetings, to recruit more, sell more literature, keep up subscriptions. Naturally, these efforts largely fail, since in ordinary times, apart from situations like the

Resistance, most people refuse the degree of political engrossment characteristic of the communist. So the complaint in all the parties is that only 20–25 per cent of members even attend cell meetings, supposedly the basic requirement of membership. As to militant activity and giving money, the complaint is: 'ce sont toujours les mêmes'! The constant agitation to politicize members gives life in the party its air of self-centred futility. The PCI has carried the policy so far as to enrol its sympathizers, becoming a mass party by the expedient of issuing cards to hundreds of thousands of its voters, who then are constantly nagged and harassed to show more activity in the party.

The delineation of various modes of being communist—the political mode in regions traditionally Jacobin, the existential mode among Red Belt workers, the ideological mode among students—is useful as pointing to familiar sorts of 'typical communist'. Yet no exhaustive list of such modes can be given; there is no way of measuring their prevalence; and they overlap. Thus however suggestive they may be, they belong with other efforts to reduce political choices to personal character traits.

In contrast, one can describe precisely the roles that the party allocates to members to play, because these are characteristic of communism and are distributed in function of its political action. They include (or, as we shall see, used to include): the professional revolutionary, mass leader, labour agitator, conspirator, popular tribune, democratic soldier, etc. They are often described in psychological terms by unsympathetic outsiders, usually in an ironic tone (thus: 'nihilistic', 'saint', 'pitiless destroyer of historical culture', 'midwife of a new and humane society', 'combative disciplined soldier', 'philosopher-theologian', 'clarifying, explaining teacher'.)[62] In fact they are not moods but *party lines* decided upon by the leadership in successive historical situations. There is one psychological point to note, however. It is that communism used to be singular among western parties because of its sudden changes of policy, in accord with the Leninist theory of tactical flexibility, and these changes presented themselves to members as abrupt switches from one role to another— from the role of conspirator to that of parliamentary democrat, for example. This requirement of versatility or 'disponibilité' proved psychologically unacceptable for many members—hence the phenomenon of fluctuation; but it gave others, a minority, the fascinating illusion of omnicompetence and an old-man-of-the-sea resilience.

The degree of versatility required and the number of roles offered have diminished since Lenin wrote the original repertoire for his party of a new type. The role of professional revolutionary of Lenin's *What is to be done?* is no longer available in the West European democracies, or even in all the dictatorships: Spanish communists are required to collaborate with the Catholics and much of the Right, just like Italian communists, while Turkish communists are required to co-operate objectively with the ruling regime, just like French communists at the time of de Gaulle. Already in the Stalinist era, the various Leninist roles were being overshadowed by the role of disciplined trooper in a rigidly organized army. Yet that role today is rejected by the West European communists as 'Chinese' and, instead, prominence is given to the roles of parliamentary democrat, unionist, and party organizer. The reasons for that will appear in an account of party policies and do not belong with a consideration of the characters of party members.

As much as (or more than) personal character dictates political affiliations, membership of a political party develops certain traits of character. Activity in any party develops the partisan character, and this is especially true of activity in the CP because it is singularly political. There are other traits that are developed by communism, but before describing them it is needful to emphasize that one is not saying that all communists are like this (and even less, that this is why they are communist). For one thing, one must remember the phenomenon of fluctuation: most people are communist for too short a time to be influenced in these ways, and they probably quit the party because they could not be so influenced. The following traits of personality and habits of thought are those that the party cultivates and exacerbates in members who stay in long enough, and notably in members who get on in the party.

THE SENSE OF THE ENEMY. All political parties cultivate the ability to recognize a privileged opponent, who is identified under all his disguises and pursued with hatred and scorn. In the process they provide members with a respectable outlet for aggressiveness and suspiciousness. The extreme Right and the CPs are unusually vehement in cultivating this sense of the enemy. This leads to a habit of ruthlessness, implacability, and vengeance that marks communism. For example, during the Resistance the French communists were the only party in favour, against the explicit, reasoned instructions of de Gaulle, of killing Germans; and at the Liberation they exceeded all others in the intransigent ferreting out of collaborationists. These wartime proclivities have been perpetuated through the long peace, because for communists it was never really peace, so that a military sense of the enemy remained seasonable. 'The enemy was like Satan, always the bearer of the most deadly menace and yet always conquered and crushed.'[63] Antagonistic references to protean enemies like imperialism, Atlanticism or fascism occupy a large part of communist writings, with particular emphasis on 'unmasking' them in situations where non-communists might not suspect their presence. 'Oh, the bastards!' had become the daily answer to absolutely everything, the password, the alpha and omega. Every act of commission or omission by the others was commented, defined, and pilloried by an inevitable, 'Oh, the bastards!'[64]

THE SENSE OF THE TRAITOR. Political parties develop, as their surface tension, an esprit de corps that is expressed in the notions of party-ness and party loyalty, and hence in a loathing of backsliders. Communism carries this to a paroxysm, illustrated in the trials—in Moscow and Prague but also within western CPs. The vengeance with which people who ostentatiously leave or are expelled are pursued and slandered is redoubled if they dare to break silence by speaking to, or just being spoken of, in the press or radio-TV. If the person has any public notoriety, the 'bourgeois' press is bound to take the case up, as happened when the PCF expelled Tillon (see p. 133)—whereupon the traitor's guilt is clearly established. Everyone in the party fears the traitor as a leper; even his wife and children must be avoided. If it is true that this attitude is being relaxed and that members of the PCF can take the risk of talking to ex-members,[65] this will be a significant evolution in party morality. Already the western parties have made no use in recent years of the other function of the sense of the traitor, the invocation of treacherous leaders to cover changes in party line. The notion of the purity and infallibility of the party could be bolstered by the defence mechanism of discovering that its mistakes were deviations due to infiltration of the leadership by police agents or fascism, as in the Barbé-Célor affair (see p. 131), in the PCF, and in the Tillon affair. But the traitor mentality is kept alive by the practice of maintaining dossiers on party members, which leads to mutual spying by members who regard each other as traitors *in potentia*. These dossiers, in the bolshevik tradition, contain only implacable criticism and are based on constant watchful observation, in accordance with the principle that 'he who begins to doubt has already ceased to be a loyal member'. So the merest peccadillo has potential significance. This breeds the sense that no man can be right alone against the watchful, infallible party but it also multiplies the guilt feelings that lead to the moral collapse of communists on trial before other communists, in the western parties as much as in Prague.

THE SUITABLE LIE, THE UNSUITABLE TRUTH. These military modes of thought applied to politics come from Lenin, who said that 'philosophy is politics carried on by other means'. Thus, there can be a politics of truth: there can be strategic truths that need to be defended by tactical lies. Naturally, the communists did not invent the notion of lies told in a good cause (the Christian churches have long used it), but by politicizing everything and then conceiving politics as a military engagement with a ubiquitous enemy, they generalized the practice of subordinating mere facts to other, more important considerations. There is a camp of peace and socialism locked in struggle with a satanic enemy and endangered by its own traitors: anything you say might be used against it. No matter that what you say is true, for there are a host of little truths that keep the Great Lie of capitalism going; and there are little lies that help forward the Great Truth of communism. So the facts become subordinate to the consideration that one 'must not give comfort to the enemy', 'not discourage Billancourt' (a working-class suburb of Paris), 'not be the objective accomplice of' such and such, 'not fall for the provocation' of such another. When the Khrushchev report in 1956 confirmed that Stalin had in fact committed crimes that western communists had denied, there were those among them who nevertheless maintained that they had been right to be wrong.

ESOTERIC COMMUNICATION. Many groups, starting with families, have their secrets, their allusions and their code words, so that they can practise what has been called esoteric communication. Since the original model for the western CPs was an illegal revolutionary party operating under the Tsarist repression, these characteristics are more highly developed than in parties with a democratic history. Secrecy, jargon, fetish words, studied ignorance, and allusiveness are forms of communist cohesion. There is reason to think that they became more pronounced as the communist project looked less and less plausible in Western Europe. Secrecy and ignorance then served as a defence, to isolate the party from an uncongenial environment. Secrecy is marked in the Finnish party, but it is the habit, too, in the supposedly more open Italian party. The PCI did not reveal what stand Togliatti had taken at the 1957 conference in Moscow until 1959, and his resignation was kept secret for eighteen months. This secrecy extends to members of the party, not just to outsiders; facts about the party are the property of the politburo—and then not of all its members.

This lack of communication is reinforced by the use of jargon. Strange as it may seem, communists do use among themselves the jargon they use in conversing with enemies. Communists in the same party talk this way, and parties exchange communications in it. The result is that they live in a slogan world where language is hermetic, frenzied (everything is a symptom of the crisis of capitalism, for example), and ultimately uninformative. A leading feature of this jargon is the constant repetition of fetish words, such as 'monopolies', which means competitive businesses, or 'masses', which means small communist groups, or 'western European working class' which means the CPs. The origin of these fetish words is in the Stalinist popularization and emotionalizing of Marxist terminology, but it has also been suggested that there is here an application of Pavlovian 'conditioning'. When one recalls the immense over-valuation of Pavlov's theories under Stalin (they were materialist psychology, against Freudian idealism), the suggestion is not absurd, especially since Pavlovian techniques seem to have been consciously applied in the communist trials.[66]

Communist communication is further complicated by allusiveness. Names are not named, policies are not stated, parties are not identified, persons unknown are denounced or referred by the names of other persons thought to agree with them (e.g. Chinese are called Albanians). This can lead to spurious agreement and real discord among communists because, although the function of allusiveness in all groups is to mark off the initiates who understand from the outsiders who do not, there is ample proof that it has been carried so far by communists that they sometimes fail to understand each other. For example, one of the most important concerns of communism in recent decades was the Sino–Soviet split, and yet discussion of it was carried on in such 'an abstract and shadowy way', said the Dutch party, that no one understood.[67] Coming from the party of Paul de Groot, one of the oldest Stalinist hands, the admission is striking. Yet it did not prevent the CPN from attacking a certain mysterious 'modern revisionism' without mentioning Moscow.[68] The Danish and Italian communists also admitted they did not understand references to the Sino–Soviet split.[69] There were signs of confusion in other parties.

The ravages of secrecy, jargon, and allusiveness could be repaired by resort to non-communist sources of information, but studied ignorance of what outsiders say is part of the same complex. Communist intellectuals living in free societies must find it impossible to remain ignorant of what everybody else knows about their party and about the communist world, so that their pretence at ignorance may be taken as deliberate self-delusion. But many other members of CPs, workers and militants in particular, would not read the capitalist press on the Soviet invasion of Hungary in 1956 or on the repression in Prague in 1968; since the party papers said little or nothing, they could remain ignorant. Ignorance is compounded by the absence of horizontal communication in CPs. If one federation dealt with another, rather than with the central leadership, or if members fraternized with members of other cells, this would lead to accusations of fractionalism, groupism, or even anti-party activity. The dependence on vertical communication reinforces ignorance and maintains esoteric communication. The point about esoteric communication is that it is much less efficient than normal communication. Consequently, for all the reasons just given, CPs are political mastodonts, slow to move and late in adapting. It can take three months for a secret decision about a new party line to percolate down to the lowest rungs of the party—by which time the election or political crisis that the new line was meant to deal with has passed. Communist leaders in the west now admit that if their parties are to function as participants in western politics, instead of as total opponents, they will need to increase the circulation of ideas within their ranks.[70]

CHILIASM. The faith in the Revolution, as the coming of a golden age, has so often been parodied as a communist delusion that it is not always noticed that this attitude has largely receded among western communists. Stalinism was the last affliction of political magic in the communist parties. The communist psychoanalyist referred to above (p. 53), who believes that the expropriation of the monopolies will inaugurate the erotic society, is an oddity today. Nevertheless, when one weighs the practical essence of communist programmes, namely the nationalization of a few more industries, in economies that are already 'mixed', against the enormous benefits that are supposed to flow from it, one must suspect that a taste for political magic lingers.

VENERATION. 'Reverence is a communist emotion', said Jacques

Fauvet, and indeed the parties have shown a weakness for veneration, for hero worship, for 'the cult of the personality'. One might understand, as a neurosis, the fascination of Stalin or Mao for westerners (especially for power-worshipping intellectuals), but the literal adulation of men as devoid of charisma as Maurice Thorez or Palmiro Togliatti is baffling. It will be dealt with later in connection with the function of the party boss. Here it need simply be noted that the parties cultivate the feeling that they are families, refuges, from which one cannot escape without becoming orphan, fraternities that do not require a man to desert his real family but will absorb it and in return constitute an enlarged family where veneration of the father is quite in order. Mother worship of female leaders like La Pasionaria (secretary, later president, of the Spanish party, who lived so long in Moscow that she became known as La Pensionaria) was supplemented by veneration of leaders' wives. Khrushchev in his secret report was typical in mentioning Stalin's rudeness to Lenin's wife *before* such lesser crimes as genocide. The practice extended to the PCF, where insults directed at Jeannette Vermeersch were party crimes. This veneration has receded in recent years but it has been so constant in the affairs of CPs that one hesitates to conclude that it has disappeared for ever.

COMRADES WITHOUT COMRADESHIP. Although communists call each other 'comrade' and 'tu', ex-communists often complain that there was no comradeship, no friendship in the party, only a superficial palliness accompanied by political watchfulness. Friendship, even between brothers-in-law or actual brothers,[71] is suspect as groupism, fractionalism. This is relevant to the speed at which the parties disappoint new recruits, some of whom joined the party in the hope of finding friendship. Whether they seek simple human warmth in the often difficult conditions of urban life, or some vaster notion of human fraternity to be attained by socialism, the CP usually disappoints such people. The atmosphere of mutual spying, the preparation of dossiers supposedly to assist in the selection of militants for promotion, and the politicizing of every human relationship exclude comradeship.

Notes

1 *LM*, 23 Feb 1973.
2 E. V. Jensen, *De politiske partier* (Albertslund, Denmark, 1969), p. 16.

3 Lars Svaasand, 'The communists in postwar Norway', paper presented at the European Consortium for Political Research's Workshop on Communism in Western Europe, Paris, 1973 (hereafter ECPR Workshop), p. 7.

4 H. Schmaltz-Jørgensen, ed., *De politiska partierna i Norden* (Stockholm, 1970), p. 100.

5 The literature on the subject is recalled by Bengt Matti in Åke Sparring, ed., *Kommunismen i Norden och den världskommunistiska kris* (Lund, Sweden, 1965), pp. 108–9.

6 President Kekkonen was quoted by Maximilian Smidt, 'Skandinavien: von ganz links nach links', in R. Hill et al, *Kommunistische Parteien im Westen* (Frankfurt, 1968), p. 200. On the prior socialist tradition, A. F. Upton, *The communist parties of Scandinavia and Finland* (London, 1973), pp. 341–4.

7 Lennart Lundmark, *Koloni i Norr: Om 650 års utsugning av Norrbotten* (Stockholm, 1971), pp. 72–87.

8 Mattei Dogan, quoted by Svaasand, pp. 6–7.

9 Ibid.

10 Hans Hinterhäuser, *Italien zwischen Schwarz und Rot* (Stuttgart, 1956), pp. 53–9.

11 Anders Ehnmark, *Rapport från det röda Emilien* (Stockholm, 1969), pp. 30–42.

12 Fauvet, pp. 166–7.

13 In Arnold Toynbee et al, *The impact of the Russian revolution* (London, 1967), pp. 58–60.

14 Lewis S. Feuer, 'Generations and the theory of revolution', *Survey*, no 84, pp. 182–8.

15 G. Lord, 'Le PCF: structures et organisation d'une fédération départementale', ECPR Workshop.

16 *LM*, 16 & 17 May 1973.

17 Bon, p. 242.

18 *LM*, 10 Mar 1973.

19 *Le Nouvel Observateur*, 28 May 1973.

20 *Dagens Nyheter*, 27 Oct 1972.

21 Annie Kriegel, *Les Communistes français*, 2nd ed. (Paris, 1970), pp. 29–34.

22 *VIII Congreso del PCE*, pp. 71–2.

23 Annie Kriegel, 'Léon Blum vu par les communistes', *Preuves*, no 182, p. 43.

24 *LM*, 6 May 1972.

25 Enrico Berlinguer, *Per un governo di svolta democratica* (Rome, 1972), p. 73.

26 *LM*, 30 Dec 1972.

27 Bernard Muldworf, *Vers la société érotique* (Paris, 1972).

28 Pertti Suhonen, 'Religious involvement and voting in the People's Democratic League in Finland', ECPR Workshop, p. 9.

29 T. W. Adams, *AKEL: the communist party of Cyprus* (Stanford, 1971), pp. 66, 113–16.

30 *Der Spiegel*, 19 June & 13 Nov 1972.

31 In addition to the books of Garaudy, one may cite Mario Gozzini, ed., *Il Dialogo alla prova*, 2nd ed. (Florence, 1965), the *Gespräche der Paulusgesellschaft* (1965–7), and the proceedings of the Semaine de la pensée marxiste, Jan 1972.

32 Neil McInnes, 'The Christian-Marxist dialogue', *Survey*, no 67, 1968. For a consistently incredulous commentary on this 'meeting of minds', one may consult the articles of Hervé Leclerc & Claude Harmel in *Est et Ouest*.

33 *LM*, 12 Aug 1972.

34 Ibid., 21 Sept 1972.

35 Ibid., 29 Sept & 4 Oct 1972.

36 Giorgio Galli, *Il Bipartitismo imperfetto: comunisti e democristiani in Italia* (Bologna, 1966), pp. 157, 181.

37 Toynbee, p. 61.

38 Galli, p. 329.

39 Laurens & Pfister, pp. 216–23.

40 Annie Kriegel & Michel Perrot, *Le Socialisme français et le pouvoir* (Paris, 1966), pp. 207–8.

41 Galli, pp. 132–5; and Giorgio Galli, *Il difficile governo* (Bologna, 1972), pp. 196–7, 210–11.

42 Sigurd Klockare, *Från Generalstrejk till Folkfront* (Stockholm, 1971), pp. 192–3; Ulrich Wagner, *Finlands Kommunisten: Volksfrontexperiment und Parteispaltung* (Stuttgart, 1971), p. 18.

43 Daniel Tarschys, 'New Left, old guard and neo-Leninism: Swedish communism in the era of "acentrism"', ECPR Workshop, pp. 5–6.

44 Sparring, p. 22.

45 The statistics in the tables are drawn from Bon, p. 243, Laurens & Pfister, pp. 183–4, *Le Nouvel Observateur*, 28 May 1973, and *Le Monde*, 23 Feb & 10 Mar 1973.

46 At the XIX Congress of the PCF, Nanterre, 4–8 Feb 1970 (*Cahiers du communisme*, Feb–Mar 1970). For the debate about the 'new classes', Jean Duflot, *L'Italie du Manifesto* (Paris, 1971) and 'La conquête des couches nouvelles', in Laurens & Pfister, pp. 181–208.

47 Barjonet, p. 138.

48 David Caute, *Communism and the French intellectuals* (London, 1964) and *The fellow-travellers* (London, 1973); Leopold Labedz, 'The destiny of writers in revolutionary movements', *Survey*, no 82.

49 Torbjörn Säfve, *Rebellerna i Sverige* (Uddevalla, Sweden, 1971), pp. 76–7.

50 For classical Soviet doctrine on the question, and its evolution, László Révész, *Export der Revolution* (Bern, 1971), pp. 30–51.

51 *Cahiers du communisme*, May–June 1966.

52 J.-P. Bernard, *Le Parti communiste français et la question littéraire: 1921–1939* (Paris, 1972).

53 Francis Cohen, editor of a PCF review for intellectuals, replied scornfully, in *L'Humanité*, 9 June 1973, to an appeal to save *Samizdat* (*LM*, 8 & 10–11 June 1973).

54 Werner Hofmann, *Stalinismus und Antikommunismus: Zur Soziologie des Ost-West-Konflikts* (Frankfurt, 1967). Hofmann's optimistic conclusions were soon invalidated by the invasion of Czechoslovakia.

55 In an interview to *Nuovi argomenti*, no 20, June 1956, reprinted in *The anti-Stalin campaign and international communism* (New York, 1956). The reference is to pp. 120–1.

56 *Anti-Stalin Campaign*, pp. 169, 177.

57 Artur London, *L'Aveu* (Paris, 1968).

58 Jean Ellenstein replying to Medvedev's book on Stalinism in *Le Monde*, 3 Nov 1972, and a propos of his own history of the Soviet Union, ibid., 1 Aug 1973.

59 Berlinguer, pp. 91–2 (italics added).

60 Almond, pp. 268, 292.

61 Kriegel, *Les Communistes français*, p. 47; Morin, p. 51.

62 Almond, p. 56.

63 Morin, p. 102.

64 Ibid.

65 *Unir*, no 70, pp. 2–3.

66 London, p. 502.

67 *De opvattingen van de CPN over internationale discussie en internationale conferenties* (Amsterdam, 1969), pp. 1–2.

68 *24ste Congres van de CPN* (Amsterdam, 1972), pp. 78–81.

69 Sparring, p. 70. Even Palmiro Togliatti, one of the masters of communist prose, confessed in his Yalta testament that he did not always understand it: 'Sometimes the state of affairs ends up being scarcely comprehensible. In several instances one gets the impression that there are differences of opinion among the ruling groups [of the Soviet bloc] but one cannot say it is so for sure nor what the differences are. Maybe it would be

better in some cases if there were open debate, even in the socialist countries . . .' (*Il Partito communista italiano e il movimento operaio internazionale, 1956–1968* (Rome, 1968), p. 245).

70 Georges Marchais promised at the Arceuil meeting of the central committee of the PCF in March 1970 'to improve the circulation of information' at the level of that committee and 'to develop . . . the information of the whole party'. Yet among the causes of the 1973 electoral defeat was identified tardy and inadequate knowledge of the party line (*LM*, 29 Mar 1973).

71 Tillon, p. 24.

3 Structure and power in communist parties

The twenty-one conditions set by the Comintern in 1920 to the admission of CPs included the requirement to adopt a party structure invented by Lenin. The main features of it were a maximum of centralization and an iron discipline reaching down through an elaborate hierarchy to the members organized in cells. The majority of West European socialists rejected the rigours of the Leninist system from the beginning, but discipline, centralism, and the iron chain of command had great attraction for a minority, those who became communists. They held that such a structure would repair the weaknesses of European socialism, ever prone to division, sectarian squabbling, and disorderly compromises with the other parties. More than half a century later, the Leninist structure continued to be defended on those grounds, especially in places where social democracy has shown the least capacity for organization, unity, and tenacity, i.e. in Italy and France. The excesses and the ruthlessness of CP discipline must always be considered against the background of the pathetic incompetence of socialists in those countries to agree, to organize, and to persist. It is in reaction against that that communism has made its way within the Left. Organization and structure were its raison d'être, and though Togliatti denied that they were its *only* superiority over socialism,[1] whenever communists have objected to them, as Garaudy, Ernest Fischer, and others did, the answer has been sharp: 'The whole history of our party is marked by the resolute struggle against social-democrat hangovers in the matter of organization.'[2]

Actually, the notion that unity alone is efficacious for change in social life is the merest prejudice, as the undisciplined multiplicity of the Protestant faith demonstrated against the static unity of Catholicism. Social democracy, too, has wrought immense changes in West European society in an atmosphere of confusion, disagreement, factionalism, and opportunism—that is to say, in a climate of liberty. In contrast, the Leninist machine has not worked. It has been politically ineffective. Has it even made any difference in the west, scholars ask, outside the dreams of the Leninists and the calumnies of their opponents?[3] It would be too much to say that the Leninist model of absolutely centralized and disciplined structure was never more than a formal fiction in the western parties, but it has been shaken repeatedly by crises and undermined by currents of indiscipline. Moreover, communist engrossment with the dogma of party structure has led to an organizational obsession that constitutes as great a barrier to political effectiveness as socialist indiscipline.

These observations preface an outline of formal party structure, and they suggest that one should not take it too seriously. For one thing, the formal structure masks the real dynamics of power in CPs, which we shall describe later. Secondly, the myth of monolithic unity scantily covers the reality of currents and fractions, struggles for power and clashes of ideas behind the fictitious unanimity.

The PCI can exalt its Spartan democracy among the young by pointing to the helots of Christian Democracy and socialism, but in its inner life it cannot help reflecting the plurality of positions and interests characteristic of a pluralistic society, to which in the last ten years have been added the ever increasing dissensions of the international communist movement.[4]

The fascination with party structure turns out to be another symptom of the political obsession we have seen in communist front organizations and in communist psychology, part of what Vittorini called 'the supersaturation of politics in communist culture'. Administrative questions about party organization come to have priority over 'ideology', i.e. the ethical substance of politics. An unwieldly, complex, slow, and opaque structure ends in political paralysis. When currents of opinion clash within the party, the true Leninist-Stalinist is the bureaucrat who seeks to remain neutral between them, so as to preserve the Leninist instrument that will serve its purpose one far-off day—the day that never comes. Speaking of such a clash of opinions within the PCI in 1962, Degli Esposti said:

Between those two positions stands Togliatti, the sceptical Togliatti who sides with neither of them, for whom what really matters is the monolithic unity of the party, his own authoritarian control, and the rigorous maintenance of democratic centralism which means nothing but dictatorship inside the party at every level and in every committee. What matters is the rigid structure that enables the party to keep its revolutionary potentiality intact, at the very moment when its political tactics would indicate more pliant and open attitudes. . . . Togliatti is a Stalinist.[5]

Hypertrophy of the political instinct leads to missing the point of politics. The administration of the revolutionary structure, the party apparatus, becomes the privileged occupation while European history flows by outside, unnoticed. The bureaucratic structure becomes autonomous, its own finality, a political party reduced to the pure state and to uselessness. The answer to every political problem comes to be seen in some new organization, or a new committee, of which, however, the function is not to discuss the problem and possible policies but to implement orders. The essence of Stalinism is in Stalin's observation, 'To govern is not to write resolutions and distribute directives; to govern is to control the implementation of the directives.' Thorez was quoting Stalin when he said, 'The political line once determined, it is the work of organization which decides everything, including the fate of the political line itself, its realization or its defeat.' One would have thought that what decided success or defeat was the nature of the policy, its relevance or its acceptability, but, for the communist, organization is the only real political problem. Policy is revealed, it is not discussed or adjusted. All that is left for politicians is 'the work of organization [which] is getting men to implement a political line'. Consequently, 'When the party suffers defeats, they are automatically attributed to organizational deficiencies and not to political errors. These deficiencies then supply the subject matter for vigorous criticism and self-criticism.'[6] Bernstein, the first revisionist, said that the movement was all, the goal nothing. The communists are arch-revisionists because for them the party is all, the revolution nothing.

Formal Structure

The formal structure of a large CP is set out in the organigram; a smaller party would have fewer intermediate levels corresponding to regions and federations. These latter divisions usually coincide with the administrative or electoral divisions of the nation. The theory is that each level elects the level next up the hierarchy. In fact, the best way to understand the organigram is to invert it and replace election with co-optation (except for the choice of members themselves). If each level really elected the next, that would be democratic, but CPs practise democratic *centralism*, which means that the delegates of each level are nominated by the level above. The nominating or co-opting level sends emissaries down to meetings of the 'electing' level, and these men ensure that the right people are elected. That applies even to the intermittent sovereign, the party congress, and to the permanent central committee, which is why they will be discussed later along with other intermediate structures. First we shall look at the operation of cells; then at the way in which delegates to the intermediate structures are selected and trained; then at the summits of power, the politburo and secretariat. Finally, we must consider three organs that do not appear in the formal organigram: the secret apparatus, the party boss, and the finances.

```
Locality cell    Workplace cell  ────→   Bureau, secretariat
            ↘       ↙
            Section assembly        ────→      ,,        ,,
                    ↓
            Regional Assembly       ────→      ,,        ,,
                    ↓
            Federal Assembly        ────→      ,,        ,,
                    ↓
            Party Congress
                    ↓
        ↙    Central Committee       ────→   permanent specialized
Political            |                       sections
Control Committee,   ↓
Cadre Committee,    Politburo
etc.                 ↓
                 Secretariat
```

The Cell

The first French communists were called 'les cellulards' so curiously did their formation into cells strike the socialists. In Leninist theory, the cell is the basic constituent of communist flesh, because it is the means of *encadrement* of the member, the means by which the leadership guides and inspires him. In particular, the workplace cell was intended to distinguish the communist from the old socialist parties with their territorially based structure. The workplace cell would mark and maintain the new party's proletarian character and it would provide the means to combat the other force active at the workplace, the trade union.

The cell has proved hard to acclimatize in Western Europe's soil, especially the workplace cell, and there are signs that it is wilting in the face of neo-capitalist distractions. Many of the tens of thousands of cells claimed by the parties exist only on paper, many more meet only infrequently, and all leave the bulk of the work to a minority of militants. Nevertheless, the cell serves the function Lenin had in view and it constitutes the CP. Without the cell, there would be no CPs and if and when they lose their specific nature and become more like other western political parties, the process will begin with the decline of the cell.

A cell has a minimum of three members and will usually undergo binary fission when it exceeds 30 members, but cells of 60 exist in the PCF and of 100 or more in the PCI. Once a year the cell elects a bureau, a secretariat, and other office-bearers, the activist minority that will attend most meetings and keep the thing going. The functions of the cell are to meet regularly, to implement instructions passed down from above notably as to party campaigns, to print a cyclostyled cell paper, to sell the official party newspaper locally, to recruit new members and chide backsliders, to raise funds (of which they may keep for their own administrative needs everything over a set target sum that is to be handed on to the federation), and to conduct discussions on party affairs and on national and international politics. A communist cannot discuss those matters anywhere else without the agreement of his cell (not even at party congresses or elsewhere in the party); the cell remains the forum for all debate. Sometimes outsiders are invited to address cell meetings but usually their proceedings are private, not to say conspiratorially secret.[7]

The level of discussion varies from place to place (and from time to time, for there are waves of activism and of lethargy) but it would be mistaken to assume that, because the CPs are machines for the manufacture of unanimity, the cells are composed of docile puppets. Quite the contrary, some cells debate furiously till the small hours of the morning, with genuine conflict of opinions and with criticism of party decisions. Sensitive subjects such as the Sino-Soviet split or the invasion of Czechoslovakia are not avoided—at least, not once the 'bourgeois press' has taken them up. Freedom of general political discussion increased noticeably in the cells of the PCF and the PCI[8] in the 1970s. The leadership has little to fear from those discussions because, in the virtual absence of communication between different cells[9] and given too the careful filtering of influence upwards by means of co-optation, there is little chance that dangerous thoughts can spread. An oppositional paper complained that 49 per cent of cell members could be outspokenly opposed to PCF policy but the leadership could still claim unanimous endorsement without being challenged.[10] Nevertheless, it would be more reasonable to expect responsiveness among the leadership if cell discussions revealed widespread opposition.

Cell activities gain in intensity at election time; and when the party launches a political campaign; and before or during party congresses; and when the party is shaken by internal crisis. Yet the greater part of the large fund of energy, devotion, and sociability that the cell taps is used on its own domestic affairs, just to keep itself going. It is only when members are up to date on their administrative chores, on recruiting and fund-raising, that they can stop to ask: what is to be done? It is precisely at that moment that advice comes from above, so that the properly political work of the cell is guided. Nevertheless, it is free to choose its subjects if it wishes to. Usually it is not long before the administrative obsession returns, and it is back to collecting subscriptions to the membership card. Cells in Italy are sometimes composed mostly of young men, so that a favourite activity is drives for female membership. Brawls with the 'fascist bands' of the MSI (Movimento sociale italiano) or Ordre Nouveau or similar Rightist groups are another recurrent occupation.

In efforts to adapt the Leninist cell to western society, the parties have repeatedly experimented. The PCI had women's cells, and it and the SEW tried youth cells, but the women's cells became gossip clubs (the way Swedish cells were once known as 'beer clubs'), while the youth cells threatened to become a party within the party; hence both were disbanded. In 1972 the PCF, as a part of its drive to attain 20,000 cells in 1973 (against 19,518 in December 1972, of which 5,376 were factory cells, 8,917 regional cells, and 5,225 rural cells) decided that cells could be constituted on housing estates ('council housing' blocks), in offices, schools, and universities. The factory cells, which have almost disappeared in the huge Italian party, are recurrently pushed with great vigour, and not only for the above-mentioned reasons of Leninist doctrine. The tiny DKP has 408 of them, putting out cell papers with half a million copies a month, because the party sees them as the way to achieve 'unity at the base' with workers who vote SPD (Sozialdemokratische Partei Deutschlands); i.e. they are an instrument of political rivalry. The PCF sought to multiply and activate its factory cells after 1968 (there were 3,800 of them in 1961 and 5,200 by 1971) in order to counter the ultra-Leftist (and later Socialist) challenge to its influence over workers. The factory cells also serve CPs by keeping an eye on the activities of communist-influenced trade unions. On the factory floor, even unions affiliated with the CGT or CGIL are far from being communist-dominated, so that the parties find it useful to have their own antennae in the workplace. Still, calls for the multiplication and reactivation of workplace cells are so much a constant of party history that there is no reason to believe that current campaigns in that sense will have any more success than in the past.

The cellular structure of the parties is becoming increasingly unsuited to a society that has television, weekenders, cars, and similar uses of leisure time. It is unsuited also to an age of lower political commitment, even among communists. It is necessary to recall that the decline is from a great height: communists used to give up most of their free time to party work, and if they now give much less, they are still more active than the members of other western parties. The fact remains that a majority are no longer active at all. Only 10 per cent of PCI members attend section meetings; 20 per cent of Finnish communists go to the cell; and no more than 25 per cent of French communists do so. Marchais admitted that some PCF cells met 'once or twice a month' in 1973, but in fact many meet only once a year, to elect the militants who will run them the rest of the time. Cell papers sometimes appear only once a year.

The parties have reluctantly adjusted to this situation. The Swedish party openly devalued cell work in the 1960s and now most VPK members belong not to a cell but to the next body up the scale, the *lokalorganisation* or section.[11] The PCF has removed from its statutes the requirement of militant activity (as distinct from membership) in a cell. The PCI has virtually let the cells disappear (only 'a few thousand' remain of the 57,000 it had at its peak and almost none of them are at places of work). The party is now organized in sections, which might contain over 1,000 members and which meet only every two months. They are kept going by a handful, maybe seven or eight, militants who meet several times a month. Plainly, this is the transition from the Leninist party with its cells to the ordinary party with its constituency groups, that is, from a party based on militancy to one based on electoralism. Hearing of one section where out of 160 members only 10–20 were active, Aldo Natoli exclaimed at its meeting:

Does such a party correspond to the Leninist idea of a party? According to the statutes, 140 comrades of the Balduino section do not belong to the party because they are not active in an organization at the base. This is a phenomenon that is seen throughout Rome and that is common through the whole party. In much of the party, the organization at the base has completely disappeared.[12]

Natoli saw that this put a new meaning on the electoral successes of the PCI, since numerical growth was not accompanied by an increase in organized political force as understood by Leninists.

> The really organized force of the party is today a tiny minority, and we are witnessing a continuous process of atrophy. There have been vast social changes in the country but no corresponding adjustment in the party. Today, the direct link with the masses that existed fifteen years ago has shrunk terribly and it exists almost exclusively at the electoral level. What has been accentuated are the characteristics of a party of opinion and what has diminished is our character of a working-class party of combat and struggle.[13]

In Spain, where one might have thought the cell to be as well suited to the needs of clandestine operation as it was in Tsarist Russia, the PCE around 1960 changed its statutes to remove the requirement that new members adhere to a cell. This was held to be the way to attract members from the middle class and the intellectuals,[14] but in rural areas too, where Spanish communism has been weak because it had no socialist soil to grow on, the cell has given way to loose groups of dozens or hundreds. Surrounded by mere sympathizers, these groups stand around most unconspiratorially in Spanish village plazas, just like other peasants.[15]

This development was foreseen by Auguste Lecoeur when, as organization secretary, he was charged with such problems in the PCF. The solution he put into effect was to become the pretext for his downfall in 1953. Lecoeur was an uncultivated ex-miner who showed enough organizing ability during the Spanish Civil War and the Resistance to be co-opted to the leadership by Jacques Duclos in 1942. At the Liberation he became mayor of Lens, an MP, and Secretary of State for Coalmining when the communists were in the government. One day in 1950 Maurice Thorez informed him that he was to become organization secretary of the party; the party ratified the decision by 'electing' him months later. Lecoeur held that delicate post for four years, when he learned, as casually as he had heard of his appointment, that he was to be purged. After an inadequate and uncontrite act of self-criticism, he quit the party and published a book[16] in which he denounced, with all the authority his former employments bestowed, the manipulation of the PCF by a small clique of officials around Thorez and his wife. His later career took him via the socialist party (at one of its meetings he was badly beaten up by a communist commando) to Right-wing anti-communism.

Among the crimes heaped upon Lecoeur's head at the time of his expulsion (which came soon after the death of Stalin and the downfall of Beria, with whom Lecoeur may have had secret connections) was Zhdanovism. Indeed, Lecoeur had never let his ignorance prevent him ruling on what the party line required of painters and writers, but others in the leadership had done as much and more, and continued to do so after Lecoeur's expulsion. More plausibly, Maurice Thorez intimated that Lecoeur, his favourite and dauphin, had 'tried to bury me before I was dead' by using his control of the apparatus, which came with the post of organization secretary, to by-pass the politburo and secretariat. The explicit charge sheet, however, was based on a letter that went out to the cells in 1951 under the unusually per-sonalized title, 'A letter from August Lecoeur, secretary of the party, to secretaries and treasurers of cells'.[17] It concerned adherents who did not attend cell meetings and did not keep their subscriptions up to date. It said:

The job of political instructor is to be given several of the most politically conscious cell members, to whom the task should be allotted of sponsoring [literally: acting as godfather to] members who come irregularly or not at all to cell meetings. These political instructors will have the job of visiting such members at home to keep them up to date, to have discussions with them, to persuade them to come to meetings, doing so without roughness, with patience, using humane and political arguments.

The suggestion was approved by the politburo and the secretariat, and hence of course by the central committee and a majority of federation secretaries. But when Lecoeur was to be destroyed, the plan was dis-covered to be opportunist, to put quantity before quality, to split the party into a minority of activists and a majority who stayed at home—that is, to dissolve the cellular structure and to make the party, like any other western party, an amalgam of voters and stair-climbers. Thorez said that Lecoeur had even proposed dropping the very word 'cell' and removing from the statutes the obligation to militate actively in a cell.

To the suspicious eye of a party boss trained in Stalinist chicanery, the army of political instructors under the command of the organiza-tion secretary could suggest the base for a *putsch*. Yet Lecoeur could reasonably answer that a CP could not hope to recruit westerners 'by millions' and still insist that they militate actively in a Leninist cell. The PCF, like the PCI, came to agree with him. Later organization secretaries, including men who had voted Lecoeur's expulsion, secured a change in the party statutes such that adherents would not need to militate actively in a cell. They virtually reinstated the division between political activists and honorary members who (in the words of an opposition faction) 'are dispensed from activities and meetings, who receive at home the visits of "instructors" come to inform them of the work of other members, and to collect, if they can, symbolic subscriptions'.[18] That may overstate the case in the PCF, but not in other parties. The Spanish party exempts women from all militant activity.[19] The Swedish party, after experimenting in the 1960s with Lecoeur's system of second-class or 'supporting' members, officially so-called, found it did not boost membership and, instead, gave up the cell.[20] Thus are western parties suffering erosion at their Leninist foundations.

The Militants and Permanent Officials

At the level above that, the edifice is sounder. That is the level of the militants, who are present as the active minority in the cell and who become a majority as we go higher up the structure, gradually blending into the class of permanent officials or *apparatchiki* as we rise. In bolshevik theory, every member of a CP should be a militant but the parties have long been reconciled to the fact that only a minority of members militate, that is, perform some function, fulfil some responsibility, to which they are nominated by the party. These men and women are the nerves of the party, connecting the mass organized in cells to the brains of the party leadership. Looking at them, typically, as instruments of the party boss, Stalin called them the 'men who understand the political line of the party, who consider it their own line, are ready to apply it . . .; without whom the correct political line is in danger of remaining on paper'. They are the steadiest part of the structure. That stability is especially notable towards the top, where the militants are mostly permanent officials, people on the payroll of the party or on the payroll of other bodies to which the party nominates them to do its work. Their steadiness could be due both to the political conviction that secured their promotion and to the distaste for losing a congenial employment in a political élite, i.e. in the tertiary sector of the economy.

Attempts to measure the proportion of militants in CPs are hampered by the fact that the parties seek to exaggerate the number of militants and to understate the number of permanent officials. For example, Enrico Berlinguer said in 1972,

. . . it is time to give up this talk about the monstrous communist apparatus that is supposed to dominate the party. The truth is that out of a million and a half members we have only a few hundred comrades who have dedicated their lives to permanent work for the party. There is no other great Italian party with so small a number of 'functionaries'. The force of our party really arises from the immense and often heroic sacrifice consented by hundreds of thousands, by millions, of men . . .[21]

So 'a few hundred' permanent officials and 'hundreds of thousands, millions' of militants. Rather less extravagantly, the PCF claimed (in 1961) to have 100,000 militants and (in 1973) to have 550 permanent officials, including 50 MPs. The much smaller Finnish party, slightly more honestly, admitted to 480 permanent officials. Outside observers think that Berlinguer's 'hundreds of thousands, millions' of militants should be cut down to 80,000, and that the PCF's 550 permanent officials should be increased to 14,000.

Such enormous discrepancies suggest, of course, that people are not using words the same way, and it is easy to see why. 'Militant' is a flattering title that the parties bestow much too lightly, so as to suggest the great reserve of dedicated force behind them; 'permanent official' (or worse *apparatchik*) has an unpleasant ring in workers' ears, as suggesting a man who has got off the production line on to an easy job at their expense. It is easy to exaggerate the number of the first, since the humble cell member who gets stuck with the job of selling party pamphlets becomes the 'militant in charge of party literature'. It is easy to understate the number of the second, since the larger CPs have the possibility, licit or illicit, of placing members on other payrolls.

Estimates of 15 per cent of the French and Italian parties engaged in militant activity were probably always exaggerated but not absurd for the time they were made (1951), a period of intense political commitment. Galli thinks PCI militants were never more than 8 per cent, in the agitated 1950s, and that this proportion fell to 5 per cent by 1966. Since the PCI declined in size meanwhile, the number of militants would have fallen from 200,000 to 80,000 or 90,000. When the PCF claimed to have over 100,000 militants, it was clear from its manner of arriving at that figure ('30,000 cell officials, 25,000 section officials, 3,300 federation officials . . . 1,400 mayors, 21,000 municipal councillors, 150 *conseillers généraux* . . . tens of thousands of communists in the mass organizations . . .') that there was considerable double counting, since one man could hold two, three, four, or more of such posts. Indeed such polyvalent activity is characteristic of communist militants and probably the rule among permanent officials. It is deliberate policy in CPs to stack as many jobs as possible with the limited number of completely trustworthy militants, because that makes it possible to block all the channels of communication leading from the base towards the leadership.[22]

As the number of militants is thus corrected downwards, it approaches the number of permanent officials, which must be corrected upwards, but which, ultimately, cannot be estimated with accuracy, so great are the parties' possibilities of dissimulation. The generous estimate of 14,000 permanent officials for the PCF includes[23] not only those few hundreds that figure on social security declarations as party employees but the many thousands who hold a job, by party appointment and on party conditions, in the scores of communist-owned commercial businesses, in newspapers and publishing companies owned by the party, in dozens of affiliated trade unions and front organizations, in party-sponsored social works from holiday homes to canteens, and in scores of communist-run municipalities. Not all the employees of such bodies would work mainly for the party. Still, the municipal chauffeur who calls each day at party headquarters to drive leaders about at the expense of his communist-governed municipality is doing useful party work. There are many others, including all those with management jobs held on party sufferance, who must be counted as permanently in the service of the party. In the Red Belt of Italy, their number runs to thousands.

Special mention must be made of one class of permanent officials who figure on another payroll: communist MPs and members of other elected bodies whose public office is a full-time paid job. When Berlinguer spoke of a mere 'few hundred comrades' in permanent employ, he was obviously not thinking of them, since as he spoke the party had 177 deputies and hundreds more in the Senate and in regional and local bodies. Yet for the communists, a parliamentarian or mayor is an agitator and militant of the party before he is a representative of his electors. He is on a party assignment, and if it ends, by his failing to secure re-election, he is provided with another full-time job. This is a practice found in few other parties and in none on a systematic scale. When their MPs are not in office, they are available for much useful party work. They can offer, as well as their official salaries which are made over to the party, whatever facilities attach to their position.

Selection and Training

Even in a democracy, no political party elects its office-bearers as democratically as it expects the nation to elect *its* representatives. Nor could we hope that a party should or even could function that way. A political party works by representing, at one and the same time, a particular set of interests and a characteristic view of the public interest. Democratic head-counting is one way of periodically adjusting the contest between parties but it would be no way of working out how a particular interest and a special conception of the 'general interest' should be formulated and advanced. This latter is an affair of informal and uncodifiable tendencies within the overriding tradition represented by that particular party. Complaints of undemocratic or oppressive behaviour within the party mean that one tendency is taking too narrow a view of the common tradition, so that demands for 'more democracy' in such cases mean a recall to the informal conditions of co-operation. They do not mean that from then on everything should be settled by a vote and every representative of the party literally elected. If parties were democratized in that sense they would sacrifice much of the individuality of their policies, whereas they function, on the contrary, by stressing particular points of view and by concentrating support around foci of opinion and interest.

It is necessary to state these platitudes before looking at the selection of communist office bearers, because the CPs conduct an elaborate parody of democratic election from top to bottom, and yet their policy is determined by a ruthlessly narrow-minded view of the socialist tradition. The elections are a show. Selection is made by simple co-optation from above. But the moment to discuss the internal democracy, or lack of it, of the CPs is not at the point of making that assertion, which does not say anything special about the *communist* party, but when discussing the treatment of tendencies, fractions, and currents in the party, which we shall come to below.

A selection of candidates for promotion is made at higher levels on the basis of the biographies of members, which are kept religiously up to date, and of the regular reports from the cells.[24] Aldo Garosci was not exaggerating when he said, 'the [Italian] Communist party has a more complex and up-to-date personnel file system than an army'.[25] The criteria for promotion are officially devotion, initiative, discipline, and responsibility; one must add an aptitude to follow the present party line and to adjust to any change in it, plus a conformity to the party's current image of itself. A list of people meeting these requirements will be presented to a cell, a section, or any other level when it has to select its office-bearers or its delegates to a higher level conference. Usually there is no choice of candidates, though in recent years the two bigger parties have allowed some choice and have consented to secret voting. That changes little, however, since the names on the short list only get there after approval from the higher echelon, and that higher echelon deputes (or instructs) militants to influence and actually to take part in the vote. Thus there are never any surprises.

If the system worked entirely in that way, there would be no surprises right to the top. In that case the CPs would be governed by seasoned militants, probably of mainly working-class origin, who had made their way through all the echelons. In reality, the co-optation becomes more blatant and the use of short-cuts commoner, the nearer to the top. The secretary-general has always found ways to bring his protégés into the leadership without the need of long progression through the ranks. As a protégé shot up meteorically, his wife would often follow. Marcel Servin and Laurent Casanova (and his wife) rose almost as quickly, by grace of Maurice Thorez, as they later fell into disgrace, by the same agency. Georges Marchais arrived at the top with a band of local followers, some of whom moved straight, and not via the politburo, into the secretariat. The critical step in such irresistible ascensions is 'election' to the central committee. The practice of admitting to that committee specialists, technicians, and journalists provides a way in which brilliant young men (usually of middle-class origin) can leap ahead of the seasoned *apparatchiki*.

Political parties often offer courses in indoctrination to members and some make them compulsory for militants. Few do so as systematically as the CPs; it was only in 1973 that the Gaullist party, in power since 1958, started its *écoles des cadres*. It is in regard to the emphasis on teaching, on training, and on conversion to a world view that the overworked comparison of the CP with a religious order is least inappropriate. Drawing on its international connections if it is small, or using a large part of its own revenues if it is bigger, a CP seeks to indoctrinate members at every level, from the neophyte cell militant to party newspaper editors and campaign managers. However, lest one lend support to the myth of the CP as a diabolical *ecclesia docens* or a military academy among political parties, one must point out two things. First, only a minority, perhaps 15 per cent, of members ever receive any systematic schooling beyond prescribed reading of four or five brochures. Secondly, much of this effort is wasted because of the large number of drop-outs among the 'students'. One reason for that (and another sense in which the effort is largely wasted, even on those who do not drop out) is that this is not schooling at all but indoctrination of a fairly coarse sort, the rote learning of a predigested pap of slogans of which many are remote from social conditions in Western Europe. Those who submit to this indoctrination acquire well anchored convictions such as can resist considerable shocks.

The policy of schooling CP militants originated in Soviet Russia in the 1920s. The point then was to create the nucleus of professional revolutionaries who would plant the 'party of a new type' in the inhospitable soil of Western Europe. Schools were started in the west, as for example in Bobigny, a Paris suburb, for training Bolsheviks, while the International Leninist School in Moscow offered courses of a year, or even two and a half years. Some eminent communists, such as Waldeck Rochet, former secretary-general of the PCF, and Aksel Larsen of the Danish party, issued from Soviet schools. Linguistic difficulties always hampered these schools, and, later, a schooling in Soviet Russia (or East Germany) came to seem incompatible with the nationalist image the parties sought. Hence the emphasis was more on local schools. The Swedish party used to have schools of its own located in the Soviet Union and in East Germany during the 1950s and 1960s; the Swedes provided the instructors and the host country offered the material facilities. These schools were closed when the VPK sought to assert its independence.[26] The DKP on the contrary continues to use East German schools in addition to its own. At the base, the neophyte West German communists go to weekend schools that the party holds in forest bungalows and holiday homes in Lower Saxony and the Rhineland Palatinate. If their 'studies' progress, they attend the party's Karl Liebknecht School in Essen or the Friedrich Engels School in Wuppertal. Full-time militants can then be sent to East Germany to study in the Franz Mehring Institute in Leipzig or an affiliated institution in Berlin-Biesdorf for three, six, or twelve months. Finally, senior cadres go to Moscow, to the Social Science Academy of the central committee of the Soviet party, or to the high school of the central committee of the Communist Youth.[27] The West German party is singularly pedantic in its stress on 'learning' (it set aside 1972 as Party Study Year) but all the parties make similar arrangements.[28] Some of the elementary brochures used in

PCF schools are available, and can be seen to be jejune propaganda.[29] The persistent political failures of the parties, and the gap between party doctrine and western realities, suggest that the intellectual quality of the 'instruction' does not improve at higher levels.

The Intermediate Levels

Since the communist militant spends most of his time operating in, or climbing up the ladder of, intermediate organs, for him they are the very texture of the party. Yet their function is the subordinate one of transmission of political signals: transmission of the party line downwards and, no less important, of information about the base (and about the nation generally) upwards to the leadership. The nullity of these intermediate levels is admitted in Article 5 (d) of the PCF's 1964 statues: 'The decisions of superior échelons are binding on inferior échelons.' That is to say, power is wholly centralized.

Thus more important than the details (the PCF has 2,500 sections grouping an average of eight cells each and employing a total of 25,000 section leaders, putting out 400 section papers, etc., etc.) is the fact that the number and activity of the intermediate levels vary in accord with a constant principle: each unit at every level must be kept to a manageable size, one might almost say a manipulable or manoeuvrable size. For that purpose, the parties do not hesitate to invent, or dispense with, new intermediate levels: town committees that supervise sections but have no upward electoral power; or regional organizations of various purviews in between sections and federations; or a federation of federations for an important area such as Paris. In that way, the structure of the party expands or contracts in accordance with its size and with the supply of militants, so as always to keep the channels of communication firmly under control from the level above. A section secretary responsible for seven cells might have to spend every night of the week at some cell meeting, but that is preferable to letting cells get so big they could not be manipulated.

Each level, and notably the federation, elects under the surveillance of the echelon above it not only its bureau and secretariat, and its statutory committees concerned with cadres, finances, propaganda, etc., but also a varying number of informal or ad hoc committees specially devoted to trade unions or farmers or women or culture or whatever politically matters there and then. The level with the most substance is the federation or *Bezirkskomitee*. There are 103 in the PCI and 97 in PCF, corresponding roughly to national administrative divisions. Since those are often also electoral divisions, this creates the danger of the federation deviating towards the status of the constituency organ of other parties, producing its own notables as candidates for elections. That tendency is resisted in the CPs which will 'parachute in' a candidate chosen by the centre, over the head of a federation notable. The rule is that electoral candidates are chosen by the central committee (and remain responsible to it), though there might be consultation with the federation before the choice is made. The federations of the PCI have been pressing for more autonomy in recent years, in parallel with the devolution of responsibility in the Italian political structure generally. They have been vouchsafed some independence in matters of purely regional concern, notably in the Red Belt, and their initiatives are sometimes endorsed by the centre. For instance, when the federation of Bari created 'students' democratic leagues', these were so successful that the PCI decided to generalize them.

The Swedish federation, or *partidistrikt*, was more successful in that in 1967 it won the right to appoint and pay its own permanents and to choose electoral candidates, though the centre still sometimes has a say in the latter decisions. In Sweden not only the state but the municipalities subsidize political parties, and so the VPK federation gets money that it keeps to itself, as to 90 per cent, and that increases its autonomy. In contrast, the PCF leadership in 1973 appointed fifteen 'animateurs' to control the federations grouped into provinces (more or less as the French government appoints superprefects and 'administrative inspector-generals on special missions'), thereby increasing the subordination of the elected federal committees to the centre.

The central committee is nominally the parliament of the party. It is elected by the congress and in turn elects the party's government, the politburo, and its cabinet, the secretariat. However, the congress that elects it is stacked by the leadership, often to the point of containing a majority of paid party employees.

It was to stop that prefabrication of congresses that the VPK ruled in 1967 that central committee members could not vote at congresses unless they were delegated by a federation. Election by the congress, whether by acclamation or supposedly secret ballot, is of a list prepared by the leadership, usually allowing no choice. Thus the central committee is just another intermediate level. It is the largest body in a CP, and shows characteristic communist 'fluctuation': a third or a half of its membership can change at each congress. Its numbers vary around 100 in the Spanish, Italian, and French parties and 45 in the Finnish and Swedish parties. It includes non-elected specialists and a number of clandestine members, who may be active army officers or senior government officials whose communist role is kept quiet, or else representatives of other CPs, notably the Soviet party, sister parties in ex-colonies, or sister parties that have federations in the territory in question among exiles or immigrant workers.

The central committee meets in camera once to ten times a year, for one to three days, to 'debate' an agenda prepared by the politburo. That agenda is seldom questioned and the leadership's decisions seldom challenged. Few western parties have yet had the experience of the Soviet party at the time of Khrushchev, when the central committee was court of appeal against a decision of the politburo. Unanimity still reigns in the west. To be sure, there was genuine debate in the PCI central committee on the occasion of the trial of the *Manifesto* heretics in 1969, and the proceedings were promptly published.[30] Also, up to his expulsion from the PCF, Roger Garaudy used to raise objections in the central committee. Still, in claiming to encourage debate in the PCF central committee in 1973, Marchais spoke as though this would be an innovation.[31] In general the central committee is a rubber-stamp parliament that serves to comment upon, 'enrich', and approve leadership decisions before they are passed on down the line.[32] As though to signify their submissiveness, members of the central committees of western parties used to have to deposit their passports with the secretariat, at a time when passports were needed for travel inside Europe. They still cannot leave the country, or publish, without authorization.[33]

The provincial branch parties of Belgium and Spain also belong with the intermediate levels. They are puppets, but, as concessions to irreducible ethnic divisions, they show how far a CP will compromise with its environment at the expense of Leninist doctrine. In March 1971, the PCB, which had operated two ethnic 'branches' since 1966, followed the lead of other Belgian parties and formally split into Flemish and Walloon wings; Brussels went under a federal committee. The congress, the central committee, and the politburo all split into linguistic wings, and it was decided that motions at any level would have to be approved by a majority in both wings. The secretariat, the real seat of power, retained its unity, even though 'elections' to it had to be approved by both wings. However, since there were five Walloons to one Fleming in the party, and all five deputies were Walloons, the Flemish wing was really an intermediate level.

The PCE has set up such puppets in Catalognia (Partit socialista de Catalunya), in the Basque country (Partido comunista de Euzkadi), and in Galicia (Partido comunista de Galicia). Though they are modelled on the PCE and although they are sometimes treated as equals—Santiago Carrillo took their representatives with him to Peking in December 1971 when re-establishing links with the Chinese party—they are creatures of the party. The Galician and Basque parties are admitted to be so; the Catalan party is nominally independent.[34] Their leaders are appointed by the PCE. Their existence is intended to disarm provincialist suspicion of the PCE's Castilian centralism, as well as to combat local oppositions on the Left. These latter are especially dangerous for communism in the Basque country.[35]

On the other hand, the Breton CP set up in 1971 is not a branch of the PCF but an opponent. The PCF is Jacobin in its nationalism, and though it approves such minor concessions as German-teaching in Alsace and Moselle, it expressly disapproves Breton separatism.[36] The reunited Irish party divides its central committee into branches representing Ulster and Eire, but it favours reunification of the country. The CPGB has 'area branches' for Scotland and Wales but it is unitarist.

The Seats of Power

The names and numbers vary from country to country, and even from time to time (for the Leninist model is no stereotype), but the rule is that a central committee of about 40 in the smaller parties and 100–200 in the bigger parties 'elects' both a politburo of 9–20 (variously known as bureau politique, ufficio politico, Praesidium, dagelijks bestuur, comite ejecutivo) and a secretariat of three to seven members. The PCI's central committee also elects a thirty-four-member *direzione* which acts through the politburo and the secretariat. The secretariat may be of the party or of the central committee or a combination of secretaries of both. Its members usually all belong to the politburo too, and it has a *primus inter pares*, a secretary-general. Elections to these offices take the form of approval of a list presented by the outgoing office-bearers, so they are in fact co-optations. The power relations between secretary-general, secretariat, and politburo are shifting but the rule is that the smaller unit is the more powerful. If the secretary-general is pre-eminent, that is party autocracy, known as the 'personality cult'; if the secretariat is pre-eminent, that is collegiate rule; if the politburo governs, that is party oligarchy. All forms have existed but the tendency everywhere has been towards the pre-eminence of the secretary-general. At all times, power is extremely concentrated, a trend repeatedly encouraged by the Comintern as necessary to avoid relapse into the political ineffectiveness of the social democrats. Another reason why the Comintern would wish to see power concentrated at this level is that this is where Soviet influence makes itself felt most, often in the physical sense: clandestine representatives of Soviet power have sat, and may still sit, in the politburos of some western parties.

The politburo functions ostensibly as the government of the party; only in the PCI is it formally subordinate to the *direzione*. It meets once a week and it calls meetings of the central committee. It fixes the agenda for such meetings and it presents reports to them which are invariably accepted. After 1956, during the phase of de-Stalinization, there was a swing towards actual government by the politburo, at the expense of the secretariat. Consultation of the larger body was held to mark a break with tendencies towards the 'cult of personality', or rule by the secretary-general. Since then the pendulum has swung back. The Dutch party, which abolished the secretariat in 1967, revived it in 1972. Everywhere, the minority of the politburo who also sit in the secretariat have regained pre-eminence. The PCF secretariat now fixes the agenda for the politburo, and the secretaries who compose it are in effect secretaries of state, each responsible for a particular domain: propaganda, administration, intellectuals, and so forth. In the clandestine parties, of necessity, the power of the secretariat is absolute. In all parties it enjoys a virtual monopoly of information, both about the party and about the international communist movement, and a monopoly if not of taking decisions, then of publishing them. Lecoeur cites instances from the time of Stalinism when politburo members were kept in ignorance of vital facts by the secretariat. But then both Lecoeur and Marty[37] cite instances from the same period when even members of the secretariat were kept in ignorance, for the totality of power does not lie in the secretariat either. Part of it (not all) is reserved to the single person of the secretary-general, the party boss.

We have arrived at the summit of the CP organigram, but not because the secretary-general has absolute power. He has extensive power and privileged access to information but he has to share them

5

with a small oligarchy of bureaucrats. To see who these people are, we do not come down the same face of the pyramid again, for they might not be members of the secretariat or of the politburo. They work on the hidden side of the pyramid in clandestine or at least little publicized functions, to which we shall revert after looking at the role of party boss.

The Secretary-General

Trotsky said in 1906, when he was still a Menshevik,

Lenin's methods lead to this: the party organization at first substitutes itself for the party as a whole. Then the central committee substitutes itself for the party organization, and finally a single dictator substitutes himself for the central committee.

Dictatorship is not too strong a word for the position occupied by some secretaries-general within the party (and hence within the state if the party were in power). More moderately, we could say that in all CPs the secretary-general has managed to assert pre-eminence based on his unique access to information and on the characteristic tendency of all CPs to heap upon the head of a 'poetic universal' or legendary hero the qualities imagined in the perfect communist. Newcomers to the office have consented for a time to govern collegially, but senior incumbents have shown a habit of taking decisions that seemed to be personal and at least were not arrived at after consultation with the regular organs of the party.

Togliatti marked his return to Italy in 1944 by taking such a decision, that of reversing the PCI's policy of refusal to collaborate with the king, in favour of entry into the government. Matters remained thus until his death, for just five months before dying in a Soviet sanatorium, Togliatti secretly disposed of power in the party, as though it were his personal property, by making it over to Luigi Longo. In a letter to Longo on 19 March 1964, Togliatti said that his health and 'other motives' (perhaps a reference to his fear of a struggle for succession) made it necessary for him to relinquish effective power, but he urged that this fact be kept secret for six months or a year and that the central committee and central control commission appoint Longo ad interim. He even drafted a communiqué in that sense, to announce the news to the central committee (charged with 'electing' the secretariat).[38] In fact, his health recovered and Togliatti exercised power till his death, but his designated successor took over then and made the mistake of publishing the secret letter of appointment a year after Togliatti's death. Longo probably needed to shore up his new-found authority, but the secret transmission of the highest elected office detracted from the PCI's claims to be a de-Stalinized democratic party.

Thorez similarly had the habit of taking *in petto* a decision after morning consultations in his residence with certain chosen members of the bureaucracy, and then presenting them ready-made to the secretariat when he went into the party office in the afternoon. When in 1952 the decision in question was to purge a member of the secretariat (at the time of the Marty-Tillon trial), the fact was kept not only from the accused but from another member of the secretariat, Lecoeur. Then when illness removed him to a Soviet hospital in 1950, Thorez, who without informing the politburo had had his wife, Jeannette Vermeersch, admitted to its ranks, transmitted the power of regency to her. As the one with access both to Thorez's Moscow bedside and to the highest echelons of the party, she gained that monopoly of information, domestic and international, that marks the great party boss. When she was absent in Russia, the PCF's ability to take any decision vanished, or vacillated. This was not to be wondered at in a party that had been known from, at the latest, 1944, as 'the party of Maurice Thorez' and even as 'the property of Maurice Thorez'.[39] Thorez's increasingly luxurious residences, rather than the party headquarters, became the exact location of authority in the party. Even when he was staying at Bazainville, fifty kilometres outside Paris, that was where the politburo had to meet. So when his end approached, Thorez too disposed of authority by passing it on to his chosen successor, Waldeck Rochet. Since the latter suffered a stroke that permanently incapacitated him, he was not able to pass on the job of secretary-general. The PCF did not, for all that, have to face the unaccustomed task of choosing its new leader. Georges Marchais was imposed by hidden authority, which some observers situated in Moscow.

These monarchical practices are seen in the CPs of the smaller democracies, too. Aksel Larsen was the complete Stalinist secretary-general of the Danish party from 1932 to 1958, in which time he acquired such power that when he was dismissed on Moscow's orders, he left the party and took most of its membership and its voters with him into a new party.[40] In Sweden, the decisions to modernize and then to re-Leninize the party were taken by president, i.e. the secretary-general, C. H. Hermansson. The only serious challenge Hermansson faced during these daring, difficult, and eventually unsuccessful operations was when his predecessor, the former party president Hilding Hagberg, called for a rectification of the party line in 1968. The Dutch party was for years the creature of its boss, Paul de Groot, who was one of the western leaders who most ardently denied that the 'personality cult' had ever raged anywhere but in Russia. In fact, de Groot conceived a passionate hatred for the de-Stalinizer Khrushchev and that, as much as any rational political consideration, led him to take the Dutch party out of the international communist movement, as though it were his property. In his great age, de Groot passed the job of leader to Henk Hoekstra, but remained an 'honorary member' of the politburo and keynote speaker at the CPN congress.

Veneration for veteran leaders is known in many political parties, especially the socialist parties. Thus it was normal that veneration should lead to such honours as elevation to the specially created post of 'president' or 'chairman' for Dolores Ibarruri in the PCE, Luigi Longo in the PCI, Waldeck Rochet (after his stroke) in the PCF and Kurt Bachmann in the DKP. It was less normal that the examples set first by Lenin and then more crassly by Stalin should have been imitated, in the cult of the mediocre and uncharismatic personalities of the western party bosses. The cult of Togliatti, though fulsome and based on distortion of the PCI's history and his role in it, was kept within the bounds of western European political practice, except for the brief period when he was adulated as 'The Best One'. The PCI has effected the canonization, as it were, of one of its founders, Antonio Gramsci, in a sentimental and inaccurate literature in which Togliatti always figures as the friend and disciple of the saintly Antonio.

The Spanish party gave freer rein to its tendency to uncritical adulation of its leaders, Jose Diaz and Dolores Ibarruri. Some of the tributes to the latter in Stalinist times resemble the sickliest Mariolatry. When the personality cult was denounced by Khrushchev in 1956, the PCE frankly admitted that it had sinned in the same sense,[41] though this was said to be against the will of the notoriously modest recipients of that adulation. Old habits soon returned, however. When the party split after 1968 into two groups led by Carrillo and Lister, much emphasis was laid in each side's attacks on the other on the degree of autocracy practised by those two men. The proceedings of the eighth congress of the PCE are notable for the fact that almost every speaker began and ended his speech with a ritual invocation of 'el camarada Santiago Carrillo', and that almost all speakers appealed to his authority for their opinions.[42]

The party that went farthest in the cult both of Stalin and of its own boss was the party that still denies that it ever practised that cult and which has not yet published the 1956 Khrushchev report denouncing it. Secretary-general of the PCF from 1930 to his death in 1964, Thorez began his own cult in 1937 when he commissioned a hack to write his autobiography, *Son of the People*, which became a standard text to be studied by French communists thereafter. The adulation of Thorez, the 'first Stalinist of France', assumed grotesque proportions after the war—perhaps because of the need to gloss over the fact that he had deserted and spent the war in Moscow—culminating in a veritable delirium of mysticism in 1953. Lest that term seem excessive, a few texts can illustrate it. An address to Thorez, absent, voted by the national party conference in 1953 states,

From this rostrum in Gennevilliers hundreds of regards re-create thy presence . . . that tranquil gesture of the hand when thou explaineth . . . thy presence gives a face to the hope of all of us. And we feel thee present in each one of us. We are hundreds here who realize in this hour that thou hast given our lives a meaning, our party the style of grandeur etc. etc.[43]

Of the numerous pathetic contributions to this cult made by Aragon, the party poet, one might recall the poem 'He is Coming Back' (Il Revient) written for the return of Thorez from Russia in 1953, or passages from 'L'Homme communiste' such as the claim that the French working class had

produced an image of itself which, better than Roland in the hours of the feudal romance, better than Napoleon surging up from the ruins of the Bastille, incarnates the force, wisdom and destiny of that class of a new type, in a man, in a hero of a new type, a real hero, Maurice Thorez.[44]

It seems unthinkable that such colourless bureaucrats as Berlinguer and Marchais should ever become the object of a similar cult, and indeed that might not happen as long as the forms of collegial direction are respected in the Soviet model. If Brezhnev or a successor were to lay claim to special pre-eminence, he would find ready imitators among the western leaders, for their personal 'image' is kept polished ready for show. Georges Marchais, for example, rates six large photographs in *L'Humanité* (12 Jan 1973) for a press conference. He issues declarations of his own on political subjects at the same time as the party makes *its* official statement, and he fills his reports to the central committee with flattering references to his own prescience.

The glorification of an individual is a curious phenomenon in a bureaucracy. Bureaucracies produce *grands commis*, eminent public servants, but not heroes. The secretaries-general of CPs are not, and cannot be, charismatic personalities. Any show of personal style or independence would have disqualified them for the job. They have to be 'typical', ordinary, mediocre, preferably with working-class manners. They are not fiery revolutionaries. They are organizers, committee men, intellectuals with a taste for organizational in-fighting and a gift for ruse, ruthlessly ambitious and yet of limited ambition, like the bureaucrat, for the highest post they can obtain is one of subordination to a higher, external or occult authority. Berlinguer's nickname in the PCI is 'iron bum'. Indeed, the capacity to outsit everybody else in committee meetings that fill the day is the first requirement in an aspirant secretary-general.[45] That such men can nevertheless attain to personal glorification tells us nothing about them but something about the communist movement. Another bureaucracy-tempered-by-co-optation that brings ordinary men to the top and then glorifies them is the papacy. The comparison here is not with Catholicism or any other religious movement but with the specific Roman institutions of the papacy. What that comparison is intended to suggest is this.

The CP is an attempt to discipline chiliasm, to canalize revolutionary aspirations. Its emphasis on theory, and on the 'science' of socialism, its stress on due process, hierarchy, and discipline, its mock elections and congresses, its horror of Leftism and unruly action, all speak for its efforts to institutionalize, to rationalize, and to bureaucratize a powerful movement of revolt and a swelling hope for utopia that have led the West European working class, in earlier years, into bloody tragedies. Now, bureaucracies that seek to organize rational activities such as the administration of the law or the creation of wealth can, for all their imperfections, remain rational right to the top. But a bureaucracy that seeks to tame the irrational, to organize the quest for utopia and salvation, must break down even when it works. That is, supposing it manages to contain the heresies and deviations and outbursts of impatience that it is designed to combat, it nevertheless fails at the top, where the fundamental irrationality bursts out in worship of the careerist mediocrity who has become boss. That unworthy vessel, who may be sincerely modest, finds he has become what Vico called the poetic hero, vested with all the imaginary virtues that prefigure the coming golden age, charged with the magic that can bring it to pass. Thus have cynical popes been sainted, and men like Stalin, Thorez, and Togliatti sincerely loved and adored by millions of Europeans.

The Secret Structures

By definition one knows little of the hidden face of the pyramid, so that this section should be as short as the chapter on snakes in Iceland. It is important to see, however, that the powers of the secretary-general are exercised in accordance with party organs that are informal or little known, or staffed by clandestine officials, or outright secret. If he is not in accord with them, it can happen that he has to back down or even be deposed. Like Khrushchev, Aksel Larsen was deposed, in 1958, by a vote engineered in the Danish party's central committee by powerful opponents. Hermansson had to accept a new party line in the Swedish party in 1972 at the dictation of a neo-Stalinist opposition near the head of the organization. Even the adulated Thorez is said to have had to abandon, in 1960, his natural inclination to support the Chinese and Albanians, as the true Stalinists, against Khrushchev, because of tenacious opposition in the PCF.[46]

The location of this sort of opposition is not in the subordinate organs, which the secretary-general can manipulate, but in other parts of the structure. The party congress 'elects' along with the central committee such organisms as a 'political control commission' and a 'financial control commission' which operate secretly and exercise immense power. The political control commission is especially important. It was invented by Lenin with the intention of creating an independent forum, outside and independent of the executive authorities of the party, where political disagreements between communists could be settled, and discipline could be restored bloodlessly. In practice, the western parties' political control commissions have developed into watchdogs that supervise the whole party, including even the secretariat, and which wield some of the power of the secret police in communist states.

Various other central commissions and central sections prepare decisions and see to their implementation, each in a particular domain: economy, foreign relations, propaganda, youth, and so on. They operate so discreetly that their membership is usually unknown. Special mention should be made of the central cadre committee and the committee for ideological supervision which look after the apparatus and the intellectuals respectively. All these bodies, like those of the formal structure, have clandestine members who may also occupy functions in the state, in the army, in front organizations (like Benoît Frachon who headed the CGT for years before he was openly admitted to belong to the PCF ruling triumvirate with Thorez and Duclos) or even in other CPs. Thus it can happen that men whose only known dignity is that of simple member of the central committee can belong to the governing oligarchy.[47] It is this informal oligarchy, rather than the formally elected party hierachy, that will later be referred to as the local bureaucracy of a western CP.

It used to be notorious that a CP had an *alter ego*, a twin secret party. At least, this was one of the requirements set in the 1920 conditions for admission to the Comintern. Since then, it has been part of the fascination of a CP that it was both party and conspiracy. Along with prosaic politics it provided the romance of the underground. It was a legal organization that overnight could be transformed into a *maquis*, using previously prepared command posts. Naturally, evidence is lacking, but the indications are that, if the western parties do play this game, they are not very good at it. It is only in exceptional circumstances that the secret parties become visible in the democracies. When Togliatti was the victim of an assassination attempt in July 1948, the PCI was instantly able to cut Italy in two at the middle and to isolate certain cities. The Interior Minister, Mario Scelba, said that this was not only the result of spontaneous demonstrations but also of the action of a pre-existing secret militia. However, the point is that, in face of the firmness of the government in Rome, this action ended quickly. The strikes were called off and the secret structure appeared to back down.

In conditions where the party was forced to fall back on its own secret bases, its performance has been poor. Mussolini managed to round up the PCI in 1926 without trouble, and the domestic relics of the party were dismantled by the fascist police so regularly that they were abandoned as too dangerous. Hitler wiped out the German party with no more difficulty; all traces of it had disappeared by 1936. The Finnish security police were 'well on top' of the party during its illegality between 1921 and 1944, despite the advantage of the nearby Soviet sanctuary.[48] The leaders of the PCF were picked up in 1939 with so much ease that a historian remarks, 'one is astonished that a party for which illegality is, as it were, second nature should have been so unprepared for clandestinity'.[49] The record of the com-

munists under the German occupation is another matter; it exemplifies legitimate illegality, the situation of what Mao called 'the fish in
water', and it was common to other non-communist resistance
organizations. Since the war, the communists have again shown little
aptitude for secret organization. Police authorities reckon with being
able to round up any underground organization within six months or
so, and the communists have not provided anything more resistant
than other oppositional forces.

Since the CPs are expressly modelled on a clandestine organization, the Bolshevik party set up in 1903 under Tsarist oppression, one
might expect them to be able to do so. More than that, one would
expect that a CP forced into clandestinity would become absolutely
obedient to Moscow, on which it would rely for financial support,
that it would show an exemplary unity forged in the difficult conditions of underground activity and, finally, that it would incline to
ultra-revolutionary policies. As it happens, there is no clandestine
party that answers that description. When the Finnish party emerged
at the end of the war from a generation of clandestinity under the
control of the 'barricade communists', it opted at once for peaceful,
moderate policies and reduced its Left extremists to an ineffectual
minority.[50] Some illegal parties have defied Moscow more readily than
a legal party like the PCF. All have split or been outflanked on the
Left by those more revolutionary than they. All propose moderate,
non-violent policies. All are regularly dismantled by the police.

We are speaking here of the parties of Spain, Portugal, Turkey,
Greece, and West Germany. They differ as to their attitudes to
Moscow. The Turkish party counts as a mere Soviet agency.[51] The
Portuguese party is also loyal to Moscow; it approved the invasion of
Czechoslovakia and it is the only West European party, apart from
the DKP, to cite the 'leading role of the Soviet Union' in its greetings
to sister parties. The KDP, that is, the illegal West Germany party,
was as dependent on the East German SED as are the Turkish and
Portuguese communists on Moscow. In fact, it was run by people
holding office in a central commission of the SED and it drew its
money and literature from the eastern republic.[52] It toed the line its
masters set. In contrast, the Spanish party became the first clandestine party to defy the Soviet Union, expressly to disapprove the
invasion of Czechoslovakia, and to dispense with Soviet aid. The
Greek 'interior' party also parted company with the Soviet Union,
not merely to the point of denouncing that invasion but also by condemning the Soviet rapprochement with the military regime in

Athens. Both the Spanish and Greek parties found solace and support in Rumania.[53]

As to unity, the Spanish and Greek parties have split in two, partly because of dissension about the conditions of operation in clandestinity. The Turkish party is chronically prone to scission, being little more than an intellectuals' debating club. Most have been outflanked on the Left. The underground KPD, and then its legal successor the DKP, faced a Maoist opposition that was so virulent and effective that it was suspected of benefiting from Bonn's assistance. The Turkish communists are decried as collaborationists by an ultra-Left guerrilla force. The Spanish party is despised as revisionist by a Marxist-Leninist faction and by the Basque ETA movement. The Greeks had dissidents who attacked both the pro-Moscow 'sectarians' and the 'revisionists' of the interior party. The Portuguese party faced the violent competition of a Marxist-Leninist party and of the Revolutionary Brigades based in Algiers. Excluded in 1970 from the 'liberation front' which has its seat in Algiers, the PCP was denounced as 'social fascist' by the ultra-Left and as class-collaborationist by the Trotskyists.[54]

That outflanking is perfectly understandable because none of the clandestine parties advocated revolutionary policies. The Spanish party preaches collaboration with everyone save the Caudillo himself, not excluding the Army and the Church, while lamenting its own Leftist past.[55] The Turkish party does not oppose successive authoritarian regimes in Ankara but behaves like the Third World CPs that shore up dictatorships tolerated by Moscow while combating democratic forces that might prove favourable to the United States. The KPD was indeed preaching the revolutionary overthrow of the German Federal Republic at the time when it was outlawed in 1956, but throughout its clandestinity it advanced moderate policies and repeatedly offered collaboration with the Social Democrats.[56] The clandestine Greek party favoured collaboration with other Leftist and democratic forces. The Portuguese party joined progressive Catholics and radical socialists, in the abortive 1973 election campaign, advocating collaboration in a united front government.[57] It is patriotic and collaborationist.[58] It joined the government of the military junta after the downfall of the dictatorship in 1974. Its two ministers participated in an administration that preached national unity, labour peace, cautious decolonization, and continued membership of NATO. Inevitably, opposition pullulated to its Left, and the PCP collaborated in its repression.

Lastly, all these professional revolutionaries got rounded up by the police with a monotonous regularity. It might be true that they withstood oppression better than the *other* anti-fascist forces but it is hard to be sure. They have as much interest in pretending that this is so as authoritarian governments have in presenting *them* as the only organized force in the opposition. In reality, the Greek communists seem to be weak and divided. The Spanish communists are arrested so often that it is said that much of the party strength at various times was to be found in Burgos prison. Carrillo admits that it is next to impossible to carry on clandestine activity in the Spanish countryside and besides, he adds in a disabused tone, Spanish communists talk like women.[59] The situation of Spanish communism within the country is so unsteady that the party cannot gauge its own strength. The illegal KPD was decapitated over and over again by the West German police, using if necessary irregular methods. Prosecutions ran to tens of thousands a year and only the privileged sanctuary beyond the Elbe kept the party alive till it regained a legal cover in the DKP.

The Portuguese party, when it was clandestine, was best at avoiding arrest but it was never able to get stable enough foundations to train its militants, to educate them in communist theory or to retain its leaders for long. When Dr Caetano, the Portuguese premier, said in 1973 that the PCP was the best organized opposition in the country, he might only have been following the authoritarian practice of tarring all opposition with the communist brush. The PCP emerged from clandestinity in 1974 with only 2,000–3,000 members but it claimed to enlist 100,000 adherents in its first month of freedom. It thereafter gave the impression of being the best organized political party, not only by staging impressive mass meetings and by disciplining its own troops, but by actively colonizing ministries, municipalities, business enterprises, and trade unions. A similar initial success could well await the PCE, if it emerges from clandestinity in favourable circumstances. In Turkey it is quite impossible to judge the strength of the party. The real communists, being a non-proletarian Soviet agency that does not oppose the government, are usually not disturbed but there is ruthless oppression, not only of ultra-Left bands claiming Marxist convictions, but of the Turkish Workers' Party, which is officially described as communist. In truth it is opposed by the communists. But then in Turkey the word 'communist' is a simple term of abuse. A football referee, having been called 'communist' by a player who disagreed with one of his decisions, took the matter to the Football Federation, which severely reprimanded the player. In general 'communist' means 'the dregs', 'a man who shares out his wife'.[60] In Spain 'communist' can mean variously clumsy, untrustworthy, dishonest.[61] Thus clandestinity produces little but the reputation of working like the hidden one, the devil.

Finances

Contemporary political activity consumes great means, in man-hours and in materials of communication, and yet it goes on outside the economic process. Hence it is parasitical. It cannot sustain itself and must rely on other, productive sorts of activity. Thus political parties can be shown by their opponents to have tainted or discreditable or compromising sources of funds, as is attested by the recurrent scandals in all democracies about parties of all colours. No party can prove that none of its funds are, in that sense, tainted because even if they all came from individual subscriptions, there would always be doubt about how voluntary or disinterested such contributions were and about who really made them (since many would be anonymous) and where they got the money from. Accordingly, it is safe for any party under attack on this score to offer to reveal all its finances, provided every other party does likewise. The CPs, whose finances have aroused a disproportionate interest among opponents, have offered to reveal all, on that condition. Their offers have never been accepted.

There are two reasons why CP finances should arouse special attention. For opponents to the Right, a contribution to those finances from the Soviet Union would confirm western communism's dependence on 'Moscow gold', that is on foreign support without which it could not exist, being an exotic or even anti-national growth. For Leftists, including many people still in a CP, an accumulation of funds, even if of lawful origin, and their rational investment for party advantage would constitute capitalist behaviour, inconsistent with the proletarian ethic of the party. The first sort of criticism would be indeed telling, though one would have to note that other West European parties and trade unions (not to mention whole governments) have secretly accepted, and even depended on, foreign financial help in this century. Mostly, that help has been American since the war but it was not only communists that accepted Moscow gold. Soviet financial help went to the Left wing of the Italian

Christian Democrats too.[62] European socialist parties and anti-communist trade unions were assisted by United States government funds, whether these were channelled through the CIA or through American trade unions. At a time when the PCF kept its account at the Soviet bank in Paris, the SFIO kept its account at the Franco-American Bank. Still, though pots have called kettles black, the communists have been particularly irritated by allegations of their dependence on funds from Eastern Europe. They thought these accusations so damaging that they have not been slow to make similar accusations about *their* Leftist opponents. Indeed, sinister allegations about foreign finance are a constant in Leftist political polemic. Dissident groups inside CPs are regularly asked where they get the money for their activities.[63] The PCE leadership hinted that the pro-Soviet Lister faction was receiving Moscow gold.[64] Thorez said his pro-Chinese opponents were getting 'buckets of money' from somewhere in 1967, and Marchais freely spoke of the 'Peking gold' that his enemies were receiving. As usual, a pretence at accuracy quite discredits such allegations. Marchais, for example, said that 'tiny groups [*sic*] in the Bouches du Rhône department had a bank account with about 100m. old francs in it'![65] Anti-communist calumny was never more reckless. But then that was at a time when the communist mayor of Vierzon, in central France, claimed that Trotskyist Leftists were descending on his region 'in Red helicopters' and 'in canoes loaded with bombs'.[66] The resources of political malice seem to be as limited on one side as on the other.

The second sort of criticism, about running capitalist businesses for CP advantage, comes mainly from ex-communists. Others might welcome such facts as evidence of 'integration' of former revolutionaries into the market economy. In any event, these charges come from people little acquainted with business and hence inclined to underestimate the difficulty of, firstly, making a profit at all and, secondly, diverting that profit past auditors and tax officials to dubious political uses. After all, the vigilance of West European governments is extreme wherever CPs are concerned. When it is further claimed that such businesses make the CP the richest party in the country (or even make the PCF the 'richest party in Europe'), this would seem to be at variance with the evident dire financial straits of the communist press.[67]

Some CPs have produced their budgets, but these are not informative because the main entry on the revenue side is gifts and donations from anonymous sources,[68] whereas the expenditure side is known to be lightened by putting militants on other payrolls. However, certain sources of funds can be specified.

MOSCOW GOLD. This is held to be the principal source, not only by opponents but by ex-communists.[69] In so secretive a party, even highly placed officials would not have sure information on the point. There is evidence that only the secretary-general and one obscure but powerful member of the central committee know the facts in the PCF.[70] There is consequently no reason to take literally outsiders' guesses that, for example, the PCI gets 34 per cent of its income from Eastern Europe, especially since another guess puts the figure at 85 per cent. It might be true that small parties, such as the CPGB, the SEW, and the DKP, which clearly live beyond their means, are largely dependent on Soviet aid. It is important to note that Soviet help need not consist of bank drafts. Party officials and communist MPs get free vacations in Eastern Europe. Also, East European organisms subscribe to western communist magazines and papers, on a scale sufficient to make them profitable. It was when it lost these eastern 'readers', after criticizing the Soviet 'normalization' of Czechoslovakia, that *Les Lettres françaises* was obliged to stop publication.

MEMBERS' SUBSCRIPTIONS. This should be easy to verify, but we have seen that CPs are evasive about their membership. When the PCF said it got 18m. francs from subscriptions in 1971, this was variously interpreted to mean that 217,000 members paid a lot or that 458,000 members paid less.[71] This is not reliable accountancy. It seems certain that no CP lives on regular subscriptions.

DONATIONS. The parties say this is the largest single source, and that these gifts are collected in special fund drives (for election finances, for a new headquarters, for the newspaper, etc.) and at the numerous fêtes arranged by the party and the federations. Collections are constant in the party cells and the better-off members are expected to give generously, especially on such occasions as the fêtes held to support *L'Humanité*, *L'Unità*, *De Waarheid*, etc. The May Day sale of lilies of the valley brings the PCF 1m. francs yearly. However, the donations are mostly anonymous and the big ones always are so. Thus the source is obscure and might lie, ultimately, in Eastern Europe.

THE STATE. West European governments probably contribute as much as Moscow, at least to the bigger parties. The Italian, Swedish, and Norwegian parties receive direct public subsidies, along with other political parties that enjoy parliamentary representation. Communist newspapers in Sweden and France get state subsidies along with some other organs of opinion. (The Swedish party is probably unique in having raised a loan, in 1967, from a capitalist bank, the Stockholm Enskilda Bank). However, all other states where the CPs have elected members support those parties, because communist MPs put their parliamentary stipend into a central kitty, from which they receive only the pay of a skilled worker. For senior officials, that pay is supplemented by perquisites such as housing, canteens, banqueting facilities, transport, bodyguards, etc., which may well add up to more than parliamentary pay. This means that the state is financing the *party* via deputies' salaries. When the parliamentary contingent is large, this assistance can be precious: 7m. francs for the PCF in 1971, and 1,100m. lire for the PCI in 1970. Similar contributions come from the salaries of permanent communist mayors and councillors. The state is mulcted too by the practice of putting permanent officials on its payrolls and by using public officers for party propaganda. Communist-run municipalities employ party workers, patronize party-owned businesses, provide premises and, it is alleged in the absence of proof, divert public funds to party works.[72]

COMMERCIAL ENTERPRISES. The PCI denies skimming off funds from the extensive networks of co-operatives in the Red Belt, but the Italian, French, Austrian, and Finnish parties all run commercial enterprises. These include substantial printing and publishing firms, advertising agencies, and shipping lines. (The beaujolais 'cuvée PCF' served at party congresses is, however, what the trade calls a 'buyer's own brand'.) The favourite party business is export-import with the communist countries, in which, along with travel agencies specializing in that region, they long enjoyed a virtual monopoly. That commerce enabled them to earn legitimate profits and to receive donations from western business men anxious to trade with the east. It also would enable them to disguise the receipt of political funds from Moscow. The freeing of east–west trade impaired that monopoly, but PCF-affiliated businesses such as Interagra were still able to earn substantial commissions from East European purchases of food in the west in 1972–3. Naturally these party businesses are managed capitalistically[73]—so much so that a PCF publishing house took legal action to protect its copyright in a book written by a man it had later expelled as 'a police spy'.[74] However, no European party has been known to back up its predictions of the imminent crisis of capitalism by selling shares short in the stock exchange, as did the American CP.[75] The parties stick to safer trades, such as supplying the thousands of communist-run municipalities. The PCF has consulting companies that advise communist mayors on their procurement and contracting problems and which channel such business to communist-controlled firms or to private capitalists willing to pay a kickback. This practice is common to French political parties and is not a communist invention. Nothing in CP financing is. The German Social Democrats had worked out most of these financial techniques before this century began. The communists brought a meticulousness and method to the administration of their funds that gives them an advantage over parties that are slapdash in the use of their parasitical revenues.

Purges, Trials, Dissidence

It has been difficult for the western parties to maintain even the semblance of the Leninist formal structure. True, it has been rare for communists to riot against their leaders, as happened in Rome in December 1969. On that occasion, prolonged discontent in the Roman sections came to a head when it was learned that some members were to be expelled for dissidence. A mob of communists several hundred strong marched on the federation headquarters, sought to prevent the federal committee sitting, occupied the premises, and shouted insults to the leadership through megaphones.[76]

More commonly, refusal to accept the Leninist model has led to persistent clandestine opposition groups and repeated attempts to legitimize 'currents' within the party. Punctuated by trials and purges, secret or open, these efforts have sometimes culminated in direct challenges to central authority and in demands for 'more democracy in the party'. The political colour of these internal opposition groups has always been ambiguous and it would be naïve to regard them as democratic or social democrat or as less authoritarian than the incumbent leadership.

Indeed *Unir*, the first opposition paper inside the PCF since the Liberation, took an ultra-revolutionary line when it first appeared in

October 1952. After the Paris street riots of May 1952 against NATO and its commander, General Ridgway, the PCF was retreating to a more moderate, 'popular front' line, which the *Unir* dissidents said meant 'abandoning the revolution'. When the Khrushchev report in 1956 spread unease in the party, *Unir* attacked the leadership for refusing to de-Stalinize. As we shall see below, there is only an apparent contradiction between supporting both revolution and de-Stalinization. The Budapest repression in late 1956 started another internal opposition paper, *L'Etincelle*, which assailed the leadership for both sectarianism and opportunism. After achieving a readership of 8,000, *L'Etincelle* merged with a Trotskyist opposition paper, but the joint publication appeared only sporadically after 1957. *Unir* continued to prosper and in 1973, aged 21 years, it claimed a readership of 15,000. Its editors published an unofficial history of the party.[77] They supply members with material highly critical of the 'Marchais clique' that runs the party, charging it with excessive subservience to Moscow, lack of inner-party democracy, and compromises with social democrats.[78] They see themselves as the true revolutionary communists, whereas the party that they refuse to leave has fallen into the hands of 'sectarian opportunists'.

These internal dissidents are dismissed by the PCF leadership as ineffectual and as financed, variously, by the government or the Trotskyists. When discovered, they are expelled but on some other pretext. They have never been brought to trial. The function of a formal trial in a CP is not to put down dissidence of that sort as long as it does not threaten to oust the incumbent leadership by winning control of the party apparatus and as long as it does not systematically dispute the Leninist principle of centralized authority. Those things —an attempt at a bureaucratic *putsch* or a challenge to democratic centralism—are sufficient for a purge and even a set trial. They are not necessary for a trial, however: a trial, that is, can serve other functions or even serve none at all, from a local political point of view, but can be dictated from abroad.[79]

The Italian and British parties have never had a Moscow trial within their ranks but the PCF has had a series of them. The technique was imported from Moscow on the occasion of the first PCF trial, that of two members of the secretariat, Henri Barbé and Pierre Célor, in 1931. That trial was prepared in Moscow by Marty and in Paris by the Comintern secretary, Manuilsky.[80] The last great purge, that of the same Marty and of Tillon, took place simultaneously with purges in the Finnish, West German, and Norwegian parties and in direct connection with trials in Eastern Europe. The significance of these events was understood only after 1969, when it became clear that trials and purges were related to the degree of Soviet influence over a western party rather than to local events, and certainly not to any psychological need to release pent-up anxiety.[81]

At the time, in the 1950s, the victims of the purges did not understand what was happening to them. They were not enlightened by their prosecutors, whose accusations were usually absurd, e.g. that the accused were police agents or spies or conspirators. So they clutched at explanations, such as that they were being made scapegoats for a policy that had failed and was now being abandoned (like the violent opposition to NATO in 1952) or that they were Jews, or that they had fought in the international brigades in the Spanish war, or that they had played too eminent a role in the Resistance for Stalinists obliged to give the credit of victory to the Red Army alone. Yet other people who could have been persecuted on those grounds were left alone or even played a leading role in the prosecution. Any such circumstances might make a communist a suitable victim but the cause of the search for victims lay elsewhere.

It lay in Moscow. Tito had been condemned in June 1948 for straying from strict obedience to Stalin into the deviation of 'national communism'. Stalin thereupon ordered a purge of 'nationalist' elements in other East European parties. In their absence, a purge of almost anyone would do instead, as a way of demonstrating entire submissiveness to Stalin. These trials spread from party to party, including the western parties—a fact to be set against protestations that western communist rule would be 'different'. They spread for two reasons. One way to bolster absurd charges against arbitrarily chosen victims was to allege collusion with foreign communists, who had a similar background, e.g. in Spain or the Resistance, in some imaginary anti-Soviet enterprise. That made it needful to stage a purge in that other CP. Secondly, leaders in any party who saw a purge as even possible would hasten to name someone else as victim lest Beria's envoys pick on them.

Within four months of Tito's condemnation, Gomulka was sacked as secretary-general of the Polish party, expelled in 1949, and brought to trial in 1951. In May 1949 the Hungarian foreign minister Rajk was arrested in Budapest and condemned to death in September. In December Kostov was executed in Sofia. Arrests meanwhile began in the Czech party, culminating in Slansky's condemnation in December 1952. The wave spread eastward too, but what matters is that it also spread west in 1949–52, either at the direct instigation of Beria, chief of the Soviet secret police, or by mimicry. Servin, himself later purged, said à propos of the Rajk trial, 'It would be singularly illogical to suppose that the French party is immune from similar attempts at penetration by the enemy'.[82]

Thus it was that the KDP, still legal at the time and indeed represented in provincial West German governments, abandoned its slogan about 'a German road to socialism', acknowledged complete Soviet hegemony, and staged a purge that reached, in March 1950, its deputy president, Kurt Müller.[83] The Finnish party literally decimated its membership between 1948 and 1951, boasting that it thereby attained ideological purity and greater strength. In Norway the secretary-general of the party, Peder Furnbotn, was sacked in October 1949 and his 'followers' purged the next year. Furnbotn, a hero of the resistance to the Nazi occupation, became 'a former Gestapo agent', and a communist MP added that 'if we came to power, such people would be brought to book by our criminal police—so that they could be condemned to be hanged'. In peaceful Oslo, communists publicly exchanged threats of murder and accusations of attempted assassination, while armed communists occupied offices and raided homes. Curiously, Furnbotn, like Marty and Tillon, remained a devoted admirer of Stalin for years after his exclusion.[84]

In April 1950 the PCF had purged its central committee of dozens of Resistance militants, but the progress of the trials in Prague in the last months of 1952 made a trial in Paris seem increasingly appropriate. The chosen victims were two members of the politburo: André Marty—'Our glory, our honour, that is, André Marty', as Thorez had said as lately as March 1949—a former secretary of the Comintern with a revolutionary record in Spain, France, and Algeria, and Charles Tillon, a Black Sea mutineer in 1919, a Spanish war veteran, leader of the partisans under the Occupation and former minister. Such pre-eminent communist merit, far from making them improbable targets for grotesque accusations, only served to show Stalin the extent of the French party's devotion. Abraham, after all, sacrificed his son.

In a Moscow-style trial these men were accused of fractional activity, ultra-Leftism, anti-Sovietism, and a variety of other misdemeanours. By December 1952 Marty had been marked for expulsion because he had protested and counter-attacked, though lamely, like a man dazed and confused, whereas Tillon, who had gone to earth, was merely dismissed from the leadership. It was only in 1969, after reading London's *L'Aveu*, that Tillon at last understood what had happened and how his affair was related to the East European trials. Then he attacked the PCF leadership, and was expelled.

The copious literature on this affair has sought an explanation in the, admittedly colourful, personalities of the accused, but in the end, this was nowhere to be found except in Eastern Europe. Whereas there Stalin or Beria designated the victims, in western parties some latitude was allowed the more agile to select a sacrificial offering before they themselves were chosen as villains in the necessary, the suitable trial. Such a trial sought to establish not facts but simply to demonstrate the party's submission to Moscow and its abjuration of 'national communism'. The *leitmotif* was 'anti-Sovietism is anti-communism' and, though there have been no similar public trials in the PCF since then, that principle still holds, as Duclos recalled in 1972.[85] That principle, and its application in disciplinary actions, is enough to cast doubt on the supposition of a different or 'better', i.e. anti-Soviet, variety of western communism. At all events, the Leninist structure is held to be fortified by a purge in the face of the enemy, and a good communist need ask, in relation to any particular purge, no more.

The Leninist theory was apparently confirmed in the most serious Leftist revolt that any western CP has faced, the challenge to the Leninist structure of the PCI by dissidents grouped around a paper, *Il Manifesto*. The PCI met the challenge by giving the dissidents a fair and formal trial before expelling them. In the next Italian general elections, those of May 1972, the rebels were annihilated, as the PCI had predicted, whereas the party made gains.

The *Manifesto* movement canalized the discontent with the PCI leadership that welled up during the 1968 strikes and student unrest and in reaction to the invasion of Czechoslovakia later that year. The movement received encouragement in the more liberal management of the PCI's twelfth congress in Bologna in February 1969, which suggested that currents of opinion, which had always marked Italian communism, would be legitimized, against Leninist precept.[86] The *Manifesto* rebels, who included deputies and a former editor of *L'Unità*, charged that the PCI was excessively subservient to Moscow and insufficiently revolutionary. It was at one and the same time Stalinist and reformist. Against that 'sectarian opportunism', the *Manifesto* group preached reversion to spontaneous undisciplined ultra-Leftism, exemplified by the Chinese cultural revolution as they understood it. Such a policy, they considered, would attract to the PCI the forces of discontent revealed by the 1968 disturbances and would restore to the party its revolutionary aspirations.

At their trial, party notables made no attempt to deny that PCI leaders were co-opted, not elected, and that the multiplicity of intermediate levels in the party served to isolate them from the membership in the cells. The most effective defence of that Leninist structure came from Pietro Ingrao, leader of the so-called Left current in the PCI, whom the *Manifesto* rebels might well have expected to endorse their attack on the party's social-democrat backslidings. Ingrao admitted that there were new oppositional forces in Italian society but he argued that they needed to be harnessed by a Leninist discipline, because their romantic ideas about self-government in soviets ignored the hard facts of the state and the nation, and because they underestimated the resistance of bourgeois society to change. The subsequent expulsion of the rebels may well have been a sop to Moscow, for the PCI was then seeking to smoothe over the disagreement about the Czech invasion, and the rebels had called for a new revolution in the Soviet Union. Luigi Longo had promised that there would never be any excommunications from the PCI, but the *Manifesto* had assailed the principle of Leninist structure.

Short of that heresy, diverse currents such as are seen in most western political parties persist in western CPs too, however inconsistent with Leninist theory. Unanimity does not prevail in the DKP or in the Swiss party, to judge from dissenting votes. The Dutch party is torn by strife between 'revisionists' and 'adventurists'. The worst case of disunity, however, is the Finnish party. Long reputed the most Leninist of the western parties, in the end it split into two parties, each with its own press and its own electoral tactics. The rift began in 1956 in connection with de-Stalinization, and it was exacerbated by dissension over Khrushchev's dismissal in 1964. Then the de-Leninization of the Danish and Swedish parties tempted the more liberal of the Finnish communists, and they were encouraged to oppose their Stalinist colleagues by the experience of working with non-communists in the SKDL electoral machine, and in the government with socialists. (After eighteen years in the wilderness the Finnish communists were in a coalition government from 1966 to 1971.) Prague completed the breach between the factions in 1968.

The two sorts of Finnish communists called each other Revisionists or Liberals and dogmatics or neo-Stalinists respectively. The latter were led by Taisto Sinisalo and comprised a third to a quarter of party strength. The more liberal faction was led by Arne Saarinen and comprised two-thirds to three-quarters of the party.[87] Their disagreements were responsible for tensions within the SKDL and for its declining electoral support. The dispute prevented the communists from rejoining the government coalition they had left in 1971 on the insistence of the neo-Stalinists. It was carried over into the Finnish trade unions, to the point of the two factions putting up rival candidates for union elections. The substance of the dispute, to which we shall return below, was party discipline and loyalty to Moscow.

Soviet intervention in the affair was blatant (Helsinki had one ambassador recalled for crass meddling in Finnish affairs). It did not succeed in mending the split, much less in assuring the predominance of the neo-Stalinist wing. Since the word Finlandization has been coined to denote decisive Soviet influence abroad, it is worth noting that the Finnish communists, backed by massive support from across the border, have never won sole power and, within their ranks, it is not the most pro-Soviet communists who prevail. Finlandization operates in other ways.

The PCI too, for all its desire to be a 'party of a new type' is, in the manner of all Italian parties, chronically divided against itself. Quite apart from the *Manifesto* rebellion, the PCI has been potentially two parties for a decade. Giorgio Amendola and Giancarlo Pajetta, members of the secretariat, had suggested the recognition of 'majorities and minorities' and of 'trends' (but not of 'factions') from 1961, but this was rejected at Togliatti's insistence as incompatible with the Leninist structure. The existence of such trends became public at the Bologna congress in 1969 and has not been hidden since.[88]

The principal ones are the so-called Right associated with Amendola and the Left around Ingrao, with Berlinguer's 'autonomists' holding the ring, elaborating the bureaucratic compromises. The Amendola current favoured collaboration with the socialist party leaders in efforts to secure reforms in Italian society. It feared that a successful Left-Centre coalition (of the socialists and the Christian Democrats) would isolate the communists. At the same time, it sought to remain on the best of terms with the Soviet leadership and for that purpose it was ready to mute PCI criticism of Soviet actions in Czechoslovakia and to delay internal democratization of the PCI. These opinions all had the solid support of the communists of the Red Belt, comfortably installed in power in the provinces and municipalities of Emilia Romagna.

The Ingrao Leftists in contrast were willing to be much more outspoken in their criticism of the Soviet party. They rejected Amendola's collaborationist, reformist proposals as social–democrat deviation. They hoped to marshal the ultra-revolutionary, maximalist energies of the Italian Left and to attract to the PCI the new dissidents outside the party. They were ready to push the demands for inner-party democracy, though on that score they were outflanked by the *Manifesto* rebels and eventually co-operated in their exclusion. The Ingrao Left disdained pacts with the socialist leadership and preferred to seek the collaboration of the Leftist base of both the socialist and Christian Democrat parties.

Neither of these currents ran its full course. Amendola's ideas would have led, at length, to a genuine revisionism, that of a social democratic party friendly to Soviet Russia. Ingrao's ideas naturally tended towards revolutionary verbalism and neo-Trotskyism. It was both necessary and very easy for the Berlinguer bureaucrats to reconcile these incoherent and half-hearted lines of thought, in a series of shifting and ambiguous compromises. There was no urgent necessity for the PCI to resolve these 'contradictions', since its role was not that of a Leninist party at all. On the contrary, it proved electorally advantageous to appeal to a variety of clientele at once. The dualism of reformism and maximalism is as old as European socialism; the CPs are like the pre-1914 socialist parties in never coming down on one side or the other for long. As long as it is far from office and as long as it is content to bump against an electoral ceiling that will keep it far from office, the PCI can hold the ground it has won from the old socialist movement while allowing its schizophrenia to become apparent in two *correnti*.

If these examples of disunity dispose of the myth of the 'monolithic' CP, they are not intended to bolster the other myth about progressive liberalization of the Leninist party. There is no secular trend towards de-Leninization of the western parties. Demands for 'more democracy' inside the parties are put forward by Leftist dissidents, dissatisfied with their leaders' compromises with social democracy. This is the Stalinist paradox of western communism. Leninist rigidity is defended by party bureaucrats anxious to stay on good terms with Moscow while they seek local office in alliance with socialists. On the other hand, 'more democracy' is demanded by Leftists who refuse that sort of integration into western democracy and who are disdainful of socialist leaders. For them 'liberalization' of the party would not mean its 'social-democratization' but its radicalization. In short, Stalinism within the party goes with a penchant for reformist alliances; the cry for more democracy within the party comes from Leftist revolutionaries.

An exception is the split in the Finnish party, where the liberals or Revisionists were less clamorously pro-Soviet than the Stalinists; they condemned the invasion of Czechoslovakia, for example. The instructive thing is that Moscow long refrained from condemning the liberals, but it did condemn the Stalinists for splitting the party and ordered them back into the party in 1969. It prevented them from formally setting up a rival communist organization.[89] Massive Soviet intervention left the liberals in precarious control, and was apparently never intended to secure the victory of the Stalinists so much as to get the party back into the cabinet. The Stalinists' activities were, if not unwelcome to Moscow, less important to it than the presence of a reformist CP in the Finnish government. Only in mid-1974, when the decade-old split had reduced the Finnish party to political impotence, did Moscow abandon its prudent pretence at neutrality. It took sides with the Stalinist minority to the point of insisting that restoration of party unity must come before co-operation with social democrats or a return to the governing coalition.

Internal critics of the Leninist structure regularly demand: 1. attenuation of the vertical structure by means of horizontal communication between cells and sections; 2. secret voting with a choice of candidates for promotion, instead of co-optation or dictation from above; 3. diminution of the role of party permanent officials by some system of leadership rotation. Taken abstractly, such suggestions might appear reasonable, but an attack on the 'dictatorship' of the incumbent leadership has prefaced the rise of every illiberal faction in the communist parties. Thorez began his long career as party boss by exclaiming, 'Que les bouches s'ouvrent! Pas de mannequins dans le parti!'[90] Earl Browder was assailed by the Stalinists in the United States party for exercising a dictatorship. The Finnish Stalinists in 1969 accused the 'liberals' of bureaucratic centralism. The Soviet-sponsored Lister faction in the PCE discovered that Santiago Carrillo was practising dictatorship in the Spanish party, but only after he had criticized Soviet intervention in Czechoslovakia in 1968.

Condemnation of the excesses of bureaucratic centralism is a regular feature of communist polemic and can originate with the most authoritarian Leninists. That is, the Leninist structure is admitted by

most communists to have objectionable features but they are
criticized only when it is tactically suitable. If the dissident minority
simultaneously pleads for adventurous, ultra-Left policies and scorns
collaboration with democratic socialists, it is bound to be suspected of
working towards a new form of totalitarianism and intolerance. If
the minority is found to be secretive and sectarian within its own
ranks, as was the case with the *Manifesto* group, that suspicion is
confirmed.

If demands for liberalization of the Leninist structure are tactical,
so too are such concessions to those demands as the leadership is
obliged to make from time to time. It would be mistaken to put those
concessions end to end and arrive at the conclusion that, as Marchais
has said, the PCF is 'a liberal party', or even 'the most democratic
party in France'.[91] That Roger Garaudy was allowed to address a
PCF congress before being expelled, and to read out a speech that was
later seized in Prague,[92] or that Pierre Daix was allowed to reply to
criticism of his ideas in a party publication[93] indicates something
about the political climate created by electoral collaboration with the
French socialists and by the intense interest of the 'bourgeois' press in
those affairs, but it does not change the fact that the practice of
co-optation was growing in the same party as Georges Marchais
consolidated his rule.

There are forces pressing for relaxation of Leninist discipline but
there are contrary forces too. The men who control the party
apparatus know that by 'democratizing' it they would risk losing the
support of Moscow without any certainty of gaining new electoral
support or new members. After all, democratic socialism is already
organized as a party in most West European countries, and the communist movement has always sought to mark itself off from it. To
that end, the discipline of the Leninist party and the myth of its
monolithic unity are a positive advantage. Millions of West Europeans
who know at first hand how the party really works stay in it—for
longer or shorter periods—because they prefer an arbitrary or alien
discipline to the democratic votes of the ignorant, the indifferent, or
the adventurous.[94]

That de-Leninization of a CP can have unexpected results is shown
in the history of the Swedish party since 1962. Defeat in local
elections in that year was ascribed to the party's links with Moscow,
which had just ordered the building of the Berlin Wall. There began a
long and secret struggle inside the party to break its links with
Moscow and to democratize its structure. This battle between the

'traditionalists' and the 'modernists' culminated in the victory of the latter, led by C. H. Hermansson, in 1964. Thereafter the party became patriotic, it simply ignored Moscow, and it dismantled much of its Leninist structure. The name was changed, from communist party to 'Left Party—the communists'; the cell was devalued; onerous party work was abolished; lower echelons won a measure of autonomy from democratic centralism; the power of the party bureaucracy was curtailed and factions were, perforce, tolerated.[95] The traditionalists averred that these measures, formalized in new party statutes in 1967, would convert the party into a revisionist, social democrat party. The ultra-Leftists judged (at first) that this had indeed happened.[96]

In reality, something rather different happened. The party attracted ultra-Leftists of the sort that pullulated in Europe at the end of the 1960s. Whereas other Leninist parties fought the ultra-Leftists as 'infantile',[97] the VPK wooed them, and actually subsidized one of their weeklies for a time. Consequently, the VPK itself was radicalized, not social-democratized. A sharp Left turn marked its 1969 congress, which heaped abuse on social democrat reformism and practised energetic verbal revolutionism. The consolidation of the hold over the party of these Leftists, who had replaced the modernists as the party Centre, was seen at the 1972 congress. The Norrbotten Stalinists, who had feared seeing their party fall into the hands of the Revisionists, found themselves struggling with people they called 'Maoists', 'Trotskyists', and advocates of civil war. They were reduced to defending co-operation with social democrats and the peaceful, parliamentary way to power, along with party discipline and loyalty to Moscow. Even the ultra-Leftists, who had usurped the old title of 'communist party', conceded that the radicalized VPK had turned Left and was making new gains among the youth[98]—without specifying, what the Norrbotten Stalinists saw, that this was the middle-class youth of the prosperous south. The process of de-Leninization and subsequent radicalization[99] has not yet run its full course. The VPK is an incoherent, transitional phase where it preaches revolution while keeping a socialist government in office and effecting a certain reconciliation with Moscow.

Dynamics of Power in CPs

Apart from its formal or static structure, a western CP consists dynamically in the stable equilibrium of three distinct forces: Soviet power, the local party bureaucracy, and communist workers. Each of these is complex and has its own internal conflicts. Each depends on the other two, whether for power, votes, representation, legitimacy, money, or inspiration. Their shifting relations explain the evolution of the western parties.

The first, Soviet power, is the only one recognized by anti-communists and many ex-communists, for whom the parties are entirely at Moscow's orders, for whom the local officials are puppets while communist militants are unpatriotic or misled workers. Although the parties have mostly served Soviet foreign policy, the Soviet power in question here is not the relatively ineffectual Foreign Affairs Ministry in Moscow but, rather, the Soviet CP. In so far as an organ of the Soviet state, as distinct from the party, does intervene in the affairs of western parties, it is more commonly the Soviet secret police. It is because 'Moscow' is complex and divided that a western party can complain of having to stage a trial on Beria's orders that hampers its propaganda against the Indo-China war (here the secret police are obstructing Soviet foreign policy) or that approval of the invasion of Czechoslovakia would ruin its criticism of NATO (there the Soviet party would get in the way of Soviet foreign policy).

The second force, the local party bureaucracy, is also divided, as we have seen in disposing of the idea of its monolithic unity, but it is solidly united in its attachment to the Leninist party machine. Its roots are mainly in that machine, which is why it is called a 'bureaucracy' and why it emerged relatively recently when the western parties had matured from revolutionary sects into national institutions. It has bases, moreover, outside the machine, in the municipalities and regional authorities long governed by communists, notably in the suburbs of Paris and the Red Belt of Italy, as well as in the numerous business enterprises and front organizations controlled by the party.

The third force consists of that segment of the working class that is deeply attached to the myth of the Bolshevik Revolution. This is a minority of western workers (most of whom incline to conservative or social democrat support of neo-capitalism), and it is a minority even of those who vote communist. It is a minority of the party membership, maybe as low as one-fifth in the PCF. It is a layer of lower party functionaries and militants, along with workers who, while not always militant, are capable of intervening in the life of the party that represents for them the utopia of proletarian liberation. This group, which is often attached to communism in its Stalinist form, provides not only some of the votes, money, and influence the local bureaucracy needs in order to survive, but also a significant part of the legitimation of the Soviet ruling class itself. That class exercises an Asian, modernizing dictatorship over the Soviet Union in the name of a western, proletarian ideology, so that it needs, as urgently as it needs money and weapons, the ideological support of a genuinely proletarian and potentially revolutionary minority inside western capitalism. If that minority were to defect, whether to social democracy or to Chinese communism, or to withdraw its support of the CPs backed from Moscow, then the Soviet ruling class would face a want of legitimacy that could have revolutionary implications in Russia. By then, of course, the local party bureaucracies would have found that their backing from Moscow had become a fatal liability. Once workers lost faith in the Soviet utopia, the local party would be a Soviet agency, like the DKP or the Danish rump party.

The relation between these three forces in the first decades after the Bolshevik Revolution was that the local party had no political substance of its own but was the meeting place of western proletarian utopianism and Soviet power. In it, the 'eye of Moscow' ruled, by transmitting the decisions of the Comintern or, when that internationalist mask was discarded, those of Stalin himself. The party nevertheless won some local political relevance when it was shown that it was not only a Soviet agency but was vested with the faith of those western workers who believed in the Bolshevik Revolution. Soviet intervention through a mere sect of the revolutionaries would have meant nothing (as Chinese intervention in Europe through the 'Maoists' meant nothing a generation later) in the absence of workers who welcomed it as word from those who had dispossessed the possessors.[100]

After the Second World War, and especially after Stalin's death, the local parties acquired a weight of their own by finding sources of power, votes, money, and respectability other than the utopian workers and the Soviet Union. This was most evident in those large parties that made the classic transition from a propagandist sect to a proletarian party and then to a national party—a party that, however far from office, represented one possible future for their nation. Yet even parties that remained small found their own niche; they found ways in which they could exert local influence, and thus support a small party bureaucracy. The Leninist machine at that point began to recognize its own interests and to conceive its own political ambitions. It did not, for all that, become self-subsistent, for it could not dispense with Soviet aid or with the loyalty of the pro-Bolshevik workers. But it could become one force among three, whereas previously it was the meeting place of two forces.[101] In so far as it sought to liberate itself from those supports, it encountered the resistance of Soviet power and of a segment of the workers. It is this stable equilibrium that characterizes the present situation of the western parties and which accounts for their vulnerability as well as for their resilience.

It is in seeking to help each other gain a greater measure of independence of Soviet power and utopian workers that the parties practise 'polycentrism'. The Sino-Soviet quarrel made it possible to negotiate with Moscow rather than be manipulated by it, since their support—and the legitimation their worker-clients could offer—were vitally necessary to the Soviet ruling class in its confrontation with the other great communist power. That quarrel was the occasion for them to win a modicum of independence, but they were usually not concerned with its substance. The fragmentation of the international communist movement and the party splits and feuds that have accompanied the Sino-Soviet quarrel were not based on it and did not involve the same political issues. They occurred because members in each local party bureaucracy saw that they were confronted by a weakened Soviet power, reduced to negotiating diplomatic support among western communists. The independence that the local party officials sought in that situation was bureaucratic, not ideological. It did not arise from some new variety of Marxism-Leninism but from the desire to use the existing Leninist party machine for purposes of their own.

In particular, in taking their distances from Soviet power while trying at the same time to hold the support of the Stalinist workers, party officials made no concessions to social democracy. Their desatellization was not democratization; neither did it further their integration into western parliamentary democracy. On the contrary, the bureaucrats sought to preserve the Leninist apparatus in all its rigidity, taking as their model the Chinese, Albanian, and above all Rumanian parties which asserted their independence of Moscow without liberalizing their rule. It would be naïve to mistake the autonomous 'national-communist' party for a liberal foe of Soviet ideology. It maintains the power of the co-opted Leninist functionaries while placating the most retrograde elements of the local working class, those who dream of a 1917 in Western Europe.

This tendency in the western parties is resisted by the Soviet parties for various reasons. Firstly, it is inconvenient, in that it conflicts with the use of those parties as agencies for the defence of Soviet foreign policy. For example, when the PCF conceived its own political (and specifically, ministerial) ambitions, it decided in 1965 to support François Mitterrand against Charles de Gaulle in the presidential elections, whereas the Soviet Union preferred to see de Gaulle remain in the Elysée Palace. When, later, Moscow similarly wished to see Chancellor Willy Brandt stay in power, it could oblige the DKP, a mere agency, to commit political suicide by asking its followers to vote in the 1972 elections for the social democrats, whom it had been damning as traitors for months. The PCF could not be reduced to that. Brezhnev could only deplore the fact that the French communists shortsightedly 'put their own particular interests first'.[102] That was inconvenient, but no more. After all, the western CPs for all their utility as parliamentary lobbies and as street demonstrators, are not the only means of influencing western governments. Nor are they intended to carry through a revolution in Western Europe, because that would only present the Soviet Union either with an additional defence liability or a genuinely revolutionary challenge to the prestige of the Soviet ruling class.

The point at which the autonomy of the western parties becomes threatening rather than inconvenient is when it calls in doubt the revolutionary legitimacy of that ruling class by attacking its domestic policies or its dealings with other CPs. Fortunately for Moscow, the western parties are restrained in that sort of challenge not only by a measure of continued dependence on Soviet power and prestige but also by their own working-class clientele. For that segment of western workers that make up the core of communist membership, Moscow is still the incarnation of the revolutionary myth. For it, anti-Sovietism is anti-communism, and dogged philo-Sovietism is the feather in the cap that distinguishes the true faith from the dull, flat, stale ordinariness of social democracy. Their existence gives the Soviet party a weapon to curb velleities of autonomy in the local party by threatening to unseat the local leadership or to found a rival CP true to Moscow.

It is between these shoals that the party bureaucracy steers towards political autonomy, towards the use of the self-perpetuating Leninist machine for bureaucratic purposes. The goal is not some 'national communism', firstly because none of the western parties intends to install communism any more than the Soviet Union requires it to try to do so; secondly, the debate about national ways to communism is camouflage or 'esoteric communication'.

Ever since Karl Marx told the First International that the revolution he foresaw would not run an identical course in each capitalist country (he was in Holland, on a visit from England, so the range of differences he had in mind might not have been great), all the Marxists have conceded the possibility of national roads to socialism. Indeed, Lenin trod the first such road, and one well outside the range of differences that Marx contemplated.[103] Every western communist leader can claim to have said, at one time or another, that the Soviet road was not the only road open to his country. For example, the Swedish party was talking of a 'Swedish road to socialism' from autumn 1946.[104] The KPD had spoken of a 'German road to socialism' from June 1945—in a document printed in Moscow and brought to Berlin by communists who had lived in the Soviet Union since 1933.[105] Clearly, this 'national communism' was a Soviet suggestion. Not so when Togliatti said in 1956 that 'the Soviet model cannot and must not any longer be obligatory',[106] but Thorez sought to create confusion by remembering then, after a lapse of memory of ten years, that he had said in 1946 that 'the way is necessarily different (from the Russian way) in each country'.[107]

Since everyone has said this, one cannot tell, apart from the political context at the moment, whether it is a banality or a sign of rebellion against Soviet power. When Stalin's Cominform in June 1948 condemned national roads to socialism as a 'bourgeois nationalist deviation', while Tito defended them, and when Khrushchev, on a visit of reconciliation to Belgrade in 1955, conceded that Tito had been right, then the meaning of the phrase is precise: it means rejection of Soviet power within a foreign CP. Yet when western leaders approve Soviet 'normalization' of the Czech party after 1968 (which led to rule by Husak, who denies that national roads exist) and simultaneously insist that the western road would not be the Soviet road, the phrase has lost all force, and is again a timid echo of banal national differences.

Most assertions by western communist leaders of their right to a national road are balancing acts between these two senses. Consequently they often fall, and into incoherency. Thus the secretariat of the PCI in November 1961 admitted that in such discussions 'the basic problem . . . concerns the autonomy which the [Italian] party must enjoy'. Then, as though dismayed at its own frankness, it added that 'no one has tried to interfere . . . with our party's autonomy', and it went on to protest that the PCI's 'full and effective autonomy' was consistent with solidarity with the Soviet Union.[108] These intimations of autonomy expressed in 'esoteric communication' are mysterious to communists themselves unless they know the state of relations between the local party and Moscow at that point. What is quite clear, in contrast, is when a western party goes too far.

When a member of the politburo of the Austrian party wrote in a journal sponsored by party notables that 'the Soviet model . . . of party and state rule is not a socialist model at all, for any country, not even for the Soviet Union',[109] then a western party was directly attacking the legitimacy of the Soviet rulers. When members of the central committee of the Italian party called for revolution in Eastern Europe, for 'the formation of a Left revolutionary alternative inside the socialist camp' aimed at 'the overthrow and replacement of the ruling groups of the USSR and of the other socialist countries by a new historical block of social forces led by the working class', and when they confided to a 'bourgeois' magazine that 'not a few of the leaders of the PCI agree with us in considering the Soviet leaders to be a group of bandits, but to say so would create serious diplomatic embarrassment', then they have gone too far, even if they protested lamely that 'we have expressed ourselves badly'.[110] Well short of such rebellion, Soviet power in western CPs has made itself felt against the stirring of autonomy that began with the secret Khrushchev report on Stalin's crimes in 1956, increased with Khrushchev's dismissal in 1964, and reached a crescendo with the invasion of Czechoslovakia in 1968.

Stalin was the last Soviet leader to exercise that power virtually without challenge. Khrushchev, already, found that he had to render an accounting to the western party officials who were dispatched to Moscow after his secret report and again after the Hungarian affair in 1956. By 1960, when Khrushchev apparently imagined he could use the Servin-Casanova faction to unseat Thorez and secure a PCF more amenable to Moscow's desires, he found that he had in fact to buy Thorez's support against the Chinese at the meeting of eighty-one parties in Moscow that year, at the cost of letting Thorez purge Servin and Casanova. Khrushchev's successors in turn had to give an accounting to the western parties for their unceremonious dismissal of 'Mr K.', an event that riled the party bureaucracies more than the Hungarian oppression.[111] By the time Brezhnev sought to exert, to the full, Soviet power in foreign parties, less than half the world's communists were still loyal to Moscow. Brezhnev apparently imagined that Moscow's power was supreme in the West European parties at least, because when Dubcek said that these parties would support him, Brezhnev blustered, 'Those who would dare do that—we have the power to reduce them to the state of groupuscules.'[112] He proceeded to test that power, with the following varied results.

The Spanish party, once the servile agency not only of the Soviet party but of the NKVD (the Soviet secret police), had already shown its discontent over the dismissal of Khrushchev. In 1968 it openly supported Dubcek, whose regime in Czechoslovakia it saw as a model of what it was proposing to its prospective non-communist allies in Spain. Its central committee in September 1968 accordingly condemned the invasion by the Warsaw Pact nations, and it expelled a pro-Soviet minority from its ranks. The PCE took an aggressively hostile stand at the Moscow meeting of seventy-five parties the next year. Moscow thereupon encouraged the dissident minority, meanwhile joined by General Enrique Lister, to form a rival CP. This acquired a certain substance since it attracted 10–15 per cent of the membership, not only among exiles in Eastern Europe but among Moscow-true communists in Spain and the émigrés in France. Supported by Poland and the new Czech government, the rival party held meetings in Moscow, put out a paper with the same name (*Mundo obrero*) as the official organ, spent money lavishly, and tellingly (though no doubt hypocritically) assailed Santiago Carrillo's rigid Leninist rule. The Carrillo party received material help from Rumania and moral support from the PCI and, more cautiously, from the PCF. It toyed with the idea of taking Peking's side in the Sino-Soviet quarrel but preferred to lapse into isolation within the world communist movement, an isolation baptized 'autonomy' and covered over with strident internationalism. It claimed by 1973 to have overcome the Soviet-backed dissidence. Its case is instructive as showing that even a small party once notorious for its subordination to Moscow, and still ill placed to secure its rear under the Francoist dictatorship, was able to defy Soviet power in its own ranks. It defended an autonomous policy of seeking an alliance with non-communist forces on a reformist platform, while maintaining its rigid Leninist structure.[113] Meanwhile it encouraged similar tendencies in CPs in Greece and Australia.

The Austrian party, the KPO, similarly chose the Czech invasion as the occasion for its open bid for independence. The invasion was immediately condemned by the politburo and then by the central committee. This challenge to Moscow was all the more serious in that the KPO, though small, has—or had—a certain audience in the old Austro-Hungarian empire, notably in communist Hungary and

Czechoslovakia, and in East Germany. Yet it was necessary for the KPO to make that challenge because the credibility of its offer to collaborate with non-communists depended on the survival of the Dubcek regime in Prague. Moscow managed to defeat that challenge by using the pro-Bolshevik workers. Senior militants, many of them unconstitutionally selected and mostly well on in years,[114] openly supported by Russian and East German money, publications, and personnel, won control of the party congress in January 1969. In the ensuing two years, that pro-Soviet majority secured the dismissal, resignation and/or expulsion of three members of the politburo, including Franz Marek, and 27 out of 87 members of the central committee, including Ernest Fischer, the party's leading intellectual. The youth organization was disbanded and replaced by a pro-Soviet rump, but in fact the party had no youth left in it. Its membership had slumped from 35,000 to 15,000, its average age had soared to nearly 60 years, and the last of its elected representation was lost. The motion condemning the Czech invasion was annulled (the only case of a western CP reversing its stand on the issue) as symbolic of the fact that two of the power centres of the party—the Soviets and the old Bolshevik workers—had wiped out the third, the party officials who had bid for autonomy.[115]

The Greek CP, living under the dictatorship of the military, sought to assert its independence of Moscow from 1967. Disagreement arose when Moscow began cultivating the Athenian colonels for the convenience of Soviet naval policy in the Mediterranean. (A similar collision between Soviet foreign policy and local anti-fascist politics had angered the PCE when Moscow resumed dealings with Madrid.) The Czech affair added fuel to the fire. In the party feud that broke out in 1968, Moscow backed the Greek exiles in Eastern Europe, who number tens of thousands, and who now constitute the rival 'exterior' party, led by Kolyiannis until the end of 1972, then by Charilaos Florakis. (That party was recognized by the PCF.) The 'interior' party, led by Antonios Brillakis, was succoured by Rumania and recognized by the PCI and PCE. Although anti-Soviet, the 'interior' party alienated the sympathies not only of Mikis Theodorakis but of other communists who in 1972 set up a third and 'truly autonomous' CP in Greece. Moscow allegedly helped the colonels track down members of the 'interior' party, who were indeed arrested with surprising facility, as were Rumania's emissaries to them. Changing tack, Moscow in 1973 sought a reconciliation of the two factions, with slender chances of success.

Similar direct, or bureaucratic, intervention using militants trained in Moscow can be shown not only in the East European parties but in such parties as the Finnish, Syrian, and Australian ones. It is admitted by all communists, save to date the French, to be a constant problem for the local bureaucracies. Luigi Longo said in a speech in Moscow in 1960 (which was released only two years later) that out of respect for autonomy 'every party must refrain and order its members to refrain from all fractional activity among the rank and file and within the bodies of other parties'.[116] To show which party he had in mind, it was in a letter to Khrushchev at the same date that Longo insisted that 'fractional subversion by one party of fraternal parties' must stop.[117] The Dutch party twelve years later[118] was still complaining of 'support for persons or groups that attack the elected and qualified leadership', and of 'interference by enemies' (it had just denounced 'modern revisionism', i.e Moscow). To be sure, the Netherlands-USSR Friendship Society was being used as a rallying point for pro-Soviet dissidents and was supplying its Soviet-financed monthly paper, replete with criticisms of the CPN leaders, to all party members. The CPN resolved not to attend international communist meetings or to invite foreign parties to its own congresses. Such meetings have been, since the dissolution of the Cominform, the occasion for direct, bureaucratic intervention in the western parties by their oldest power centre, Moscow.

Where that was not effective, Moscow could appeal, against the bureaucracies of even the largest parties, to the loyalty of the basic power centre in a party, the communist workers. The existence of numerous utopian workers convinced that 1917 saw the inauguration of a workers' paradise in the Soviet Union was necessary for the original implantation of CPs in Western Europe in the early 1920s. Their continued existence fifty disillusioning years later is due in large measure to tireless indoctrination by a local CP which needs them as a power base. Now, however, its creature threatens to turn against it when it seeks its independence of Moscow. When the PCI's biggest federation, in Bologna, began to behave in the 1960s like any other Italian party bureaucracy—patronage, corruption, capitalist friends, fast sports cars, the high living of provincial *parvenus*—the Stalinist workers grouped in soviet-style fraternities in, for example, the Bologna tramways, revolted and revived the maximalism and utopianism that were characteristic of Emilian socialism even before 1917. Again, when the PCI in 1968 condemned the Soviet invasion of Czechoslovakia, similar groups throughout Italy were roused by Soviet intervention to attack their leaders. Leaflets denouncing the 'corrupt' PCI leadership, condemning their reformist parliamentary tactics, and raking up 'unmanly' incidents from their past were distributed among Italian workers. They were held to have originated in the Soviet and Polish embassies, and it is known that diplomats from those legations stirred up militants at the base. Radio broadcasts from Eastern Europe condemned the party line. Magazines defending Soviet actions against PCI criticism suddenly appeared in Italy (e.g. an Italian version of *L'Union soviétique*). There were disquieting rumours of a plan for a new Moscow-true CP backed by a section of communist workers and led by Stalinists like Edoardo d'Onofrio, Ambrogio Donini, and Pietro Secchia. The PCI leaders never dared to reply to this Soviet subversion, which was known in the party as 'dissenso nel dissenso', though they did venture to quarrel with its Polish and East German agents. Berlinguer pleaded with his Stalinist rank and file to give up, at last, their 'utopian views of Soviet reality'.[119] He failed to convince them, because he was not willing to say explicitly that Moscow did not want the local party to try to realize the utopian desires of the revolutionary workers but to work within the Italian political system so as to defend Soviet foreign policy more effectively. It was left to the ultra-Left during the troubles of 1968–9 to try to get the workers to see that the only result of their attachment to the myth of the October Revolution was to provide a western, Marxist aura to the Soviet oligarchy and to give Moscow the means to curb any move towards autonomy within the PCI. Faced with a campaign that shook the party to its foundations, the PCI leadership moderated its criticism of Soviet actions and gave its own domestic policy a sharp Left turn: it endorsed the workers' demands that plunged Italy into the economic crisis of 1969 in an effort to win back the confidence of its Stalinist base.

There might be no more than 20 per cent of communist workers who reject their conditions of life of western capitalism so utterly that they cling to the Soviet myth of the October Revolution or at least prefer to apologize for distant Soviet injustices rather than accept local capitalist injustices. That is enough to constitute the sinews of parties that are losing militancy and are loath to part with their proletarian patent. Indeed, this group is so politically significant that it has been courted not only by the Russians but by the Chinese, Albanians, and assorted ultra-Leftists. Since they are genuine proletarians, in Marx's own sense, they are insensitive to the appeal of Chinese communism, the ideology of a non-proletarian, peasant revolt. The numerous Chinese interventions in western parties through the 1960s all ended in the expulsion of the pro-Chinese dissidents. Only in the Belgian party did they manage to take with them as much as one-third of the party membership. After these failures, the Chinese appeared to realize that the best place for them to secure a hold over western communism was not at the proletarian base, via the Maoists, but in the local bureaucracies, via parties independent of Moscow such as the Rumanian party. To the western communist bureaucracies, Peking could offer the prospect of a new International, the International of autonomous party bureaucracies, defended from Soviet interference by Chinese patronage and from the proletarian base by the alibi of Chinese super-revolutionism. Coming from Asian communists who ruled in the name of a peasantry, the offer was not attractive to western parties with a proletarian mythology, but transmitted as 'polycentrism' under Rumanian auspices the proposal had some success.

When Togliatti first proposed polycentrism in 1956, the notion was ignored or rejected, in part because other communists could not see which of the two different things Togliatti meant: regional groupings of parties, or their individual isolation.[120] The French and Austrian communists thought he meant the first and rejected it.[121] Togliatti had to reply that he did not mean regional groupings but admitted that that idea *had* been put forward and even tentatively applied among European CPs, though not at his suggestion.[122] It was only some years later, towards the end of the 1960s, that polycentrism in just that sense of regional groupings became the defence reaction of CPs seeking mutual support in their efforts to gain independence of a Soviet power that they could not defy without losing not only material aid and prestige but the confidence of their core of proletarian followers. By that time, officials in those parties had conceived the ambition of using the Leninist machine for their own purposes, knowing that the Soviet Union would have no objection to non-revolutionary political activity compatible with its own foreign policies and that the utopian workers were well accustomed to a mixed diet of sectarian philo-Soviet rhetoric and reformist politics. The only difficulty was that effective political action entailed, everywhere in Western Europe, co-operation with democratic Leftist forces that objected to Soviet policy, both domestic and foreign, and required that communist allies dissociate themselves from it. Polycentrism came to seem a solution to this predicament.

The predicament itself was becoming untenable, because of the conflicting requirements of legitimation for Soviet and western communists. The exchange of legitimations, or of ideological justifications, had always been as important as the provision of material aid, and it was two-way. The Soviet rulers need the ideological endorsement of Marxists in capitalist lands as much as western communists need the prestige of the proletarian state that 'expropriated the expropriators'. But once the two parties began pursuing different courses, the legitimations had to be forged and the ideological endorsements censored. That was achieved by the technique of giving jointly signed communiqués radically different interpretations, and by ignoring or suppressing the other side's protests. Moreover, the quotations in the Soviet press from western communist papers (which had always been an important way of justifying Soviet rulers to their people and of encouraging western communists: good pupils have their homework read out in class) came to be highly selective and even falsified. A few examples will illustrate these elaborate procedures.

In March 1973 Brezhnev and Berlinguer met in Moscow for the first time, officially, in five years and issued a joint communiqué that contained a diplomatic settlement of the breach opened by the Czech affair. The PCI agreed not to mention, i.e. to suspend, its opposition to Soviet policy in Czechoslovakia, and the Soviet party agreed to mention specifically the right to autonomy of each CP. Into the bargain, Berlinguer sided with Soviet policy on European unification, and Brezhnev gave him back his badge of proletarian internationalist. Yet when *Pravda* printed the communiqué it omitted the reference to party autonomy and even made it seem, by a judicious selection of phrases, that the PCI had rallied belatedly to the conclusions of the 1969 meeting that approved the invasion of Czechoslovakia. In the course of an interview that was 'requested' immediately by *L'Unità*, Berlinguer pointed out *Pravda*'s errors of omission and commission. *Tass* duly reported that interview but left out the parts where Berlinguer corrected *Pravda*. But then *L'Unità* also omitted to report that on the same day that Berlinguer was in Moscow approving Brezhnev on European unity, his colleague Amendola was in Cologne defending another view of European unity palatable to some western socialists but obnoxious to Moscow.[123]

Many parties have had similar experiences. In 1968 *Pravda* had printed a resolution of a regional organization of the Finnish party approving the invasion of Czechoslovakia but overlooked the official resolutions of the party's politburo and central committee condemning it. The common programme that the PCF signed in 1972 with the French socialists was not published in Moscow, and in *Pravda*'s summary of it there was no mention of its assertion that 'there can be no model of socialism that can be transferred from one country to another'. In return, when a Soviet delegate attended a PCF congress in December 1972, he was required to re-write his speech before delivering it.[124] At the time, the French President was about to visit Brezhnev, and the conflict between Soviet foreign policy and the French party's own political ambitions was painfully evident. That was dealt with by the Soviet press omitting from accounts of speeches by Marchais all criticism of Pompidou, while *L'Humanité* omitted from Brezhnev's speeches all compliments to Pompidou. Worse, the Soviet press, which uses western communist editorials to answer allegations of injustices in Soviet Russia, took to falsifying its highly selective quotations when western communists began to tread carefully in the Solzhenitsyn and Sakharov affairs.[125] For example, condemnations of Solzhenitsyn's *Gulag Archipelago* that were put out by *Tass* in its foreign service only were printed, with ascription but without comment, by western CP papers in 1974—and were then quoted in the internal Soviet press as though those western communist papers had originally written them. A sign of the crisis in the mutual traffic in legitimation was the hours-long dispute in the Soviet party politburo about which medal to award Aragon, the literary *gloire* of French Stalinism who had criticized Czech normalization as 'the Biafra of the spirit'.[126] Censorship and falsification in the exchange of ideological justification became so dangerous that speeches of communists at other parties' congresses must now be submitted in advance. If they are not amended to suit the host, the speaker is refused the floor, as was a British communist delegation at a Polish party meeting in 1968[127] and as was an Italian communist delegation at a Czech meeting in 1971.[128] At the PCI congress of 1972 only the Russians and North Vietnamese were allowed to speak from the platform, presumably after prior censorship. Other delegations had to submit their messages in writing, and the Czech message was printed in *L'Unità* with a critical comment. Indeed, some parties now refuse to send or accept such delegations. The PCF gave notice that it would invite none (not even from Moscow) to its 1974 congress.

In these circumstances, the western CPs saw that a polycentrist legitimation might conceivably replace a Soviet one, if that latter were to be withheld or if it had to be dispensed with as too compromising. That is, co-operation with like-minded officials in CPs in the same region could offer a 'proletarian internationalist' warrant for the attempt to escape from Soviet tutelage. This idea made its way during the great rift in the world communist movement in the 1960s. The principal issue in that quarrel was the role of the Soviet party in the world movement, its traditional function as one of the three power centres in all other CPs. The other issues that came up were derivations from or disguises for that. Thus the debate about 'fractionalism' in the movement referred to Soviet and Chinese use of fractions in other CPs, in order to exercise power there. 'Revisionism' and 'dogmatism' were labels for Soviet and Chinese interventions, respectively, in other parties.

The polycentrist solution would be to eradicate both those influences and use regional groupings of communists to answer the charge that a party was thereby relapsing from proletarian internationalism into that nationalistic party-egoism that had, according to Lenin, ruined the Second International in 1914. The Rumanian party, having checked the pro-Soviet minority in its ranks by using its state power (and, specifically, by using the firing squad), actively encouraged this polycentrism. It exchanged numerous visits with the Italian, French, Finnish, Belgian, Swedish, Greek ('interior'), Norwegian, Swiss, British, and Spanish CPs, as well as the Japanese, Australian, and Israeli parties, from 1969 onwards.[129] The Rumanians even managed to secure an invitation in May 1972 from the jealously isolationist Icelandic party. It was customary at these meetings to issue a communiqué in which the Rumanians and their interlocutors praised 'autonomy, diversity, and tolerance' in the communist movement. If the visitors to Bucharest were willing to be more explicit, the communiqué would reject the notion of a 'centre' or of 'uniformity' in the world movement and would denounce foreign (i.e. Soviet) intervention in other parties. The PCE made the sense of these denunciations plain by 'recognizing' (as though it were a foreign state) the Chinese CP while Carrillo was in Bucharest in September 1971 and by sending a mission to Peking directly afterwards.

Thus encouraged from Bucharest (and even succoured by the Rumanians where their home base was threatened, as was the case of the Greeks and Spaniards), the West European CPs exchanged visits among themselves from 1969 more frequently than ever before. Their regional conclaves too increased in frequency: Rome 1959,

Brussels 1965, Vienna 1966, Paris 1970 and 1971, London 1971, and a whole series of consultations in 1973 in Stockholm, Copenhagen, Paris, Rome, and Düsseldorf to prepare a meeting in Brussels in 1974. Regional meetings on special subjects followed in Lyons and Rome. Every West European party from Cyprus to Finland attended the most important of these gatherings, even the Dutch, but the Turks were sometimes and the Icelanders usually absent. The meetings were not an aspect of the general process of political unification taking place in the European Community at the time, since they included parties from countries outside and hostile to that unification, e.g. from the neutrals. Indeed, care was taken by the communists not to seem to attach any importance to the relations between the nine (earlier six) parties from the European Community. Nor were these meetings designed for political efficacy at the European level. For *that* purpose, the Italian and French CPs would have had to treat with the West German and British socialist parties (some contacts were actually made at that level) and not with the negligible West German and British CPs. When the leader of the PCF goes to meetings of the tiny DKP, PCP and PST, as did Marchais in 1973 and 1974, he is not looking for European unity or Leftist collaboration, but for a proletarian internationalist legitimation.

The organizers of the regional meetings of West European CPs did not omit to invite parties that were entirely dependent on Soviet (or East German) backing, such as the Portuguese, West German, and West Berlin parties. Such meetings, furthermore, would endorse certain Soviet policies, such as the Russian conception of European co-operation as expressed at the 1973 Helsinki meeting on European security. But they would not endorse, or in any way prepare, meetings of all CPs, such as Moscow was pressing for in order to stage a trial of strength with the Chinese by intervening in third parties. Polycentrism, which has its parallel among the CPs of Latin America and the Arab world, was designed to show communist workers that a local bureaucracy that defied Soviet power was not thereby abandoning the proletarian universalism that has been a hallmark of the movement since 1917.

The manoeuvre was not assured of success. Firstly, Soviet power is by no means absent from gatherings that include such Soviet agencies as the CPs of Germany and Portugal. Secondly, some at least of the western communist workers realized that 'regional internationalism' was hollow oratory on the part of bureaucrats with local political ambitions.[130] They saw that when a communist official said, 'Unity is only possible in diversity, on the basis of respect for the independence of each party and for its right to elaborate its own national and international policies and to maintain the position it considers the right one each problem,'[131] then 'unity' has become as meaningless as it was in the pre-1914 Second International.

Notes

1 Palmiro Togliatti, *Il Partito comunista italiano*, 2nd ed. (Rome, 1970), p. 9.

2 M. Servin, then organization secretary of the PCF, in *Cahiers du communisme*, June–July 1954, p. 731.

3 Fauvet, p. 321.

4 Galli, pp. 92–3.

5 Gianluigi Degli Esposti, *Bologna PCI* (Bologna, 1966), pp. 244–5.

6 J.-M. Domenach, 'The French communist party', in Mario Einaudi et al, *Communism in Western Europe*, 2nd ed. (Hamden, USA, 1971), pp. 81, 88–9.

7 For a lively account of cell life in the PCI, Marcello Argilli, *Un Anno in sezione: Vita di base del PCI* (Milan, 1970). Covering the agitated period of the *Manifesto* crisis, it might not be typical.

8 *Unir*, no 82, pp. 8, 18; *Il Mondo*, 29 Nov 1973.

9 Instances of horizontal communication are reported: Argilli, pp. 23–4 & 39; Lord, ECPR Workshop, p. 35. At the level of the regional organization and upwards it is frequent, but by then it involves permanents and senior militants.

10 *Unir*, no 78, p. 8.

11 K.-V. Winqvist et al, *Svenska Partiapparater* (Stockholm, 1972), pp. 262–5.

12 Argilli, p. 168.

13 Ibid., p. 152.

14 Guy Hermet, *Les Communistes en Espagne* (Paris, 1971), p. 70.

15 *VIII Congreso del PCE*, p. 303.

16 *L'Autocritique attendue* (Paris, 1955).

17 *Cahiers du communisme*, Feb 1952. For the Lecoeur episode, Louis Couturier, *Les 'grandes affaires' du Parti communiste français* (Paris, 1972), pp. 58–65.

18 *Unir*, no 74, pp. 8–9.

19 Ignacio Gallego, *El Partido de masas que necesitamos* (Paris, 1971), pp. 67–8.

20 Winqvist, p. 298.

21 Berlinguer, pp. 95–6. In 1970 the PCI declared to the tax authorities 36 paid employees, whereas even the tiny PSIUP declared 41, while the socialist party declared 180 and the Christian Democrats 855.

22 For examples, Galli, *Il Bipartitismo imperfetto*, pp. 340–1.

23 *Unir*, no 66, p. 9.

24 Schemas for biographies and reports are found in A. Rossi [Angelo Tasca], *Physiologie du Parti communiste français* (Paris, 1948), pp. 246–50.

25 In Einaudi, p. 205.

26 Sven Landin, *Uppbrott från stalinismen* (Stockholm, 1973), pp. 38–47.

27 *Der Spiegel*, 10 Apr 1972.

28 On PCF schools, Kriegel, *Les Communistes français*, pp. 166–76 and Ronald Tiersky, *Le Mouvement communiste en France* (Paris, 1973), pp. 261–2.

29 *Est et Ouest*, no 503.

30 *La Questione del 'Manifesto': Democrazia e unità nel PCI* (Rome, 1969).

31 *LM*, 29 Mar 1973.

32 Alain Strang, 'Comment le PC a décidé de dire Non', *Journal du Dimanche*, 26 Mar 1972.

33 *Est et Ouest*, no 505, p. 2.

34 Gallego, pp. 37–8.

35 Iker, 'Nacionalismo y lucha de clases en Euskadi', *Ruedo ibérico*, no 37–8, pp. 15–36.

36 On the PCF and the 'nationalists' of Brittany and Occitania, *LM*, 2 Feb & 29 June 1971, 15–16 Oct 1972, 16 Aug 1973, & 3–4 Mar 1974.

37 André Marty, *L'Affaire Marty* (Paris, 1955), p. 41.

38 *Preuves*, no 176, p. 92.

39 Tiersky, p. 266; Marty, p. 96.

40 H. W. Andersen, *Dansk Politik i går og i dag* (Viborg, Denmark, 1972), pp. 213–14.

41 Hermet, pp. 64–5.

42 *VIII Congreso del PCE*, pp. 93, 113, 115, 146 & *ad nauseam*.

43 *Cahiers du communisme*, Mar 1953, pp. 397–8.

44 For the significance of the incantatory phrase, 'of a new type', Michael Waller, *The language of communism* (London, 1972), p. 86.

45 Annie Kriegel, *Communismes au miroir français* (Paris, 1974), pp. 129–60.

46 *Unir*, no 65, p. 23 & no 73, p. 31.

47 Observers attributed great power to three simple members of the PCF central committee: Jean Kanapa, of Czech origin, and Jacques Denis and Jean Jérôme, both of Polish origin. Their influence certainly exceeded their formal rank.

48 Upton, pp. 122–3.

49 Fauvet, p. 20.

50 Upton, pp. 238–40.

51 Guy Hermet, 'Le Communisme en Espagne et en Turquie: deux types de clandestinité', ECPR Workshop.

52 Margarete Buber-Neumann, *Der kommunistische Untergrund* (Zurich, 1970), pp. 76–8; Bärwald & Scheffler, pp. 57–8, 61–2, 72–3, 87–8.

53 Whereas the KKE split under oppression, AKEL, also operating in a Greek community, but legally, maintained its unity and thrived to the point where it embraced 4 per cent of the population, making it the world's biggest non-ruling communist party, in relation to population.

54 The Algiers radio station, Voz da Liberdade, publishes as well as broadcasting, this propaganda, e.g. *Brigadas Revolucionarias* (Algiers, 1972). Other opponents based in Paris publish *Ergue-te e Luta: Jornal operario comunista* and *Combate operario*. A characteristic attack is *O Programa do PCP a luz do marxismo revolucionário* (Paris, 1973).

55 *VIII Congreso del PCE*, pp. 30, 36.

56 W. Abendroth et al, eds., *KPD-Verbot oder mit Kommunisten leben?* (Reinbek bei Hamburg, 1968), p. 53; Helmut Bärwald, *Deutsche Kommunistische Partei: die kommunistische Bündnispolitik in Deutschland* (Cologne, 1970), pp. 17, 114–17; Richard Loss, 'The communist party of Germany (KPD), 1956–68', *Survey*, no 89, pp. 66–85.

57 *Avante*, Apr 1973, p. 6.

58 Silas Cerqueira, 'Dans la clandestinité: Antée ou Sisyphe? Le cas du parti communiste portugais', ECPR Workshop, pp. 36–9.

59 *VIII Congreso del PCE*, pp. 68–71.

60 *LM*, 13 Aug 1971.

61 Hermet, p. 187.

62 *LM*, 16 May 1973.

63 *La Questione del 'Manifesto'*, p. 207.

64 *VIII Congreso del PCE*, p. 290.

65 *Preuves*, no 193, pp. 18–19.

66 *Le Nouvel Observatoire*, 10 Apr 1972.
67 *Est et Ouest*, no 522, pp. 1-24; *Expressen*, 11 June 1972.
68 They were 20m. francs out of 45m. for the PCF in 1971 (*L'Humanité*, 23 May 1972). They were 2,600m. lire out of 5,780m. for the PCI in 1970 (*La Stampa*. 17 Apr 1971).
69 e.g. by Mme Tillon, *LM*, 7 Apr 1970.
70 Kriegel, *Les Communistes français*, p. 129.
71 *LM*, 15 June 1972; *Unir*, no 66, p. 89.
72 Galli, *Il Bipartitismo imperfetto*, pp. 219-20; Buber-Neumann, p. 15.
73 A list of KPO firms is given in *Est et Ouest*, no 495, pp. 12-13; PCF firms, Gross, pp. 43-4 & 100-3; AKEL firms, Adams, pp. 74-6.
74 *Action*, Apr 1972.
75 It lost (Philip J. Jaffe, 'The Varga controversy and the American CP', *Survey*, no 84, p. 146).
76 *L'Unità*, 6 Dec 1969.
77 *Histoire du Parti communiste français*, 3 vols (Paris, 1961-4).
78 *Des Oppositions communistes aux CIC* (Paris, 1971) is an oppositional history of this dissidence. Also *Unir*, no 70, pp. 18-23.
79 'The party needs a trial' (London, p. 160).
80 Couturier, pp. 14-15.
81 As was suggested (Almond, pp. 333-5).
82 *LM*, 20 Sept 1952.
83 Helga Grebing, *Geschichte der deutschen Arbeiterbewegung* (Munich, 1966), p. 257.
84 T. Halvorsen, 'Oppgjøret med det 2. sentrum', *Kontrast* (Oslo), no 43, pp. 30-42; 'NKP etter krigen'. *Røde Fane* (Oslo), no 6, 1973, pp. 32-8.
85 *LM*, 20-1 Feb 1972.
86 Stefano Munafó, 'Il Congresso del Partito comunista', *Mondo operaio*, Jan 1969, and 'La "riforma protestante" del PCI', ibid., Feb 1969.
87 Tapio Koskiaho, 'The Finnish communist party as a cabinet party after the second world war', ECPR Workshop, pp. 24-7.
88 Enzo Bettiza, *Quale PCI?* (Milan, 1969).
89 Wagner, pp. 24-5, 111-20; Pertti Hynynen, 'Folkfronten i Finland', *Zenit*, no 14, pp. 48-63.
90 Maurice Thorez, *Fils du peuple* (Paris, 1954), pp. 70-1.
91 *LM*, 29-30 Apr & 6 May 1973.
92 Ibid., 28 Mar 1973.
93 Ibid., 22 Aug 1973.
94 The Leninist structure is 'a mystery that fascinates and outrages our critics: the mystery of our unity and discipline' (Berlinguer, p. 95).
95 Upton, pp. 98-101.
96 Nils Holmberg, *Vart går Sveriges Kommunistiska Parti* (Gothenberg, 1965); 'Från SKP till Vpk' and 'Fem kommunister om Vpk', *Zenit*, no 14, pp. 4-35; 'Om kommunistpartiernas kris, smågrupperna och vänsterns uppgifter', ibid., no 24, pp. 4-12.
97 Romano Luperini, *Il PCI e il movimento studentesco* (Milan, 1969).
98 *Dokument nr 1 från SKP första kongress* (Stockholm, 1973), p. 24; 'Vpk-kongressen', *Zenit*, no 31, pp. 46-53.
99 'The radicalisation of the [Swedish] CP in recent years is to a large degree due to the 'Leninisation' of the erstwhile New Left and Left Socialist strata' (Tarschys, ECPR Workshop, p. 21).
100 Walter Kendall, 'Folk myths of the western world', *Bull. of Soc. for the Study of Labour History*, no 24.
101 Livio Maitan, *PCI 1945-1969: Stalinismo e opportunismo* (Rome, 1969), pp. 183-203.
102 Erick Weit, *Eyewitness* (London, 1973), p. 140.

103 Edmund Demaitre, 'The origins of national communism', *Studies in Comparative Communism*, 2/1, Jan 1969, pp. 1–20.

104 Tom Olsson, 'SKPs politiska utveckling 1943–50', *Arkiv för Studier i Arbetarrörelsens Historia*, no 2, pp. 78–95.

105 Eric Waldman, *Die Sozialistische Einheitspartei Westberlins und die sowjetische Berlinpolitik* (Boppard am Rhein, 1972), p. 58; Grebing, pp. 284–5.

106 In the *Nuovi argomenti* interview, *Anti-Stalin campaign*, p. 138.

107 *The Times*, 18 Nov 1946.

108 Alexander Dallin, ed., *Diversity in international communism: A documentary record 1961–1963* (New York & London, 1963), pp. 462–3.

109 Franz Marek, 'Zur geistigen Krise im Kommunismus', *Wiener Tagebuch*, July–Aug 1969, p. 33.

110 *La Questione del 'Manifesto'*, pp. 20, 65, 96.

111 Åke Sparring et al, *Röd opposition: Europas kommunistiska partier och Chrusjtjovs fall* (Stockholm, 1965).

112 Roger Garaudy, *Toute la vérité* (Paris, 1971), pp. 178–9.

113 Fernando Claudin, 'The split in the Spanish CP', *New Left Review*, no 70.

114 Out of 374 delegates, only 23 were aged under 30; 141 were over 50.

115 Kevin Devlin, 'Czechoslovakia and the crisis of Austrian communism', *Studies in Comparative Communism*, July–Oct 1969.

116 Dallin, p. 858.

117 *Il PCI e il movimento operaio internazionale*, p. 145.

118 *24ste Congres van de CPN*, p. 93.

119 Luciano Vasconi, 'La strategia internazionale del PCI', *Mondo operaio*, Feb 1969, p. 17.

120 He seemed to mean the first in his interview to *Nuovi argomenti*, but the second in his report to the central committee several weeks later—*Il PCI e il movimento operaio internazionale*, pp. 60 & 68–9.

121 Dallin, pp. 492–3, 528.

122 Ibid., pp. 496–7. Yet in his Yalta testament, Togliatti clearly stated that autonomy, independence of Moscow, carried risks that could be met by regional co-operation (*Il PCI e il movimento operaio internazionale*, pp. 236, 243).

123 *LM*, 16 & 20 Mar 1973; *L'Unità*, 18 Mar 1973; Wolfgang Berner & Heinz Timmermann, *Erfahrungsbericht über den Besuch einer Gruppe führender Vertreter der Italienischen Kommunistischen Partei in Bonn und Köln am 15–16 März 1973* (Bundesinstitut für ostwissenschaftliche und internationale Studien, 1973).

124 *LM*, 20 Dec 1972.

125 Ibid., 26–7 Aug 1973; *Est et Ouest*, no 516, pp. 10–14.

126 *LM*, 14 Sept 1973.

127 Lennart Ljunglof, *Världskommunismens kris efter Prag* (Stockholm, 1969), pp. 17–18.

128 *LM*, 29 & 30–1 May 1971.

129 Heinz Timmermann, 'Neue Einheit im Weltkommunismus: Bemerkungen zur Interessenallianz zwischen rumänischen und westeuropäischen Kommunisten', *Berichte*, no 2, 1972.

130 Basilio Blasco, 'Los comunistas españoles vistos por Guy Hermet', *Ruedo iberico*, no 37–8, p. 134.

131 Gallego, p. 48.

4 The communists and neo-capitalist democracy

Having identified, in the local party bureaucracy, the architects of communist policies, we shall now see what those policies are, in relation to West European neo-capitalism, to the institutions of parliamentary democracy, and to European unity and defence. A later section will look at the political alliances by means of which the communists hope to advance these policies.

Economic Policies

Because they cling to economic hypotheses put forward many years ago by Marx and Lenin, the communists have difficulty in giving an account of the West European economies of the late twentieth century. The Marxist theory of value, which stresses the contribution of one factor of production, labour, at the expense of the contributions of capital, enterprise, and (most important today) science and technology, not only leads to the proletarian bias we have seen in their ideology, but it hampers the communists in understanding the economy. The Leninist vision of western capitalism in its imperialist death-throes would not help towards such an understanding either, but it is not meant to do so. It serves, rather, as a philosophy of history or a myth: an apocalyptic prophecy that no fact can controvert but which can subsume hundreds of instances that illustrate it. The notion of capitalism being brought to an end by its own internal contradictions is beyond the reach of facts: if the economy expands and capital moves across frontiers, that establishes the culpable collusion of capitalist forces, but if there are difficulties, conflicts, and nationalist protectionisms, then that establishes the fatal contradictions of capitalism. Once the system is assumed to be within in its last critical moments, then examples are easily found to illustrate the 'crisis', even if the last moments last for decade after decade. The breakdown of the gold-exchange standard is part of capitalism's crisis, said the politburo of the PCF, but so is an increase in suburban crime, say communist mayors,[1] and so are corruption in the national radio, unsolved murders, embezzlement in business, or any other scandal. (This was the leitmotif of a PCF congress in December 1972.) Plainly, the theory of capitalism's crisis is not economic analysis but a figure of communist rhetoric. It provides those long, rhythmic sentences that begin 'The crisis is reaching new heights' and that consist of the enumeration of disparate observations: Renault workers are agitating, high school students are opposed to the military draft, university students have complaints, etc. What proves that this is not analysis is that it can be used at any moment for year after year, and it can be applied to European nations in very different stages of economic growth, to Portugal as much as Sweden. Indeed Sweden, which never had an empire, becomes on this view 'imperialist' and, despite a generation of socialist rule, 'the world's most capitalist nation'. If Switzerland is conceded by the Swiss and French communists to be 'a special case' that escapes the 'general crisis of capitalism', that is only a temporary phenomenon due to the exploitation of immigrant labour.[2]

Economic analysis being superfluous, there is no need to rationalize an economic policy. Policies are *class* actions, so that anything the present ruling class does is to be condemned and anything done in the name of the working class is to be approved. A government is never neglectful or incompetent or ignorant or unlucky but always perfectly skilful in attaining its class interests. So communists need not lay out their policy in advance. It will be simply a working-class policy. That evasion leads to opportunism. When communists were in governments, or majorities, after the war, they co-operated in the task of economic reconstruction. Thorez opposed strikes and called for higher production, the PCI was enthusiastic about reconstruction, and the Finnish party approved armed strike-breaking and the conscription of strikers.[3] But when they passed into the opposition, the communists revived the Stalinist view that capitalism tended to permanent stagnation and was unable to promote technological development or to raise living standards. The PCI shared this view but gave it up in the face of Italian economic expansion. By 1956 Togliatti was ridiculing the French communists for sticking to it.[4] The PCF indeed made 'absolute pauperization' a dogma in 1955 just when postwar reconstruction finished and the French economy launched on a long phase of expansion. The communists demonstrated their indifference to economic reality by maintaining throughout this period of prosperity that French workers' living standards were lower than in 1938 or even than in 1911; that European workers were eating less than in the eighteenth century; that if Frenchmen bought motor scooters it was only because they lived so far from work, while if they bought cars it was only because the metro was too expensive. Twenty years later the dogma of pauperization had not been forsworn and the same sophistries were used to defend it: if workers bought their own houses, that proved that rents were too high. This nineteenth-century *misérabilisme* was shown to be an antiquated mobilizer of discontents when the New Left in the 1960s successfully assailed neo-capitalism precisely for its supposed 'abundance' and waste.

Economic progress in Western Europe was too evident to be denied. In order to account for it, the communists had resort to the theory of 'state monopoly capitalism' that had been put up by Lenin before the present form of capitalism was dreamed of, in 1917, and consecrated by a resolution of the Moscow conference of eighty-one parties in 1960. It asserts that the concentration of capital has led to the domination of the economy by monopolies linked together by finance capital, which have taken control of the state and reduced it to the tasks of a mere agency, and which exploit everyone outside the small group of monopoly capitalists, not omitting colonial nations. This combination of economic and political power seemed vaguely to hint at forces large enough to accomplish the enormous changes seen in postwar Europe, but those changes could not be described in detail without calling in question the Leninist myth of capitalism's last crisis. A movement indifferent to economic analysis made no effort to establish the theory of state monopoly capitalism but was content to use it as a slogan; it was even abbreviated to SMC, as though to avoid any temptation to think. The label 'monopoly' was applied to any large firm, no matter what its market share. Suggestions that the state might have some influence over even the largest firms were rejected.[5] If firms compete, that shows the 'contradictions' of SMC; if not, that proves monopoly. The analysis is so superficial that it is clear the communists are interested in hastening to the political implications of the theory.

The implications are that the proletariat and the capitalists, who were the protagonists of the Marxist epic, disappear, leaving only 'the people', on one side, and, on the other, a very few, shadowy, faceless monopolists—15 families in Sweden, specified Hermansson, 20 families in Finland, and 90 families in Norway, said the communists.[6] In the rest of the population, all political distinctions are blurred, as have been all economic ones. Anyone is free to join a communist-led front. The aim of that front is to 'isolate the monopolists' and expose them to populist wrath. The amalgam of state and capital, 'a single mechanism', was held to be stable and stagnant, but as their political ambitions grew, the communists allowed that it could be attacked from within: by electing leaders of the front to ministerial office, where they would use state power to expropriate the monopolies. There is nothing to do with monopolies short of expropriating them, as Lenin said,[7] so that reformist proposals can be disregarded.

More precisely, reforms have no strategic interest but they are of tactical relevance. Berlinguer says reforms are proposed in order to win allies, and then those allies must be 'radicalized',[8] in the sense of being incorporated into the 'historical block' of forces under the hegemony of the CP. Kriegel has shown how the PCF regularly resists economic reforms but, when they are put through, it seeks to win control of the institutions that administer them (nationalized industries, workshop commissions, social security, etc.) and to divert them from their original purpose on the pretext of emptying them of 'class-collaboration', and thereafter to pose as their one true defender against the enemies of the 'conquests of the working class'.[9]

Thus communist economic policy becomes absolutist and conservative. It can have no impact on the system until communist ministers nationalize major industries. Anything short of that is some form of class collaboration or 'administering the affairs of the bourgeoisie'. SMC is a block, and to draw distinctions within it, for example by pointing to the divergent interests of American and European capitalism, would be to organize a 'sacred union' in defence of local capitalism.[10]

An economic policy based on those premises is designed to attract a motley of malcontents, and thus the CP becomes *il cartello degli scontenti*, the union of the discontented. Pending the great final act of expropriation of the monopolies, it welcomes on the same footing the most incompatible clientele—consumers and shopkeepers, landlords and tenants—because no economic distinction matters alongside the fundamental one between monopolists and the rest of the population. The PCF has espoused the cause not only of workers, wage-earners, and pensioners of every condition but of fishermen, professional footballers, yachtsmen, handicapped children, small shopkeepers, motorists, comic opera artists, refugees from the colonies, overtaxed managers, engineers and technicians, expropriated landowners, and even *bouilleurs de cru*, small-time bootleggers. As Galli says of the PCI, a party that is always complaining about everything will attract all those who have a complaint. Political scientists solemnly call this collection of various clienteles the exercise of the function of *tribune*, but from the Romans to Marx a tribune was understood to speak for certain definable interests. For populism and contemporary communism, the only criterion is that the interests be 'little'.

The CP's defence of little landowners and little capitalists and little shareholders has raised the question where it would not also defend little golfers and little monopolies. It is certain that all the CPs have given up the Marxist distinction between capital and labour and instead defend, when it is electorally suitable, any form of business except 'monopolist feudalism'. Since they also defend the right to inheritance and of private property in farmland, the communists come to appeal to many of the same groups as nourish anti-Wall Street populism in the United States, Poujadism in France, *qualunquismo* in Italy, Veikko Vennamo's party in Finland, or any other movement that traces social ills to vaguely delineated 'big business' and 'high finance'.

The short-term economic measures proposed by the communists consist in the encouragement of consumption, while the structural changes they propose are nationalization. The excessive accumulation of capital is the main feature of the present system, Marchais has said.[11] To be sure, communist suggestions for reduction or removal of indirect taxes on articles of current consumption, for price controls and increased wages, and for the inauguration of expensive new social services would indeed put a stop to much capital formation. If it is objected that such measures would also be inflationary, Marchais replies that monopolist profits are 'four to seven times as high as those declared for tax purposes now', so that it would be enough to expropriate them in order to finance increased consumption.

Nationalizations were opposed by the PCF inside the popular front of 1934–7, as accords with Marxist theory, but since the war the European communists have favoured massive nationalizations. Since the Italian state inherited the nationalizations of fascism, the PCI can content itself with demanding the immediate socialization of sugar and pharmaceuticals, while the VPK asks for the takeover of drugs, building materials, insurance, and armaments, and the DPK adds banks, the press, and the culture industries. The PCF's list of candidates for nationalization—which is admitted to be the pivot of its economic programme—would cover half the field of productive investment in France. Although the list was shortened at socialist insistence in the common programme of 1972, communist nationalizations would in fact be endless since the party allows that workers can ask for their enterprises to be taken over.

Given the large hold the state already has over West European economies, it is difficult to see how further nationalizations would in themselves extend public influence; and the Italian communists, at least, are keenly aware of the insufficiencies of a bloated and incoherent public sector.[12] From a Marxist point of view, moreover, simply to transfer more property to a state that respects private capital would not be socialism. However, the communist infatuation with nationalization might have more to do with electoral calculation than with economic policy. It has been shown above how many of the communist leaders had their only acquaintance with the economic process by working in state services and how many of the CPs' members and voters work in the public sector. It would be natural for a political party to seek to extend an environment it had found so congenial. Nationalized industries are the bases of communist power and the party would want to increase their number for that reason alone. The *gauchistes* had that in mind when they attacked communist power and prestige firstly in party fiefs like the nationalized Renault motor works.

However, nationalization, like pauperization, is an old-fashioned idea in the eyes of younger Leftist forces, who are more interested in workers' control or *autogestion*. The revival of these anarcho-syndicalist ambitions in the 1960s reflected disillusion with state ownership, whether in the massive and oppressive form seen in the Soviet Union or in the state-capitalist form familiar in Western Europe. The passage to public ownership had not brought liberation, and younger socialists were casting about for a collectivism without servitude. The CPs vigorously resisted these utopian schemes when they were revived, just as they had denounced the Yugoslav heresy in the 1950s. However, when the worker-base of the parties showed some sympathy for them, the party leaders moderated their opposition. Hermansson admitted that the Soviet nationalizations had been centralized and enslaving, and claimed that, in some unspecified way, western nationalizations would be compatible with workers' control.[13] The PCI allowed that Yugoslav-style experiments would be possible in the public sector.[14] Even the PCF, after roundly condemning *autogestion* as chimerical, claimed to discover its attractions when the rival CFDT trade union federation gained a wide audience by advocating it. It is too early to say whether such concessions are merely verbal. To this point, they resemble the hurried communist conversion to such popular ideas as democratic planning in the 1950s or libertarianism and the 'quality of life' after 1968. It would be reasonable to suppose that a CP in office would, just like other West European political parties, seek to aggrandize the state and refuse to surrender the least particle of economic power to the workers.

The apparent hesitation between state control and workers' control could last indefinitely, to judge from the communist ambiguity about agricultural collectivization. As recently as 1956, Togliatti was rhapsodizing about 'the great, in fact superlative successes' of collectivization in the Soviet Union,[15] but by 1961 Thorez was insisting that the Soviet model would not be followed in a communist France.[16] Today no CP recommends collectivization of agriculture, so well known are the failures and the inhumanity of the Soviet precedent. Yet none is willing to stop at the slogan 'The land to the tiller', but adds at once that a communist regime would 'encourage' the formation of co-operatives as a stage towards 'higher forms of socialist agriculture'.[17] Nothing is said about what happens when the peasants refuse to join the co-operatives. Thus there is no advance here over Stalinist policy, since Stalin too meant to 'win over' the small peasants into joining co-operatives voluntarily. Terror and famine ensued only when they declined.

A greater ambiguity than that runs through all communist economic policy. It is suggested in Lenin's saying 'We do not put forward demands that capitalism can fulfil'. That is a saying the communists recall whenever it is objected that something they propose is impractical or ruinous. They then point out that their demands are *meant* to be destabilizing: they are *intended* to ruin the capitalist economy. Of course, that point is not made as long as any particular communist policy looks to be practical and possible, as some of them are. They have not been overlooked in this brief review out of lack of sympathy. When communists point to the countless injustices and inequalities that riddle the economies of France and Italy, they often make remedial suggestions that might well be feasible. Even their imprecations against 'profit' (which are misleading, because they approve the same thing when it is renamed the 'surplus' of a socialist enterprise) are usually aimed at the most undemocratic and economically most dangerous feature of the neo-capitalist economy: the reinvestment of retained profits by co-opted oligarchies of company directors. Yet it is impossible to discuss economic policy with a party that declines to fix any criterion for the judgement of policies and that insists that its policies can be *either* acceptable *or* ruinous as it chooses. A party that is both reformist and revolutionary from moment to moment is effectively freed from rational consideration of economic policies. What it is not freed from is the consequence of collecting clienteles of assorted malcontents, which is that demands are unleashed and expectations aroused that no economy could satisfy.[18] The collection of clienteles is practised by all democratic parties, of course, but the communists have attracted the most utopian and the least compatible ones by posing as both the tribune of 'the people' in a stable system and as the revolutionary overturner of that system.

The Communists and Parliamentary Democracy

The CPs' policies towards the parliamentary system may be judged on the solid evidence of their operation within it, at least where, and to the extent that, they are free to operate. They are not always so. Although the new DKP has operated legally in West Germany since 1971, its members are still excluded from public office and public employment (even as teachers) in some Länder. In Italy they claim to have been subjected in the 1950s to unconstitutional persecution, though they courted some of this by their own violent activities. In France they maintain that their participation in the parliamentary system and in local government is limited by unjust electoral laws designed to their disadvantage.[19]

Communists participated not only in parliaments but actually in governments after the war in France, Italy, Belgium, Luxembourg, Austria, Greece, Denmark, Norway, Finland, and Iceland, but during the Cold War they were excluded not simply from governments and from governing majorities but from regular participation in bodies to which they were elected; sometimes they refused to participate anyway. These exclusions and refusals were attenuated at the end of the Cold War, and communists returned, for a time, to office in Finland and Iceland, to governing majorities in Norway and Sweden and to regular participation in parliamentary work (as well as in local government and trade unions) in the other liberal democracies.

Indeed, they returned to these things with such enthusiasm that they put out of date theories about the communist micro-society and counter-culture. It had been plausibly asserted during the Cold War that CPs constituted a separate cradle-to-grave sub-culture in Western Europe, a way of life deliberately cut off from 'bourgeois' society and intended to prefigure a socialist world (the Italians called this idea *prefigurazione*) in a reduced-scale model complete with everything except the secret police. Now the German social democrats already did this a century ago, and it was when their sub-culture deliquesced in Wilhelmian society at the start of this century that Sorel conceived the use of violence and 'scission' (cutting oneself off) to maintain the originality of the proletarian counter-culture. That notion was borrowed if not by Lenin, then by western Leninists. 'The party', said Gramsci, 'is a model of what the workers' state will be tomorrow.'[20]

It was their recurrent cultivation of communist separateness and their ability to turn in on themselves in times of political stress that led, during the Cold War, to the theory of the communist micro-society. Yet it was precisely at that time that the communist micro-society was being compromised, by the Leninist (and quite un-Sorelian) practice of 'entrism', *noyautage*, white-anting: the use of fronts to 'throw a red net' over western society. Inevitably, the effort to gain surreptitious influence over the society one was supposed to be cut off from ended in the deliquescence of the micro-society. This could happen violently, as when the Spanish communists sought to infiltrate the Francoist vertical trade unions and were exposed, or peaceably, as when communists were contaminated and corrupted by the societies, the government departments, the municipalities, the businesses and the parliaments they meant to white-ant. When they returned openly to parliamentary methods, the communists retained an intense party patriotism but they became a *secular order* by quitting the cloisters of the imaginary micro-society.

This transition was reflected in such details as official communist disapproval of the practice of automatically using 'tu' between communists or of giving the clenched-fist salute.[21] It was seen, too, in the modernization of the party's propaganda techniques, in the opening of some of its debates to opponents, in the introduction of electronics and advertising methods in campaigns, in the use of the 'star system' and 'political marketing' to *sell* leaders and propaganda themes, and in the transformation of the annual fêtes (of *L'Humanité*, or *L'Unità*, of *De Waarheid*, etc.) from the tribal rites of a micro-society into a popular fair complete with jazz, pop singers, Coca Cola, IBM stands, and modern art. Above all, the return to secular society was seen in new attitudes towards parliament and the possibility of winning office.

During the Cold War, communists' attitudes on those points had prompted the supposition that they did not really want to govern—let alone stage a revolution—but were content to operate indefinitely as tribunes of the proletariat and as spokesmen of Soviet foreign policy without (as it was variously put) contributing to, participating in, being integrated into, legitimizing or stabilizing western democracy. They were seen as a foreign body in the system, of whom Alexander Werth used to say, 'Rien n'est possible sans les communistes, rien n'est possible avec les communistes, rien n'est possible contre les communistes'.

It is certain that after they gave up insurrectionary hopes in the early 1930s, the communists settled into the role of tribune, that is, a recognized opposition status with a claim to monopoly over the right to express, canalize, and rationalize proletarian discontents.[22] As long as no other party challenged that monopoly, whether by claiming to be a rival proletarian party or by reducing discontents by means of reforms, the communists were so much at home in the role of tribune that some thought they would never sacrifice it by seeking real political power. But to see the CPs as tribunes is to notice only one of the three power centres described above: the communist workers whose utopian aspirations the parties express. In reality, the other two power centres can force the party into actions incompatible with its function of tribune.

The Soviet Union, for one thing, uses the party to defend its foreign policy. When that led the PCF into the violent strikes and street rioting of the early 1950s directed against NATO, these actions, which seemed to some workers to be insurrectionary, damaged the CGT and the workers' cause. Repeatedly, Moscow has obliged the parties to take up unpopular stands that in no way correspond to the opinions of the communist workers, as over the Hitler-Stalin pact, over Tito's Yugoslavia in 1948, over the Budapest uprising of 1956, over the Common Market, over Israel, and so on. Then, as the Cold War abated, the Soviet Union saw that the parties could better defend Russian foreign policy in parliamentary majorities or, where possible, in governing coalitions. This second departure from the role of tribune well suited the local bureaucracy, which had meantime conceived more extensive political ambitions.

Hence both those power centres were pushing the parties beyond the limited defence of 'working-class' interests towards active participation in western political systems. That active participation is to be contrasted not only with the hostile, absolute opposition of the tribune but also with the *external support* that CPs in the developing world (and in Turkey) give to governments favoured by Moscow. In consenting to participate, the western parties had merely to extend and develop a function they had been exercising, for years, more consistently than they or their critics cared to admit. Analysis of communist oratory in parliaments shows an insistence on defensive tribune rhetoric, with much vague moralizing and little reference to Marx, Lenin, or revolution, but in their votes and, above all, in their work inside parliamentary committees, the communists had long been contributing to the system. The Finnish party was in office for long periods after the war and, even when it was not, its votes were needed to install a head of state favoured by Moscow (latterly Kekkonen). The Cypriot party, AKEL, though out of office similarly helped to keep in place a head of state well seen in Moscow, Makarios. The Scandinavian parties have repeatedly exercised decisive influence in their parliaments—in commissions and corridor negotiations more than on the floor.

The PCI, too, long took advantage of the fact that most Italian legislation is cast in parliamentary commissions, where discussion is secret, where favours are traded, and where effective amendments are secured. On the floor of the Palazzo di Montecitorio the PCI seemed to practise a sterile and systematic opposition, making its votes available to any current inside Christian Democracy interested in bringing down the cabinet of the day. But off the floor, by dint of zealous attendance at commission meetings and thanks to briefs prepared by the party and its experts, PCI deputies were successful lawmakers. They had 45 per cent of the amendments they proposed accepted, sometimes by threatening the majority with recourse to public debate if they could not get their way in the commissions. Since the PCI would usually vote for a law that incorporated its amendments, even if it did not like the law as a whole, the party ended up voting three-quarters of the laws enacted in Italy between 1948 and 1968.[23] When the Left-Centre coalition in 1968–72 voted a large mass of reformist legislation, the PCI could fairly claim to be among the authors.

The PCF has been less successful as a lawmaker not only because it continued to prefer obstruction to amendment (though its obstruction declined from the epic heights of 1950)[24] but also because the other parties, notably the Gaullists, were unrelentingly hostile to its participation. The party had usually been available during the Fourth Republic to bring down a government, and, when that was no longer possible in the Fifth, it continued to use the floor of the Palais Bourbon for tribune demagogy. When it moved public amendments, they were often demonstrative and unrealistic and if perchance one of its amendments were accepted, it would not automatically vote for the whole bill. Nevertheless, the PCF was active and effective in parliamentary commissions,[25] and it can boast of a list of positive and constructive votes. The PCF indeed became increasingly parliamentarist to the point where its opposition to the presidentialist tendencies of the Gaullist and Pompidolian regimes proceeded from, or at least appealed to, a respectable conservatism. Its criticism of 'personal rule' was not merely a hankering after government-by-assembly, at the expense of the executive, but expressed an attachment to even the most antiquated institutions of parliament, such as the senate. The communists came to show a parliamentary punctiliousness that was almost comical in a party that had once so well applied Lenin's counsel to make bourgeois assemblies sounding boards for propaganda.

Thus, the communists' oppositional participation in parliamentary democracy went beyond the function of tribune, but it was still consistent with the supposition that they did not really want to govern and that, even if they did, they remained—in the eyes of others—impossible candidates for shared office. Those suppositions were advanced not only by students of the parties, who knew of the communists' fear of internal division and violent 'fascist' opposition in the event of them coming to office, but also by the general public as questioned in the opinion polls. As regards the PCF, a long series of opinion polls shows that down to 1972 Frenchmen only gradually came round to the idea that the party did want to win power and that it was increasingly fit to share it. Paradoxically, the party's rising credibility as a party of government was accompanied by undiminished, or even heightened, distrust of it. The explanation could be that the efforts of the party bureaucracy to further its political (and strictly ministerial) ambitions were seen to be making way and yet they were resented by the communist base, which needed the CP as tribune and as opposition, in order to express its utopianism, but which had no desire to be *ruled* by party bureaucrats. Significantly, the distrust of the party seemed to increase near election times, whereas its abstract right to share power was conceded at other times. The polls can be understood by allowing that voters distinguish between thinking that communists are in general 'fit to govern', and wanting (especially when it is an immediate possibility) to be governed by them. This has led psephologists to the paradox that the nearer communists seem to get to power, the harder it is for them to grasp it.

At all events, it is clear that in trying to increase its credibility as a candidate for office, the communist bureaucracy has to fight on several fronts. It has to meet the distrust of its own base, suspicious of co-operation with social democrats and of the corruption of office. In a few cases, it has to overcome Moscow's preference for a strong, bourgeois but pro-Soviet government (e.g. Gaullism) over a dubious coalition of local communists and socialists. And everywhere it has to meet the attacks of its traditional political opponents. For the French and Italian parties—the two that have a chance of achieving the status of parties of government but have not yet done so, as has the Finnish party—those attacks concentrate on these points: that the party does not really want to cease being the tribune of the workers' ghetto and to accede to office; that it would not seek power by peaceful, constitutional means; that it would not tolerate opposition and a plurality of parties once it was in office; and that if ever it got to power, it could never be voted out again. We shall examine each of these points in turn.

The Will to Govern

It might seem odd that parties that had threatened revolution for half a century should be required to prove that they really wanted power. Yet they were so very much at home in the role of the tribune who damns *all* governments that doubts arose. Besides, none of them, save perhaps the old KPD, had ever seemed to have a chance of seizing power, and all of them knew it. Since the Yalta agreement, communist rule in Western Europe (though not perhaps in Greece) seemed excluded by the great powers. Communist leaders were known to fear that if they won a large measure of power at a time of social crisis (e.g. in France in 1968), this would spark off counter-revolution, or even intervention by NATO. Finally, they feared that sharing power with social democrats would compromise them in the eyes of their worker base, as it did for the Finnish party after 1944 and again after 1966. Hence, when they saw ministerial office as possible from the end of the 1960s, they needed to prove their will to govern.

From 1969 Amendola was insisting that 'The PCI, a party of government—that is not just an electoral slogan. It means participation in the political direction of the country.' Taking power was no longer something for the vague future ('after the revolution') but something for which the party needed to groom itself within the present system and for which it needed to establish plausible strategies. The PCF, for those reasons, published its first 'programme for a democratic government' in 1971, followed by a work recalling its record in power after the war.[26]

The Peaceful Road to Power

Marx and Engels envisaged instances of a bloodless transition from capitalism to communism, but Lenin did not. This is a crucial point in Lenin's revision of Marxism: bourgeois parliaments could and should be exploited by communists but armed insurrection was ultimately inevitable. Khrushchev re-revised the dogma (thus earning his Chinese title of Revisionist) by telling his party's twentieth congress in February 1956 that in some 'highly developed capitalist countries', i.e. Western Europe, a coalition of 'all the patriotic forces' (*sic*) led by the working class, i.e. by the CP, could win a parliamentary majority and effect 'radical social transformations'. The Swedish party had said as much in 1953. Togliatti seized upon this and it was written into the PCI's programme that year, while the PCF inserted a paraphrase of Khrushchev in its training literature for militants. Even the clandestine and persecuted Spanish party discovered between 1956 and 1960 that armed struggle would be justified only if the conditions of the masses 'reached the limit of the supportable', and it opted for legal procedures.[27]

This new line was ascribed to Lenin, on Khrushchev's authority, by the choice of an irrelevant quotation[28] and it has drawn the fire of the Chinese, the Trotskyists, and the whole far Left ever since. It has even been seen as a conversion to social democracy. Yet the doctrine was always accompanied by significant reservations. Khrushchev insisted that the transition to post-capitalism would be peaceful only as long as 'the reaction' did not resist, adding that 'it was not our fault if [in 1917] the Russian and international bourgeoisie organized the counter-revolution . . . and obliged the workers and peasants to take up arms'.[29] Thus the Bolsheviks were being offered as models for these 'peaceful' proceedings. The same qualification was made from the start by Togliatti, who allowed that violence could still arise 'from the pig-headedness with which [the reaction] tries to block the inexorable advance of the forces of progress'.[30] It was also made by Waldeck Rochet: 'It depends on the degree of resistance by the exploiters to the will of the people.'[31] The disagreement with the Chinese, said Luigi Longo[32] echoed by the PCF,[33] was not that western communists had forsworn violence but that they thought they could 'discourage the reactionaries from recourse to open violence', in which case *the inexorable* would proceed peaceably.

Another reservation was that 'peaceful' did not mean 'constitutional'. Thus, the *coup de Prague* of 1948 could continue to be held up as an example of regular accession to power, whereas it was in fact a copy of Hitlerite methods. Nor did 'peaceful' mean 'parliamentary'. In launching the new doctrine, Khrushchev had said the peaceful transition could take place only in a climate of 'acute revolutionary struggle'. Togliatti said this meant 'a hard struggle by the masses' outside parliament. Longo said that it would include 'mass pressure and clashes, even violent ones', while the Finnish party specified campaigns 'by unions and other mass organizations and worker demonstrations of various sorts'. In the years since then, the communists have never omitted these references to the 'ineluctable moments of crisis, of rupture, of acute clash',[34] that will enliven the peaceful way to power and which will include, says the PCE, a nation-wide general strike and communist control of the streets. That is why the PCF leaders consider that they remain on the peaceful road when they make minatory references to social disturbances that could carry the Left to power apart from any normal elections.

The point to note is not simply that the communists have a more elastic notion of peace and non-violence than other parties, but that they are less lucid about the inevitable consequences of their own actions. Their Leftist critics would seem to have a juster appreciation of the West European social fabric when they say, not that more violence is desirable, but that the communist version of a peaceful way to power would produce a situation of violence for which the party, with its delusions about 'inexorability' and about discouraging opponents, would not have prepared its followers and allies.

Dictatorship of the Proletariat

Arrived in power by whatever means, would a CP tolerate other political parties? The traditional doctrine, exemplified by the practice of sister-parties, was that a CP would install the dictatorship of the proletariat, which means authoritarian rule by a party acting in the name of the proletariat. A single party would rule, no political opposition could be tolerated in the difficult and dangerous phase of transition towards socialism—and none would be necessary afterwards, because there would be only one class, and hence the basis for only one party.

For a party that had abandoned the project of seizing revolutionary power by itself, this doctrine was a considerable handicap, since no other party would consent to collaborate with it for the peaceful conquest of power—at the cost of being suppressed in the event of success. Thus in May 1963, Thorez announced that 'the theory of the single party in a socialist regime was an error of Stalin's'. The need for a plurality of parties was thereafter incorporated into PCF doctrine and by 1966 it was made explicit that there would be more than one party not only during the transition phase, when at least the socialist party would share power with the communists, but also in the socialist state itself. In fact, 'all parties working for the construction of socialism' would be in the government. The DKP accepted the same doctrine by 1968, and the PCE declared that one-party rule was a deformation of Marxism good enough for backward countries but unsuitable to modern conditions. Consequently, the phrase 'dictatorship of the proletariat' disappeared from communist parlance. The PCF refused to remove it from its statutes in 1964 but it did not figure in its 'programme for a government' in 1971. The last time the expression was used by a PCF leader seems to have been 1966.[35] If other parties refer to it, it is only to insist that it would not be a 'vulgar dictatorship', nor would it resemble East European practice, but would constitute the most advanced form of democracy.

However, this concession to western political customs also had its reservations and qualifications. Marchais illustrated what he meant by a multi-party state by saying, 'In six socialist countries out of fourteen there is a single party, but in the eight others, two or more parties.'[36] The fate of the peasant, Catholic, and socialist parties in Bulgaria, Poland, and East Germany would scarcely tempt western parties into an alliance with the communists, but

Marchais thought the illustration was so convincing that he often repeated it. Moreover, even the admittedly one-party Soviet system continued to be held up as an example of democracy, free criticism, and people's control. In general, when western CPs concede that East European society has certain inadequacies, that 'mistakes' have been made there, and that upon occasion legality has been infringed there, they will not specify the oppression of political opposition and the intolerance of criticism among those 'shortcomings'.

Prospective allies wanted to know which sorts of political party would secure tolerance under a western communist government. At first, up to about 1964, it was only those 'working for the construction of socialism'. This was suspected to cover only a few parties, as became clear when the Dubcek regime in Prague in 1968, which was far to the Left of any western social democratic party, was deposed as an 'enemy of socialism'. From 1964 'democratic', and not necessarily socialist, parties were promised a role. That word also is capable of a narrow definition in communist usage and so, to meet objections, it too was dropped from 1966. Any party that 'operated within the framework of socialist legality' would henceforth qualify. It was obvious, however, that legality would change in the new regime, in such a way as to outlaw opposition that might be described as 'sabotage organized by the former exploiting classes with a view to regaining power and restoring capitalism'.

One could continue at the game (their political opponents do) of pressing the communists from one verbal concession to another, without winning a grain of certitude as to their future intentions—and without noticing that the more 'liberal' they become, the more they expose their illusions about the nature of power in western societies. It is a detail that their contemporary position—which is that communism can be attained without the dictatorship of the proletarian party but simply by way of advanced democracy—is a Marxist and Leninist heresy. What matters is that Marx condemned that view in advance because he saw its fatuity. When he told Proudhon that no imaginable extension and development of the Rights of Man, of the 'principles of 1789' or of republican democracy could possibly lead to communism, Marx was enunciating a truth that subsequent events incline us to state in reverse: no society where the Rights of Man are respected and where republican democracy is preserved would tolerate the transition to communism. The 'advanced democracy' imagined by western communists is an illusion inconsistent not only with Marxist theory but with common sense. It presupposes that economic power remains where it is today —except for the nationalization of some monopolies, which, however, leaves intact the capitalist ethos and all 'non-monopolist' business—and that the rights of political parties, trade unions, and the press are maintained, while a minority of communists (or at best a temporary 51 per cent electoral majority of Leftists) carry through 'radical social transformations' violently unpalatable to the rest of the nation. That situation would not be a transition to anything but counter-revolution, as events in Chile in 1973 demonstrated. The political conclusions drawn from the inaccurate 'monopoly' theory of capitalism blur all distinctions save the distinction between a handful of monopolists and the rest of the people. Thus they lead to a faith in the possibility of a democratic passage to communism, a faith that becomes more unrealistic the more it becomes democratic.

The Verdict of the Electorate

To the question whether a communist government could be voted out of office, the western communists have given a variety of answers, of which the clearest, least ambiguous, and most credible is, No. In Marxist theory, the transition to communism will be an epoch, like the passage from slavery to feudalism or from that to capitalism, so it would be absurd ('unscientific', say the communists) to imagine a coming and going every four or five years from one stage of history to its predecessor. However, since the communists are everywhere an electoral minority, and since their bureaucrats can hope to win office only in collaboration with other Leftist forces, their coming to the ministries would not be as epoch-making as all that. Hence those prospective allies insisted on knowing whether, arrived in power by those means, the communists would consent to quit if they lost the next elections. The replies have been confused, because a desire to maintain Marxist theory and to make their accession to office a world-historical event was being combined with a desire to reassure allies without whose help the whole question was academic. When the modernists in the Finnish party offered, from 1965 onwards, all sorts of assurances about the peaceful way to power and the maintenance thereafter of civil liberties and party plurality, they still refused to concede that Finland could change its mind after 'transferring power from one class to another'. The

Swedish party seems to have been the first to say clearly, in 1965, that it could be voted out of power in the usual way. The same year, the PCI began moving towards a similarly unequivocal stand,[37] and by 1972 it was so insistent on the point that it was plainly out of tune with the PCF. For the French party was more tenacious in maintaining that 'there can be no return from socialism to capitalism'. It used such shifts as saying that subsequent elections might change the *government* but they could never change the regime.[38] It was not until the election campaign of 1973 that the PCF conceded quite unambiguously that it would be possible for France to retreat, not from communism, but from the 'advanced democracy' which was the most that could be installed by a coalition of communists and socialists. This was put even more emphatically after that coalition's defeat in the elections.[39]

These concessions to formal democracy were accompanied by the usual reservations. All the CPs insist that the 'next elections' in question would be held according to proportional representation and after correction of such dispositions in electoral law and delineation of electorates as might disadvantage the Left. Moreover, the parties have argued so vehemently that the 'façade' of formal parliamentary democracy covers capitalist trickery, e.g. the use of state power and the capitalist press to serve class interest, that one could not expect them meticulously to observe its formal rules. That is to say, even if communists had really decided to practise parliamentary politics as they now exist in West Europe, their view of them is so cynical that one could not regard this as a conversion to virtue.

Once again, though, the question of the communists' greater or lesser sincerity in making the concessions required by their ministerial aspirations is quite overshadowed by the question of their own illusions about western society. The reason why the long debate about *l'alternance* was so confused is not that the communists were reluctant or insincere so much that they felt the whole issue was, as Marchais said, 'a false problem.' Having assumed that there existed a set of interests that were common to the vast majority of the people (everyone but the monopolists) *and* that these interests could be effectively represented by a political party, the communists thought it illogical to suppose, even hypothetically, that such a party could be thrown out of office by 'the masses'. 'This question will only arise if the Left in power does not keep its promises. . . . If the Left in power meets, in the measures it takes, the aspirations of all the working classes, the alternation of power becomes point-less.'[40] Mistakes, it was granted as a matter of pure theory, could be made by such a government, but, as has been shown, the communists assume that policies are the expression of class interests and so they never go seriously wrong from the point of view of the class in question. Thus the thought of a return, not only from communism but even from the transition phase of advanced democracy, is a useless pondering of a most improbable event. All that subsequent elections would determine is how fast the regime progressed towards communism. The basis of this self-confidence is a solidarist populism, propped up by the monopoly theory of capitalism.

Political Adventurism

The adjustments the communists have made to their doctrines on such issues as the peaceful way to power, tolerance of political opposition, and observance of western parliamentary precept have convinced some people and not others. There is plentiful debate about whether the communists 'have really changed'. Scepticism would be justified and doubt irrepressible. After all, the communists (and for that matter the Left socialists in general) have for a century past run two horses: the maximum and minimum programmes. The communists have never chosen irrevocably between getting everything at once and getting a little by stages. Leninism in fact was proposed as the science of political tactics that would combine those two. Hence the zigzags of the CPs before and in the two decades after the war—breathing fire and revolution one month, practising an exquisitely classical parliamentary horse-trading the next. Hence everything—or *almost* everything—the communists say today they have said before, and shortly afterwards they said its opposite. Whatever they say that is liberal, democratic, or tolerant jars with the whole history of their party, with Leninist theory, and with the practice of sister-parties in power. In any case, its force is abridged by the qualifications and special definitions that accompany it.

Yet rather than try to weigh their sincerity or solve the impossible puzzle of whether the communists have 'really changed', one can look at the particular forces pressing for changes in policy and the particular forces restraining it. The force impelling the parties to adopt new policies inside neo-capitalist democracy lies in the local

7

party bureaucracy. Motivated, like other political groups, by the desire for power, it cannot, for all that, simply embrace the democratic faith and it cannot even *pretend* to do so. If hypocrisy and duplicity were all it needed, it would not persist in uttering those qualifications and reservations that dismay prospective allies, as when it says that peaceful means include street violence, that opposition would be tolerated as long as it did not oppose the regime, and that the passage to socialism risks being a one-way journey. Instead, if duplicity were enough, it would promise anything at all in order to win power, and then hang on by hook or by crook. But it cannot discard its revolutionary rhetoric, no matter how urgent its desire to practise 'revisionist' policies.

One reason for that is that substantial change in communist policy declarations has usually been slower than changes in daily practice. The new line is revealed in brief glimpses, which are immediately lost in verbose reassertions of the old line. Hence the double-talk and esoteric communication of communist literature, which students decipher by attending to changes of detail that foreshadow substantial turns. This might be an instance of the general rule that a party ideology that is laid out formally in a theoretical programme will change more slowly than practical activity, so that the latter comes to have an air of opportunism, the former an air of insincerity. In addition, there are special reasons for communist ideological conservatism. The local party bureaucracy that writes policy needs the utopian workers and it needs the Soviet Union—and both of *them* require it to cover its reformist nakedness with a revolutionary figleaf. The bureaucracy is never so revolutionary as when it is seeking collaboration with social democrats with a view to ministerial office. The utopian workers at such moments need to be reassured that their tribune is not deserting them. Besides, it is exactly then that those workers must be immunized against faith in reforms lest cohabitation with social democrats cause them to transfer their allegiance (as most other workers have done), leaving the CP without a local base. The Soviet ruling class also needs from its allies within the capitalist world, in an age of peaceful coexistence, repeated affirmation of universalist revolutionary dogma. That enables it to keep alive, in these quieter times, the legitimizing fable that its only enemies are 'class enemies' and 'counter-revolutionaries', whether they be in Washington, Leningrad, or Prague. That the western CPs play the parliamentary game while they put out these revolutionary declamations well suits the Soviet ruling class, because access to the corridors of power facilitates communist influence over bourgeois governments and provides information about their intentions.

Reasons to doubt the permanence of the CPs' conversion to parliamentary practice will not, then, be found in the inconsistencies of their pronouncements or in imputations of insincerity. They will arise, rather, from the thought that so complicated a three-sided game is too hazardous to play for long. Trying to win political power in Western Europe in the name of revolutionary Marxism, but in partnership with social democrats, with the backing of a dwindling minority of utopian workers who live in the reality of neo-capitalist existence, and with the connivance of the Soviet ruling class which lives in the reality of the international power struggle, is too incoherent a project to have a solid future. Reason to doubt will arise also from the western Leninist party's own structure. A party machine that practises disinformation of its members and co-optation of its leaders while it tolerates nothing but the most narrow-minded view of the socialist tradition is not convincing in the role of parliamentary democrat. Western communists now disown Gramsci's idea that their rigidly hierarchical *party* prefigures the communist *society*, but their claim that the habit of an intolerant discipline prepares them for the practice of liberal governance seems, literally, Jesuitical. The party is even less convincing on this score because it defends dictatorial sister-parties in Eastern Europe. Reason to doubt will arise, finally, from the party's merciless intolerance of its nearest ideological neighbours, those Trotskyists and ultra-Leftists whom it denounces without scruple to factory foreman and police spy.

Against all such doubts, practice weighs more heavily. And the practice of the West European CPs is electoralist, parliamentary, revisionist. It might be objected that this refers only to the means they have chosen. But politics is about ways and means; the rest is myth. A party that works for revolution *now* is a different political phenomenon from one that consents to adopt the means of parliamentary reformism, no matter that the second insists that *its* ultimate aim is revolution too. A party that puts its finger in the parliamentary machine to the extent that the major western parties have is unlikely ever to overturn society, if only because its electoral allies would not agree. The progressive and apparently reluctant adoption by the communists of one article of the democratic faith after another illustrates this process of progressive incorporation, or integration. It was especially noticeable in the PCF after the 1973 elections, when it sought to remedy the causes of its electoral disappointments by proclaiming the sanctity of private property and civil liberties. Within six months, it was actually engaged in actions to defend small shopkeepers and ultra-Leftists.

To describe this democratic dilution of revolutionary purity is not to prove that the CPs have become 'parties like the others', or that they are now a variety of social democracy. That is possible and there is some evidence for it.[41] Yet one would also need to remember, what a score of examples from Spain to Finland have shown, that European parliaments have served as hunting grounds for parties of political adventurers. CP bureaucrats who seek political power by using the Leninist machine while placating the Soviet ruling class and the utopian workers resemble, more than a new variety of social democracy, just such a band of political adventurers. Unlike the socialist party or the other great political bodies, the CP is playing for high stakes against long odds, that is, for a revolution to be achieved by a minority with the consent of the majority. If that party is dangerous it is not because it is conspiratorial, insincere, and hypocritical but because it is steeped in populist illusions, which have replaced its faith in outmoded Marxist theory. It believes that the victory of communism is 'inexorable', and this leads it to discount and devalue the opposition it will encounter. It underestimates the resistance that any extensive change will meet in West European society, as when the PCI talks glibly of 'the reformist road to revolution', and so it risks running into violent reactions which others will think it is deliberately courting. It believes that correct policies need no opposition, as Marchais says to explain the quiet that reigns in Eastern Europe, and therefore it will, with the best of intentions, be led into oppressing critics that could not, on its populist, solidarist theory, speak for the people. 'We have no enemies among the people. Our only enemies are the tiny handful of great monopolists', says the PCF's political theorist.[42] In power, and confronted with the fact of diverse and conflicting interests among 'the people', confronted too with the dissatisfaction and resistance aroused by contingencies in the implementation of *any* policy, such illusions can be dangerous. The Jacobins had similar illusions and the consequences were so awful that in 1925 a Soviet pamphlet was still recalling the horrors of 'the politics of the guillotine'. Only, the pamphlet in question, *Problems of Leninism*, was signed: Joseph Stalin.

European Unity and Defence

Whereas the CPs used to function as propaganda agencies for Soviet foreign policy, they have begun to develop doctrines of their own on international relations. Since these new doctrines, in common with the domestic policies of the CPs, are electorally opportunist, they can differ from party to party and may even seem to conflict with the aims of the Soviet Union. One must hesitate to conclude that they do in fact conflict and first ask whether there is not a division of labour between Moscow and a CP. After all, an apparent divergence has always existed. It was implicit in the nature of the Soviet regime as a *revolutionary state*, that is, (a) a government that had to maintain diplomatic relations with other states, when it did not actually seek their alliance and assistance, and (b) the general staff of a global revolution dedicated to subverting those same foreign states. Hence, since 1917, Moscow has had a 'dual policy', treating with states according to international law while supporting local CPs that one day could overthrow them. The divergence that this implied was accepted in good discipline by the CPs, to the point of their being dissolved for Russia's advantage (as the Polish party was in 1937) or suffering persecution from Moscow's allies (as so often in the Mediterranean region). That divergence could be explained as a matter of timing: diplomacy today, subversion tomorrow—but only until 1956, when the Soviet Union adopted the policy of peaceful coexistence with the capitalist world. Therewith the western CPs lost their potential revolutionary role. They could continue to prophesy the victory of the communist system but it could only come to pass by established communist societies demonstrating their superiority, not by western CPs adding to the number of such societies by means of armed revolution.

The dual policy then became increasingly embarrassing for western CPs. The PCF managed, at the cost of the Servin-Casanova purge, to buckle under when Moscow openly supported de Gaulle, whom the PCF was still denouncing as a semi-fascist usurper. AKEL managed to hold its audience among Greek Cypriots while Moscow opposed *enosis* (for the sake of its Mediterranean policy). On the other hand, only a fraction of Greek communists could excuse Moscow's overtures to the authoritarian regime in Athens that was persecuting communists. And the PCE in its great majority rebelled when Moscow began to cultivate the Francoist regime (and when Poland supplied coal that helped break a Spanish miners' strike).

It was from tensions such as these that the West European CPs sought relief in new thinking about foreign policy. Their task was especially difficult, in that peaceful coexistence was a promise and a threat. It opened new vistas of co-operation with democratic parties, but it deprived them of their revolutionary credibility among the communist workers. Consequently, the CPs had to argue that coexistence did not involve any division of spheres of influence between Moscow and Washington such as precluded the coming to power of a genuinely revolutionary party in West European capitals. This entailed denying that even at Yalta in February 1945 there had been a division of spheres of influence in Europe between the communist and capitalist allies. It entailed denying that there was a Brezhnev doctrine of limited sovereignty in communist countries, not so much because opponents might deduce from it that Moscow could in future intervene in Western Europe to keep a CP in office, but because communist workers might deduce from it that the United States already enjoyed a parallel right to prevent such a party coming to power in the first place. Finally, it entailed denying most adamantly that the détente arrived at by Messrs Nixon and Brezhnev in the mid-1970s was super-power collusion over Europe's head and could lead to what Gaullists and Chinese called a Russo-American world condominium. In short, it entailed denying the obvious.

In this difficult situation the bigger West European CPs gave priority to foreign policy considerations that, without necessarily indisposing the Soviet Union, would carry the most electoral weight at home. For example, when de Gaulle retired in 1969, the PCF saw an opportunity to win back the votes it had lost to him, by posing as the party of the super-Gaullists and by denouncing in his followers—Georges Pompidou, Jacques Chaban-Delmas, and President Giscard d'Estaing—poor patriots who were 'smuggling France back into NATO', abdicating national sovereignty, and in general yielding to American pressure. The first difficulty of this manœuvre was that it had to be combined with the denial that there was any great-power condominium, whereas the essence of a Gaullist foreign policy is that there is always the danger of such a condominium unless smaller nations staunchly defend their independence. That point was made unequivocally by the last Gaullist incumbent at the Quai d'Orsay, Michel Jobert, in 1973-4.

The second difficulty was that while the PCF denounced these unpatriotic backslidings with a maximum of energy and bad faith, Moscow feigned not to notice them but continued to accord successive French governments the same treatment it had given de Gaulle. Indeed, it repeatedly embarrassed the PCF by delivering to Paris a resounding satisfecit just when the party had discovered some new 'Atlanticist' deviation or was actually engaged in an electoral struggle. The apparent conflict was most obvious during and after the election of M. Giscard d'Estaing in 1974, when the PCF tried to launch a 'national front', a broad alliance of patriots against the supposedly pro-American president—whom Moscow had helped to elect (by having its ambassador ostentatiously honour him during the campaign) and thereafter treated with respect. Still, given that there was a conflict between the PCF's vote-catching and Moscow's diplomacy, Moscow too would have reason to fear that de Gaulle's successors would drift back to the American connection. Thus it would be well content with a division of labour whereby the PCF denounced the possible intentions of a government that diplomatically continued to get the benefit of the doubt.

Similarly, Moscow would not necessarily be alarmed by the tactical fluctuations of the West European CPs on the question of NATO. They have long since given up the passionate and violent opposition to that military alliance that marked the Paris riots of 1949 and 1952, but then Moscow has also abandoned support of such 'peace campaigns' in favour of direct negotiation with Washington. The West European CPs combine a watchful scrutiny of NATO's development in ways that might incommode the Soviet Union, with the assurance that they would not, in office, insist on their countries quitting NATO, at least not immediately. Indeed, several CPs that have held office have done nothing to get their nation out of NATO, and parties still seeking office have given their allies certain 'assurances'. The Norwegian CP proposes a referendum on the issue of NATO.

The Icelandic communists made more fuss about the NATO base at Keflavik before and after leaving office than when they were in power from 1971 to 1974. The PCP, which had approved terrorist attacks on NATO installations when it was clandestine, approved Portugal staying in NATO when the communists got portfolios in 1974. To be sure, both these parties were insecure junior partners in fragile coalitions and thus were ill placed to insist on so important a measure as leaving NATO. Still, since that is the only sort of power the bigger CPs can hope for in the near future, they might behave similarly. However inconsistent with communist theory it might be to have communist ministers in a NATO government, the Soviet Union could derive evident advantages from the arrangement.

The variations of the PCF on the NATO theme are so intricate that the French socialists have not been able to follow, despite the fact that the piece was composed for their benefit. In December 1962 Waldeck Rochet declared that although the communists maintained their total opposition to NATO, they would not make France's withdrawal from it a prior condition of co-operation with the socialists. This 'concession' soon became pointless, because de Gaulle went on to lead France out of the NATO military organization (but not out of the alliance) in 1967. The PCF grudgingly applauded this move but argued that since not all links had been severed between French and NATO armed forces (which was true) and since France remained in the alliance, the country was still a satellite, subject to United States military strategy. It intensified its attacks on NATO under de Gaulle's successors and reported signs that they were surreptitiously accepting France's reintegration in the military organization. Accordingly, it proposed to the socialists during the negotiations for a common programme in 1970 and 1971 that France withdraw from NATO altogether, before accepting in the final version of the common programme in 1972 an ambiguous compromise:

The government will declare itself for the simultaneous cancellation of the Atlantic Pact and the Warsaw Pact. . . . While refusing to reintegrate itself in NATO, France will not deny itself the right to conclude defensive alliances as well as treaties of non-aggression. . . . The government will make plain its will to move the nation towards independence of any politico-military bloc. The problems posed by the obligations laid on France as a member of the Atlantic alliance will be resolved in that spirit.

When M. Mitterrand interpreted this to mean that the PCF had agreed to let France stay in the alliance until some other system of defence had been set up, party spokesmen retorted that this was not in the text but that, on the contrary, a Left coalition would seek independence of the Atlantic bloc.[43] The PCF has since then maintained its vehement opposition to the alliance while indicating its willingness to enter a government that was not explicitly committed to leaving it, at least not immediately.[44]

Italy's security is more obviously dependent on NATO than

France's so that the PCI has operated in a different political and strategic environment. It has, for all that, followed the same meanders towards a similarly ambiguous position. From 1969, the *Manifesto* opposition denounced the PCI for abandoning its criticism of NATO and for silently consenting to Italy's indefinite membership of the alliance. Indeed, the Italian socialists said they had the impression that the PCI no longer insisted on Italy's 'unilateral withdrawal'.[45] Yet when pressed, PCI leaders would say that they still demanded that Italy should quit the organization.[46] True, they came to subordinate that exit to the improbable condition that all military blocs were dissolved. Amendola said,

We must get Italy out of the blocs, which means concretely for us Italians out of the Atlantic alliance, but in such a way as to guarantee that this will not mean in any sense our entry into the socialist bloc . . . getting beyond blocs will provide the guarantee that Italy's withdrawal from NATO will not mean a reversal of alliances.[47]

Berlinguer added that the NATO issue could, in 1972, 'be seen in a dynamic way and not in the static terms of the Cold War years.' That meant:

This decisive question of getting free of the bonds of subordinaton that tie our country to NATO cannot be reduced to a simple declaration for or against the military pact. The struggle against the Atlantic pact will, rather, become more effective the more it is identified with a general movement of liberation of Europe from American hegemony and of the gradual surpassing of opposed blocs, up to the point of their liquidation.[48]

Italian socialists take this 'dynamic' vision to mean that the PCI would join a government that put off an exit from NATO to the Greek kalends, but when Berlinguer is specifically pressed, that is not what he says:

One can conceive of our getting out of NATO as a process, as a separation having various stages. There are more immediate problems, which ought to be faced first, such as the existence of foreign bases and our renunciation of military integration. But the process ought to result in the complete breaking of the tie. . . . If you ask me: would you accept NATO?, then I answer decisively in the negative.[49]

Since they entertain the notion of independent West European nations unarmed and unprotected, exposed to the designs of the Soviet Union (even if they suppose the Warsaw Pact 'dissolved'), it is clear that the communists have nothing that could answer to the name of a *defence* policy. Their simultaneous insistence on independence and disarmament leads to an incoherent mixture of patriotism and pacifism, because the independence they mean is vis-à-vis the United States but the disarmament is vis-à-vis the Soviet Union. Apart from the criticism of professional armies and heavy defence budgets that is common to much of the Left in Europe, the PCF specifies that it would scrap the French nuclear force.[50] It signed a common programme with the socialists that called only for a stop to the growth of that force (but not its destruction), which simply proves that the subject is as pregnant with future misunderstandings between these two partners as is the issue of leaving NATO.

Opposed to effective defence at the national level or within NATO, the CPs are even more resolutely hostile to the (admittedly speculative) notion of a joint West European defence force. Ever since the PCF joined with the Gaullists in scuttling the European Defence Community in 1954, it has vigilantly censured any suggestion for West European defence co-operation, as a reincarnation of that projected European Army. This is a point on which there has never been even an apparent divergence between the unanimity of the West European CPs and the interests of the Soviet Union, ever fearful of a new defence entity to its west that might, even though inferior in fire power to the United States forces now arrayed there, give the Germans greater influence and autonomy. The admission by Giorgio Amendola in 1973 that a common West European defence policy was 'a real problem' in no way detracted from that unanimity. Amendola went on to explain that the 'real problem' would consist in asserting 'European autonomy vis-à-vis the United States' by practising a policy of 'active neutrality' and by rejecting 'the costly, dangerous illusion of a nuclear-armed European third force'.[51]

Communists' rejection of a joint European defence is part of their general refusal to countenance supranational institutions in the region, for example such as might evolve from the European Economic Community. Their hostility to the notion of European unity has been unremitting and is common to the parties of the six (later nine) nations directly concerned and the parties of the neutral and non-member nations.[52] It is sometimes thought that there are two exceptions to this hostility, which can however easily be accounted for. Firstly, it is said that the PCI has been more 'pro-European', and has even coaxed the other parties into a more favourable attitude. Any such coaxing has quite failed to convince the PCF, CPGB, and the DanKP, which were never more outspoken against united Europe than at the conference of western CPs in Brussels in January 1974.[53] Moreover, the PCI's own position proves on examination to be anything but pro-European, as that term is used by the advocates of West European union. The PCI agreed before the other CPs to seize whatever place it could within the European institutions, such as at the so-called parliament of Europe in Strasbourg or in the lobbies and corridors of the European executive in Brussels. In that, it showed its political flair, but its object was to make more effective its opposition to supranationality and to United States influence. The PCF eventually did likewise, without abating one jot of its criticism of the Common Market and all its works.

The European organization that the PCI favours would not be a political entity but something nearer the UN Economic Commission for Europe: 'a system of co-operation between all the nations of Europe [i.e. both east and west], whatever their social or political regime';[54] or again: 'a democratic multinational organization that tackles the problems whose solution is beyond the grasp of individual nation-states: the monetary crisis, the movement of capital, the control of multinational corporations, energy, environmental problems'.[55] For the United Europe movement, this would be *Hamlet* without the Prince of Denmark, European union without a political soul.

The other supposed exception is the recurrent 'recognition' or acknowledgement by the Soviet Union (e.g. by Khrushchev in 1962 and by Leonid Brezhnev in 1972) of the Common Market as 'a concrete reality' with which Moscow is disposed to treat. This stand, duly endorsed by the western CPs, means that the Soviet Union is ready to regard the nine-nation Economic Community as a phase in the internationalization of production, a process from which the Soviet Union hopes to benefit, e.g. by importing western capital and technology and by finding western markets for its manufactures. Accordingly, Moscow is willing to promote negotiations between Comecon (the East European economic union around the Soviet Union) and the Common Market, if this is a way to secure those advantages, just as it is ready to deal with the United States, Japan, and the individual European nations as long as the Rome Treaty leaves them the right to deal singly with outsiders. On the contrary, the Soviet Union does not thereby recognize the Common Market as a unit that would be entitled, for the sake of its own political individuality, to *stop* the internationalization of production at the borders of the Nine. That is why the communists call the Nine 'Little Europe', which is, at best, a stage towards the real or Big Europe that stretches from the Atlantic to the Urals. They sometimes put this in Marxist jargon by saying that transnational economic co-operation (in which the present Soviet leadership has an urgent interest) is an objective, material base which throws up, in capitalist lands, the deplorable super-structure or ideology of European unity and defence. The communists mean to purge the process of such subjective excrescences and to promote economic co-operation within a politically disunited and militarily defenceless Europe from the Atlantic to the Urals under Russian leadership.

The Soviet Union is obliged as a great power to envisage the European question on a level with (and latterly in the context of) its relations with China. It is here that a clear disagreement about foreign policy emerges between Moscow and the western CPs, and it is directly related to their bid for local autonomy. Throughout 1973 and 1974 the Soviet Union pressed them to agree to a meeting in Moscow of world CPs. This could only be a meeting of CPs acknowledging some measure of loyalty to Moscow, and its main purpose would be (or so western communists suspected) to pronounce the expulsion from the communist movement of China and her protégés. Soviet anxiety in the matter was not ideological in origin, but concerned the moral justification of an eventual resort to force. If the CPs from the capitalist homelands of Marxist socialism would consent to join in the excommunication of China from the movement, that would facilitate Soviet dealings with an awkward neighbour. Even in the most ruthless Realpolitik, it is necessary to give a dog a bad name before hanging him. Of more immediate relevance, such a joint pronouncement by world CPs would justify an eventual intervention in 'ex-communist states' such as a post-Tito Yugoslavia, Albania, and Rumania.

The western CPs, on the other hand, would see such a meeting as a solemn reinstatement of Moscow as the one true centre of the movement. They would perhaps shed few tears for Peking's expulsion (though parties openly at loggerheads with Moscow would sorely miss Chinese and Rumanian support) but they could not agree to the restoration of 'monocentrism' without sacrificing all the gains they had made in the direction of autonomy during the Sino-Soviet quarrel. Soviet pressure was intense during the January 1974 CP rally in Brussels and when it was, apparently, unavailing, that conference was reported most selectively in the Russian press. Moreover, there followed sharply critical Soviet articles about the Finnish, Spanish, and Japanese parties, which had made too ostentatious a display of independence.[56]

If ever the meeting in question comes to be held, it will be accompanied by much ideological acrobatics, so it is worth insisting that the point is not ideological. For the western CPs it is bureaucratic, i.e. about their ability to use the Leninist machine without, when needful, a Soviet legitimation. For Moscow it is great power politics, i.e. concerning its struggle with China and its hegemony in east Europe. The further course of the affair will largely determine not the degree of autonomy the western CP bureaucracies can win, but the use they make of it. In other words, the Soviet fear of China not only makes possible that autonomy but influences its direction. As long as aggressively Leftist policies are taboo among West European CPs, because suspect of Chinese inspiration, and as long as revolutionary adventures are excluded, because liable to create dangers and new responsibilities on Russia's western front, the autonomy they secure can only be applied in a Rightist sense, in the quest for electoral alliances with and beyond the social democrats.

Political Alliances

A familiar figure of communist rhetoric combines, incongruously, populism with the quest for allies. The party is presented as the agent of 'the masses' in a contest 'that opposes a whole nation to a handful of profiteers', but then it is conceded that the masses in question are a minority of the electorate—which is 'why the communists, for their part, have as a major preoccupation the maintenance of the still young alliances . . . that permit democrats to work fraternally, etc., etc.'[57] Revolutionary minorities (including the communists, in the past) reconcile their numerical insignificance with their claim to represent the masses by means of a distinction between those masses' real and apparent interests. What the majority votes for is the people's apparent interest; what the minority wishes for it is its real, or long-term interest. But a CP that abandons the project of forcing its will on the people, in the dictatorship of the proletariat, and becomes instead an electoral machine, must aspire to win a majority of the vote *now*, whether alone or in coalition.

So the quest for alliances that will enable it to win votes or to share office becomes its supreme obsession. As the central committee of the PCF declared baldly in December 1962, 'The communists have *no higher duty* than to do everything to extend and consolidate the junction with the socialists *and other republicans*.'[58]

Ever since Lenin, the communists have called these alliances by the military name of 'fronts', and they have practised an elaborate scholasticism to distinguish fronts according to their class base. It was alleged that the 'united front' assembled all the proletariat, the 'popular front' included the middle classes too, and the 'national front' went beyond class to embrace the 'patriots' and victims of the 'monopolies' anxious to defend national independence. Since communist class theory is too coarse to be instructive, and since this 'theory' covers only political expediency, the various alliances are best distinguished on the familiar Left-to-Right spectrum of parliamentary groups.

When Khrushchev in 1956 suggested alliances with all 'progressive' or even just plain 'patriotic' forces, the PCI hastened to take this up. At its eighth congress in 1957 it 'definitively abandoned the previous identification of the motive force of an Italian revolution with the proletarian or semi-proletarian masses', in favour of an alliance between the working class and the middle classes.[59] Yet it did not attempt, any more than other western parties, the sort of social and political analysis of those vague 'middle classes' that would have been needed for a quest for allies among them. It was not till a decade later that the 'new classes' became the subject of a heated debate among communists. In the interim, the non-proletarian forces seen as possible allies were described, as by the successive CP congresses in Moscow since 1957, as the 'peace-loving' and 'anti-imperialist' forces, who should be concerned to work with the communists to ensure 'peace and security'. So this was merely defence of Soviet foreign policy, here called 'peace and security'. Only towards the end of the 1960s when the western parties had definite political ambitions, did these alliances acquire a specific, local content.

At first they were proposed to the neighbouring social democrats. Offers of collaboration with socialists were nothing new in communist history, though they had usually been followed by denunciations and rivalry. 'Socialism and communism are brothers', said Kurt Schumacher, 'like Cain and Abel.' What was new was the purpose of the alliance. In 1936, for example, Thorez had said that even a 'true popular front' meant the installation of soviets in France and of the dictatorship of the proletariat, and not 'a vulgar policy of ministerial collaboration'. Yet that latter was what the communists proposed at the end of the 1960s. The PCF called it 'advanced democracy' in its 'Champigny Manifesto' of December 1968, the month in which it began the negotiations with the socialists that were to culminate three and a half years later in the common programme of the Left. In 1969 Berlinguer called the same thing formation of a 'historical block' with a strategy of reforms, whereupon Amendola shook the PCI membership by declaring that the party was ready to practise that policy by joining the socialists in the government forthwith.

Such offers of alliance, for practical and limited objectives, involved an evident ideological sacrifice for parties that had been denouncing the socialists recurrently for a generation as the agents and dupes of capitalism if not of fascism. For the smaller parties in particular, virulent criticism of social democracy had been the long and short of their ideology. For a party like the DKP, then, to force its unwanted collaboration on socialist enemies was, if not political suicide, then quite confusing for its members and voters. Worse, it brought ridicule. The large socialist parties of West Germany and Britain did not need such 'help' and could spurn it with wounding words. These un-political gestures might suggest that the small parties were being obliged to follow a general communist policy decided elsewhere and designed to benefit only the large parties. Yet even the small parties won rewards from the strategy of electoral and parliamentary collaboration with socialists and Left socialists. In Iceland, they were the rewards of office, in Scandinavia a new parliamentary influence. In Norway from 1972 a negligible party won a role in the anti-Common Market campaign and then a parliamentary outlet for its opposition to NATO and its advocacy of nationalizations. In Sweden a small party was able from 1970 to keep the social democrats in office, to gnaw at their Left wing and to influence their legislation, no matter that the socialists pretended not to count communist votes towards their majority in the chamber. Even the DKP's offers of collaboration won an echo in the Left wing of the SPD and, more particularly, in its Juso youth federation. So for these parties, the policy of alliances towards the Right was more congenial than the isolation in a political ghetto that they had endured throughout the second Stalinist glaciation.

For the larger parties, it was more than that. It seemed to be the road towards power in Rome, Paris, and Helsinki. If they were larger, then the corresponding socialist party must be smaller (since communism grows on socialist soil) and hence more in need of support for its own ministerial ambitions. Still, even the addition of communist and socialist votes would not give a majority. In countries where the Left was split into substantial communist and socialist parties, precisely *because* it was split it had seldom won a larger part of the electorate than the old socialist parties before 1917—which was at best between 30 and 40 per cent. In France at the time the communist-socialist alliance was sealed, the two parties combined had been hovering around 40 per cent of the electorate, as had the Left vote (PCI + PSIUP + PSI) in Italy. In Finland, the social democrats and communists had scored 41·5 per cent in 1962. That circumstance led the communists to extend their offer of political alliance further towards the Right.

The desire to win office, which the communist bureaucracy now has in common with other western parties, was apparently the decisive factor in this sacrifice of ideology. One could contrast that policy of haste towards power with the slow work of building up the social democrat vote in Britain, Sweden, or West Germany to about 50 per cent. Naturally, the social democrats there first got to power in Lib.-Lab. ministries or in a *Grosse Koalition* with the Right, but the communists could scarcely invoke those precedents without conceding they were taking a path specifically condemned in their own theory. That the anxiety to win office was involved is shown by three facts. Firstly, these offers to collaborate with parties to the Right of social democracy were not made by the communists in places where a large socialist party might, on its own, win power and carry a communist dwarf on its shoulders: there were no such concessions in Britain, West Germany, or Sweden. (Twenty years before, in 1944–5, the CPGB had indeed called for a national government, but that was a reflection of Soviet foreign policy, the wish to keep the wartime alliance going into the first years of peace.) Secondly, these offers of communist collaboration were extended farther and farther towards the Right, in utter forgetfulness of Marxist precept, in dictatorships where the Left was small and embattled but engrossed with the political prospects after the dictatorship, as in Spain, Portugal, and Greece. Finally, these offers were made more and more pressingly in countries where office seemed to communists to be tantalizingly close and yet harder to obtain (in accord with the paradox mentioned above), as in France and Italy.

The Greek 'interior' party adopted a policy of broad alliance under the regime of the colonels, seeking to co-ordinate its opposition in a 'united patriotic front' with that of the forces around Andreas Papandreou. Then both wings of the KKE participated in the Greek Republic after the restoration of democracy in 1974, seeking allies to their Right. The Portuguese party, which is entirely dependent on Moscow, would have contested the 1973 elections on a joint ticket with the Catholic progressives and the socialists, if the opposition had been allowed to function. The PCP suspended the violent activities of its ARA groups (unlike the Brigadas Revolucionarias) in order to re-assure its bourgeois allies. Then it joined the government of the military junta in 1974. In this, it went to the end of a long-standing 'national front' ideology that had earned it the scorn of the far Left.[60] The Spanish party progressed from offering to collaborate with all anti-Franco forces to specifying that it would co-operate politically with 'non-monopolist bourgeois', then with 'members of the oligarchy', with the hierarchy of the Catholic Church, with the Spanish army, and perhaps even with the monarchy. Defending Church and army from Franco, the PCE disavowed the 'Leftist errors' of its own sectarian past and declared it was ready to negotiate (hinting that it was already doing so in secret) with 'any group or sector, no matter what its past, that publicly and openly takes its stand on democratic ground'.[61]

In the liberal democracies too, the communists became similarly promiscuous. The Belgian party offered in 1972 to collaborate with Christian Democrats, even those supporting the government. The year before, the two wings, 'liberal' and 'orthodox', of the long divided Icelandic communist movement found that the one thing they could agree upon was to enter a government with progressives. By then the Finnish communists had been three years in office with socialists and a centre party, and only quit when their party was rent (in part perhaps by the strains of office) into two incompatible factions. Even the comically sectarian Dutch party called for a government of communists, socialists, and 'all democrats and progressives'.[62]

Generic offers of collaboration with everyone but the devil himself came from the two largest parties, and with an insistence that increased as office seemed nearer. Indeed, the PCI and the PCF closed a chapter of mutual misunderstanding and marked 'a new start in relations between the two CPs' by meeting in Rome in May 1973 to declare their common willingness to work 'with all proletarian and democratic forces', not excluding 'forces representative of the popular masses of Catholicism'.[63] The PCF had already, from 1972, applied this doctrine in the 'union of the Left' with the ideologically motley French socialists and with a section of the Radicals. When that coalition had limited success in the 1973 elections, its scope was extended by the communists to include petty bourgeois forces traditionally hostile to socialism. By the 1974 presidential elections, the PCF was wooing the Gaullists too. The PCI went farther and faster.

At the start of the 1960s the Italian party was preoccupied with maintaining its alliance with the Nenni socialists and fearful of the isolation it would suffer if those socialists reunited with the social democrats and joined the government in a Centre-Left coalition. (They did both, for a time.) By the end of the decade the Italian communists were preoccupied with a very different problem: how far to the Right of the socialists they should accept political allies. The principal currents in the dispute, which became public from 1968-9, were represented by Giorgio Amendola, who favoured collaboration with the socialists on a frankly revisionist or minimalist programme, and Pietro Ingrao, who stood for a more revolutionary, maximalist policy but one designed to appeal to the dissatisfied progressives who voted Christian Democrat. Amendola's policy was backed by the party officials installed in local power in the Red Belt, but it alarmed the utopian workers at the base and the neo-Trotskyite intellectuals in the bureaucracy. The Leftist rebellion around the paper *Il Manifesto* was largely a violent reaction to that policy of compromise. Yet when the rebellion spread, it was seen that Ingrao's ideas could be carried, if not by himself then by others, to the point where they would frighten off the political allies the party needed if it were to win office, as well as causing deep offence in the Soviet Union. The invasion of Czechoslovakia in 1968 having taken place meanwhile, the utopian workers chose, as always, to remain faithful to the Soviet Union and they deserted the maximalist intellectuals. Hence the bureaucratic compromise, now represented by Berlinguer, could be adopted: Amendola's minimalist programme would be offered to the broader electoral base imagined by Ingrao. For that purpose, the party expelled the rebels and presented itself to the nation as the party of order, reformist, pluralist, intolerant only of Leftist excesses, ready to compromise with the Vatican over the heads of its anti-clerical socialist allies—but all this with the objective of splitting Christian Democracy or at least of winning many electors away from it. It was imagined that this line would draw away enough support to oblige a weakened Christian Democracy to accept the communists in the governing majority, which Berlinguer would have settled for in 1970, or even into the government, which he demanded from 1971. This strategy was applied in the 1972 elections. It succeeded in that it wiped out the Leftists (though unfortunately it wiped out the satellite PSIUP also, so that its rump had to be absorbed into the PCI) and won for the party over half a million additional votes—but it neither split nor 'redimensioned' nor humbled the Christian Democrats. Indeed, the Christian Democrats for a time governed in a Centre-Right coalition, the Andreotti cabinet of 1972–3, leaving all the Left out of office. That was the worst possible solution for the PCI, and it had no rest until Giulio Andreotti resigned and a new Centre-Left government was installed in July 1973. Thereafter the PCI practised what it called 'a new sort of opposition', which was in reality tacit collaboration.

It was then that the Allende regime in Chile, which the PCI had offered as a model, just as it had offered the ill-fated Dubcek regime as a model, was overthrown in a bloodbath. The party drew the conclusion that no matter whether it followed Ingrao or Amendola, no matter whether the Berlinguer compromise prevailed, it could never win a secure electoral majority, one that could withstand the sort of pressure that had brought Allende down. Coalitions of communists and socialists could rule in Scandinavia with precarious majorities but not in countries with a history of fascism and *pronunciamentos*. Accordingly, the PCI adopted a strategy that was qualitatively new, although it consisted quantitatively in an extension farther to the Right of the offers of collaboration it had been making for a decade, with a view to ministerial power. It proposed to the Christian Democrat leadership a *compromesso storico* (the phrase was meant to echo Gramsci's *blocco storico*, though it meant something very different), a historical compromise. The communists would come to power in Rome in partnership with the Christian Democrat politicians, over the heads of the Catholic progressives whom Ingrao had thought to seduce, and even, if necessary, over the heads of the socialist party that Amendola had thought to entice out of the Centre-Left.

This compromise would entail not only giving up the revolutionary way to power but even the electoral way to power, since it would not occur at the hustings but in the back rooms of the Montecitorio between leaders of the parties. But that is a detail, since such is the normal procedure of Italian parliamentary democracy, as it was of the French Fourth Republic. It entailed giving up hope of splitting or weakening Christian Democracy, and it risked frightening the socialists into thinking that Catholics and communists were combining behind their backs. Significantly, the new line was at once approved by the officialdom of the Red Belt. Guido Fanti, communist president of the region of Emilia, declared that the 'historic compromise' was already working in his fief, and he took the occasion to recall that the whole move towards power on the base of 'a new majority' had begun in Emilia.[64] Renalto Zangheri, Fanti's successor as mayor of Bologna, welcomed the new line as a break with 'frontism', in the sense of united-Left politics.[65] The reaction at the base was reserved, if not hostile. At last, all ambiguity was dispelled: the party leaders wanted office and ideology be damned.

When the party bureaucracy goes so far in its political ambitions, the question arises whether it still enjoys the support of the Soviet Union. When the PCF signed the common programme of the Left, an envoy of the Soviet party went to its congress to warn against the ideas and the policy of reformism and class collaboration. Other signs of Soviet displeasure have been detected by specialists in esoteric communications. (As to the Chinese communists, their attitude was not in doubt. The Peking papers referred to the Union of the Left as 'the French socialists and some other parties'.) However, there are just as many explicit approvals, as by Brezhnev when he endorsed western parties' 'co-operative actions with all democratic parties and forces, including the socialist parties'.[66] The policy of broad alliances has been practised by parties entirely dependent on Moscow, like the Portuguese, as well as by parties openly at odds with Moscow, like the Spanish. It could be that the Soviet leadership is divided on the issue, or in two minds. Meanwhile, it would be proper to assume that this is an issue on which the interests of the Soviet party and of the local bureaucracy coincide, so far. Certainly, every innovation of this sort is welcomed by the leaders of the other western parties, whose ambitions are the same. For example, the common programme signed by the PCF with the socialists was at once proposed to their local socialists by the Italian, Finnish, West German, and Dutch parties.

The fact remained that this policy was difficult, if not adventurous, for the western parties. It necessitated balancing the requirements of Moscow, of the local worker base and of prospective political allies. In seeking to secure the collaboration of the latter, for example, loyalty to Moscow was a constant liability, yet it could never be discarded. It was not the communist electorate that regarded the link with Moscow as a liability (as we have seen, the voters are relatively indifferent to such remote issues) but the political leadership of other western parties who were invited to collaborate with the communists. They would hesitate to join forces, with a view to a democratic change of government, with a party that apologized for Soviet practice in the matter of transmitting legitimate power, e.g. waiting for Stalin to die, killing Beria, evicting Khrushchev by surprise, etc.[67] Also it was difficult to enlist the support of the western political class while defending both Polish and East German governments that turned tanks on protesting citizenry, and a Soviet government that censored and persecuted intellectuals and artists and oppressed Christians and Jews. It was especially painful to be ogling a Catholic party and have *Pravda* recall the duty of militant atheism incumbent on communists. It was gravely compromising to hold up the Dubcek regime as an example of humane communism respectful of its allies, as the PCI explicitly did,[68] and then watch its annihilation by sister-parties. A brief condemnation of that lethal form of 'fraternal socialist help', a condemnation that was subsequently moderated and thereafter adumbrated but never repeated, was not enough to satisfy prospective allies. They had their own problems, after all, in assuring followers that collaboration with communists was not destructive of liberties, so they maintained pressure on the communist leadership to condemn the invasion and subsequent 'normalization' of Czechoslovakia; the French socialists held a congress on the question in 1973 and invited communist leaders to attend. The PCI was franker, the PCF more evasive, in responding to allies' appeals for a condemnation of the Prague purges of 1972, while the Finnish party was sundered in trying to find an acceptable stance. None of the western parties could admit that communists were being persecuted in Czechoslovakia for just the sort of socialism they were proposing to other western parties.

It was equally embarrassing for a western CP to have Soviet agencies attacking its socialist allies, as ambassador Abrassimov attacked François Mitterrand in 1972, or putting out criminally indictable race-hate propaganda, as did the Soviet embassy in Paris a year later.[69] Finally, it was a disadvantage for an opposition party to have its Soviet backers working harmoniously with the local government, as did Moscow not only with the Gaullist and Pompidolian governments but with those of the Greek colonels, of Generalissimo Franco, and of Dr Caetano.

Thus torn between its Soviet power centre and its prospective political allies, the communist bureaucracy had also to placate its worker base, alarmed by the sight of the tribune reconciled with the social democrats and Catholics whom the communist workers detest. This difficulty was met by combining co-operation with redoubled vituperation. The VPK was seldom so critical of the Swedish socialists as when keeping them in office, and it made a regular practice of addressing to the socialists the very accusations of reformism and class collaboration that the ultra-Leftists were levelling at the communists. The PCF similarly accused the socialist party of base electoralism and of the collection of random clienteles of malcontents, using the same words the ultra-Leftists used to denounce the PCF. The repeated nagging attacks of the French communists on the socialist party throughout the preparation and propagation of the common programme were felt to be 'frankly intolerable' by Mitterrand, but then they were not intended for him so much as for communist workers and militants suspicious of their own leaders. That distrust welled up from the base, through several federations, and found expression within the central committee in 1972 and 1973. In Italy, too, the offers of collaboration with the Catholic party were distasteful to a keenly anti-clerical communist base, though probably no more so than willingness to cohabit with the democratic socialists formerly led by ex-President Saragat.

Distrust of social democrats is constitutive of the mentality of the communist worker. Communism is something that happens within socialism because some workers reject the policies of social democracy, so to run these two horses in harness would be a feat. The communist militants know as well as their leaders that such running together has usually ended, in Western Europe, by the communists being duped by the socialists. Socialist distrust of communists is usually illustrated by a reference to the Prague coup of 1948, but communist distrust of socialists is based on scores of instances of trickery and treachery that are enshrined in communist folklore. For a communist worker, a bourgeois social democrat politician like Olof Palme, Antonio Giolitti, or François Mitterrand is a schemer who uses proletarian rhetoric to win office, whereupon he kicks away the ladder by which he climbed and proceeds to administer the affairs of the bourgeoisie. To be sure, the versatility of the European socialist parties in the matter of electoral alliances and parliamentary combinations might well inspire mistrust. Hermansson showed that sort of wariness towards a Swedish socialist party ever suspect of readiness to reverting to the Rightist alliances that it has used to hold office before. Georges Marchais for the same reason long demanded, but did not get, a 'contract for one legislature' that would have enabled the communists to force a dissolution if their socialist allies should seek to change partners in the corridors of parliament, as they were wont to do throughout the Fourth Republic. The shift to a presidential system only heightened those fears. A French socialist directly elected to the Elysée with the aid of communist votes could turn his coat with even less difficulty than the socialists of the Palais Bourbon, and the communist militants are acurely aware of it. The western CP with the longest experience of sharing office with social democrats, the Finnish party, is the one that has suffered most, in the eyes of its adherents, from that alliance.[70]

If anxieties of that order are uppermost in the minds of militants, the party bureaucracy is conscious of the danger that collaboration with social democrats might erode its own foundations. Its electorate is preserved by the faith that reformist activity within neo-capitalist democracy is nothing alongside the final proletarian liberation that is to be attained by following the Bolshevik way. Already exposed to the corrosive influences of the communications media, which invade the proletarian home as they never could when the faith was formed half a century ago, that belief could not fail to be weakened by the sight of communist acceptance of socialist methods. A boast by Mitterrand in 1972 (being impolitic, it was disavowed) that his party could eventually win away 2–3m. communist votes was received with amused contempt by Georges Marchais, but Marchais did not press for the constitution of 'base committees' of communist and socialist militants, while his campaign for Left unity in 1972–3 came down to one, and only one, joint meeting with the socialists. Contact can bring contagion. There were renewed efforts by the PCF in 1973 to revitalize its workplace cells, in order to counter growing socialist influence in the factories. Moreover, the principal objective of the communists in the French elections of that year (which they never expected the united Left could win) was to stay ahead of the socialists, as the major power on the Left. It would advantage the communists nothing if in their effort to win power in the state they forgot their mission of half a century: to win power in the socialist movement.

In sum, the policy of alliances with social democrats is dangerous for the CPs, let alone alliances with forces to the Right. It involves them in taking their distances from one of their power centres, the Soviet Union, in order to reassure local allies, and in arousing the well-founded distrust of their other power centre, the militant workers. It exposes them to the attacks of the Trotskyists, Maoists, and other Leftists, to whom they have surrendered the ground to their Left. There is no CP in Western Europe that has not smarted since 1968 under the scornful attacks of the Leftists. These difficulties are exacerbated when the communists accede to office in a coalition. The Finnish party found between 1966 and 1970 that to approve the devaluations that inevitably follow the coming to power of a coalition including communists, to take the unpopular measures necessary to defend the neo-capitalist economy, and to serve as minority partners, not to say hostages, of a democratic government, brought a sharp fall in electoral support. Indeed, responsibility within a system it condemned fractured the party, and made it a useless ally for the socialists.

When the CPs offer alliances well to the Right of the socialists, as the PCI did in 1973 with its *compromesso storico*, populism and desperate electoralism would seem to have led to incoherence. This policy as espoused by the Spanish, Portuguese, and Greek parties is comparable with the anti-fascist national coalitions of the Resistance and the postwar reconstruction. But when it is revived in Italy in the 1970s, it must seek to justify itself by agitating a 'fascist menace' that bears no relation to the limited possibilities of the MSI, the neo-fascist movement. If there is a fascist—i.e. a national-solidarist, populist—danger in Italy, it is not in the MSI but in the spectre of a communist-Catholic-socialist-liberal-republican-social-democrat 'national front' government that would have no opposition—except the MSI.

It is a commonplace of Italian (as of French and Finnish) politics that when a government fails to satisfy the political class, there is talk of 'enlarging the majority', by bringing in some of the dissatisfied to share responsibility. There is no thought of passing power to another party or parties, with different policies—which might indeed be unpractical in those three countries—but neither is there thought of changing the incumbent government's policies or of securing their implementation by an unresponsive administration. The lesson that broader and broader coalitions govern worse and worse is only admitted at times of crisis, whereupon there ensues a spell of authoritarian or *monocolore* government, before the process of widening the majority begins over again. Coming from the PCI, however, this familiar suggestion is open to peculiar objections. The PCI concedes that the sort of policy it wishes to implement would be unacceptable, indeed would probably awaken violent resistance, if the Left had only a 51 per cent majority. It draws the inference that the same set of policies would be practical given a bigger majority. Not at all. Only the populist prepossessions of the communists lead them to suppose that there exists any one sort of policy that would be acceptable to 'the masses', to a majority of Europeans, to 90 per cent or even 70 per cent of the population. On the contrary, majorities of that sort can be mustered, in peacetime, only on a programme of vagueness and misunderstanding. When the PCI proposed its historic compromise, it took care not to specify the programme of such a broad coalition, beyond antifascism and national unity.

The fallacy of this 'national front' reasoning is especially obvious in Italy. Christian Democracy is inadequate exactly because it is itself a *compromesso storico*, it is *interclassista*, it is a 'historical block' without common policies, of just the sort that Gramsci, Mussolini, and De Gasperi all thought would best govern Italy. To add the communists to that confusion of clienteles would not advance Italy's affairs but neither would it advance the communists' affairs, beyond giving them the opportunity to 'colonize' their ministries with party members. For one thing, Christian Democracy has shown a capacity to absorb, blunt, and divert opposition that would make it a more dangerous bedfellow than the socialists who already are dreaded by communist purists. Secondly, if from within that grand coalition the communists sought to push through their characteristic policies, they would encounter as much, and as violent, opposition as if they were in power in a Leftist coalition with a one-man majority. In fine, coherent policies compatible with the system can be implemented even by minority governments, of which Western Europe has had a number since the war, whereas incoherent policies incompatible with the nation's economic, moral, and military situation cannot, *short of revolution*, be implemented by a temporary majority—no matter how huge and no matter whether it was secured by electoral misunderstanding or by parliamentary horse-trading. And coherent policy does not arise from 'isolating the fascists' or rallying the masses against the monopolists, the handful of profiteers. Under such populist cover, the communists might be pursuing other specific goals, but then they are doing so adventurously.

It would be idle to try to predict the outcome of that or any similar adventure. Over and above the uncertainties that confront any party in the fluid politics of Latin Europe and Finland, and in addition to the large doubts one must have about the succession of the dictatorships in Spain, Portugal, and Greece, there is the circumstance of the CPs' own complex structure. Within them three different forces are at war, and are in different balance from party to party. Latterly, one of them, the local party bureaucracy, has successfully advanced its political ambitions in several countries. This has led to prophecies that the parties will be integrated into the western polity as a variety of social democracy. That is not impossible, though the Leninist party structure and the utopian workers are powerful obstacles. The third power centre in the parties, the Soviet influence, introduces an additional contingent factor that is especially unpredictable. It involves the CPs, more than any other western parties, in international affairs, that is to say, in the domain of the rigorously unforeseeable. What the Soviet Union's relations are with the United States and China will affect what it wants in Western Europe, and its influence over many of the CPs will be one way it will attempt to get what it wants there. The mere fact of identifying the forces at work and recalling their contingent interactions in the past is enough to discourage prophecy.

Notes

1 *LM*, 20 & 26 July 1973.

2 *Neue Zürcher Zeitung*, 28 June 1972.

3 Fauvet, pp. 151, 159–60; Upton, pp. 261–2; Romano Luperini, *Gli Intellettuali di sinistra e l'ideologia della ricostruzione nel dopoguerra* (Rome, 1971).

4 *Rinascita*, no 12, Dec 1956, p. 674.

5 'Le capitalisme monopoliste d'État. Conférence internationale de Choisy-le-roi, 26–29 mai, 1966', *Economie et politique*, no 143–4, June–July 1966.

6 C. H. Hermansson, *Vänsterns Väg* (Stockholm, 1965), p. 90; Upton, p. 348; Norges Kommunistiske Parti, *Program* (Oslo, 1973), pp. 9–12.

7 'There is no middle term between the two systems. Monopolies must lead to socialism' (Lenin, *Collected works* (Moscow, 1960), xiv. 217).

8 Enrico Berlinguer, 'Costruire una nuova unità internazionalista e compiere un

passo avanti per il socialismo', in G. Vacca, ed., *Politica e teoria nel marxismo italiano 1959–69* (Bari, 1972), pp. 440, 443.

9 *Les Communistes français*, pp. 243–4.

10 *LM*, 14 & 20 July 1973.

11 Ibid., 23 Dec 1971.

12 Giorgio Amendola, *La Crisi italiana* (Rome, 1971), pp. 24–7.

13 *Vänsterns Väg*, pp. 118–19.

14 *LM*, 12–13 Nov 1972.

15 *Anti-Stalin campaign*, p. 123.

16 Dallin, p. 488.

17 Barjonet, pp. 66–7; G. Chiaromonte & G. Pajetta, *I Comunisti e i contadini* (Rome, 1970), pp. 46, 60; *VIII Congreso del PCE*, p. 128.

18 For a meticulous examination of PCI economic policies, and for a demonstration of the incompatibility between *any* economic policy and 'the agitational complex', Arrigo Levi, *PCI: La lunga marcia verso il potere* (Milan, 1971), pp. 71–104.

19 Tiersky, pp. 154–8.

20 A. Gramsci, *L'Ordine Nuovo 1919–20* (Turin, 1954), p. 99.

21 *LM*, 4 Sept 1973.

22 Georges Lavau, in Bon, pp. 25–37.

23 Galli, *Il Bipartitismo imperfetto*, pp. 308–14; Pierre Ferrari & Herbert Maisl, *Les Groupes communistes aux Assemblées parlementaires italiennes (1958–63) et françaises (1962–1967)* (Paris, 1969), pp. 3–108; Franco Cazzola, 'Consenso e opposizione nel Parlamento italiano: Il ruolo del PCI dalla I alla IV Legislatura', in *Rivista italiana di scienza politica*, Apr 1972; Franco Cazzola, 'L'opposizione di un partito di governo: il PCI in Parlamento dal 1948 al 1972', ECPR Workshop.

24 For Homeric battles in the Palais Bourbon, Tiersky, pp. 177–81.

25 Ferrari & Maisl, pp. 115–206.

26 *Changer de cap* (Paris, 1971); François Billoux, *Quand nous étions ministres* (Paris, 1972).

27 Hermet, *Les Communistes en Espagne*, pp. 67–71.

28 *Rinascita*, no 5, May 1957, p. 248.

29 *Est et Ouest*, no 491, p. 3.

30 Togliatti, *Il Partito comunista italiano*, p. 128.

31 *Est et Ouest*, no 491, pp. 2–3.

32 Dallin, p. 856.

33 *Est et Ouest*, no 503, p. 9.

34 Togliatti, in *Anti-Stalin campaign*, pp. 246–7; Longo, in Dallin, p. 856; Finnish party, *Kommunistische Parteien im Westen*, p. 208; Berlinguer, p. 16.

35 *Est et Ouest*, no 489, pp. 3–5 & no 500, pp. 1–4.

36 *L'Humanité*, 13 Sept 1972.

37 For the PCI's evolution, Heinz Timmermann, 'Revolutionärer Reformismus: Bemerkungen zum Sozialismusmodell der Italienischen KP', *Berichte*, no 2, 1973, p. 16.

38 *LM*, 17–18 Sept 1972.

39 For a history of PCF variations on the theme of *l'alternance*, *Est et Ouest*, no 504, pp. 2–5.

40 *L'Entreprise*, 24 July 1971.

41 Heinz Timmermann, 'Westeuropas Kommunisten und die Europäische Gemeinschaft', *Beiträge zur Konfliktforschung*, iii (1972), pp. 5–38; and 'Frankreichs Kommunisten: Wandel durch Mitarbeit', *Europa Archiv*, ix (1973), pp. 300–10.

42 *LM*, 5 Dec 1973.

43 Ibid., 15 Jan 1972, 17 & 27 Feb 1973.

44 Ibid., 28–9 Apr & 23–4 June 1974.

45 Ibid., 18–19 Oct 1970; *Mondo operaio*, Feb 1969, p. 19.

46 *Rinascita*, 28 May 1971; *Frankfurter Allgemeine Zeitung*, 13 Apr 1972.

47 Amendola, *L'Europa*, p. 92.
48 Berlinguer, *Svolta democratica*, p. 30.
49 Arrigo Levi, 'Berlinguer's communism', *Survey*, no 84, p. 6.
50 *LM*, 28–9 Apr 1974.
51 *Rinascita*, 30 Nov 1973.
52 Neil McInnes, 'The communist parties of Western Europe and the EEC', *The World Today*, Feb 1974.
53 H. Timmermann, 'Die Brüsseler Konferenz westeuropäischer kommunistischer Parteien vom 26–28 Januar 1974', *Berichte*, no 10, 1974.
54 Amendola, *L'Europa*, p. 80.
55 *L'Unità*, 28 Jan 1974.
56 See above for the intervention in the Finnish debate. For the PCE, *LM*, 23 Feb 1974; for the Japanese party, ibid., 24 May 1974.
57 *LM*, 17 Nov 1972.
58 Bon, p. 33 (italics added).
59 Silvano Belligni, 'Riforme di struttura, democrazia e alleanze nella "via italiana al socialismo" ', ECPR Workshop, p. 15.
60 Central Committee of PCP, *Por uma grande campanha política de massas* (1973); *Avante*, Apr & June 1973.
61 *VIII Congreso del PCE*, pp. 22, 30, 36.
62 'Manifest van de CPN', *De Waarheid*, 1 Sept 1972.
63 *LM*, 12 & 13–14 May 1973.
64 *Il Mondo*, 29 Nov 1973.
65 Ibid., 6 Dec 1973.
66 *L'Humanité*, 2 Jan 1973.
67 As the PCI testily told Moscow: 'Sui problemi posti dalle decisioni del PCUS sulla sostituzione del compagno Krusciov', declaration by the PCI Directorate, 22 Oct 1964 (*Il PCI e il movimento operaio internazionale*, pp. 248–51).
68 In statements by the Directorate, 17 July 1968 and by the Politburo, 5 Aug 1968 (ibid., pp. 304–9).
69 *LM*, 1 Sept 1972 & 27 Apr 1973.
70 Upton, pp. 266–7, 351.

Index